The Campaign of
TRAFALGAR

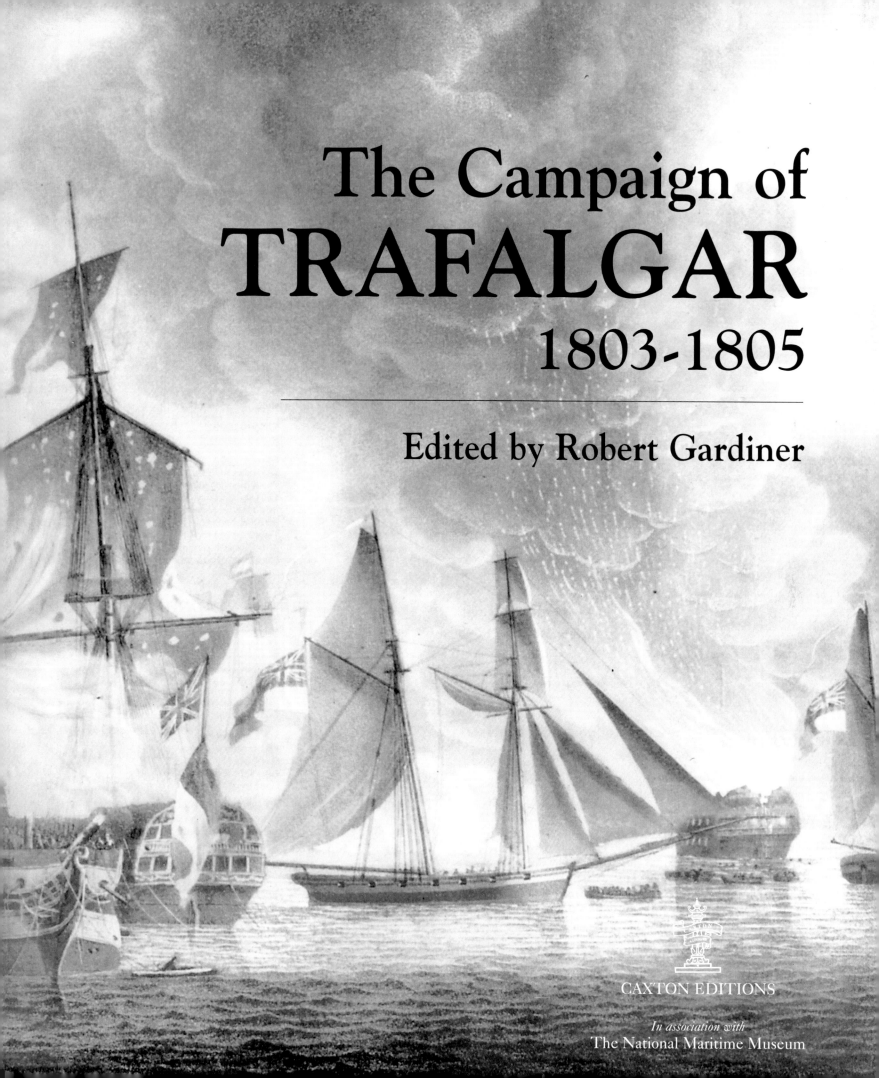

The Campaign of
TRAFALGAR
1803-1805

Edited by Robert Gardiner

CAXTON EDITIONS

In association with
The National Maritime Museum

FRONTISPIECE
The climax of the greatest battle of the age of sail. 'Victory of
Trafalgar, in the Rear. This view of the total defeat of the
combined Fleets of France and Spain ... is most respectfully
inscribed to the Right Honble Lord Collingwood...',
aquatint and etching by Robert Dodd (1748-1815) after his
own original, published by the artist, 1 March 1806.
NMM neg B2582

Copyright © Chatham Publishing 1997

First published in Great Britain in 1997 by
Chatham Publishing, an imprint of Gerald Duckworth & Co Ltd

This edition published 2001
by Caxton Editions an imprint of
The Caxton Publishing Group
ISBN 1 84067 3583

British Library Cataloguing in Publication Data
A catalogue record for this book is available
from the British Library

Designed and typeset by Tony Hart, Isle of Wight
Printed and bound by C.T.P.S.

Contributors

Roger Morris
Introduction 1803-1805
Part I: The Colonial War Renewed
Part II: The Invasion Threat
Part III: The French Grand Strategy
Part IV: Trafalgar
Postscript

Robert Gardiner
America's Barbary Wars
Cruise of the *Marengo*
HM Sloop of War Diamond Rock
Poacher turned gamekeeper
Privateering actions
Privateering vessels
An epic of convoy defence
The convoy system
Ships of the Royal Navy: the 12pdr frigate
Invasion craft – the nightmare
Invasion craft – the reality
Fulton's Infernals
'Dangers of the Sea': shipwreck
Ships of the Royal navy: gunboats and gunbrigs
A naval officer's view
Ships of the Royal Navy: the 50-gun ship
Ships of the Royal Navy: the 74-gun ship

Richard Hunter
Ship decoration

David Lyon
East indies and Africa 1803-1804
The National Flotilla
The Downs Command
Anti-Flotilla operations: the Channel
Invasion defences
Torpedoes and rockets: the attacks on Boulogne
Anti-Flotilla operations: the North Sea
French naval bases: Boulogne and the invasion ports
Calder's Action
Strachan's Action

Iain MacKenzie
West Indies 1803-1804
Vincejo at Quiberon"
The blockade of Brest
Watching Toulon
Missiessy's raid
Ordeal of the *Belleisle*

Julian Mannering
Notes on artists

E V E Sharpston
Frigate actions
Spanish gold
Lone fight of the *Redoubtable*
Counterattack

David Taylor
Nelson takes over in the Mediterranean
Villeneuve's first sortie
Villeneuve escapes
Nelson in the West Indies
The blockade resumed
Trafalgar – the opening moves
The lee line
The weather column
The final stages
Storm after the battle
Securing the Victory

Colin White
Death of Nelson
Nelson's funeral

Jenny Wright
Dance's Action

CONTENTS

Thematic pages in italic

PREFACE

ALTHOUGH THE eighteenth century lacked the kind of mass, and instantaneous, media so familiar in the late twentieth, the earlier age was just as interested in news and current affairs. This was largely satisfied by the written word – at increasing chronological distance from the events themselves, newspapers, journals and books. But even in the 1700s, the written medium was not the only source of information. A sophisticated printselling industry evolved, producing relatively cheap, and sometimes tasteless images of a nature that even modern tabloids would eschew, purporting to depict recent happenings of public interest. However, among them were also to be found fine engravings based on the works of well known artists, including remarkably detailed maps and charts of land and sea engagements, which often stand up in point of accuracy to modern research.

In this fashion the public was provided with an image of the great occurrences of the time, and the 'Chatham Pictorial Histories' are intended to recreate this impression in the naval sphere, which for an island nation like Britain was a paramount concern right down to recent decades. Of course, besides the public prints, there were also more formal representations like the oil paintings commissioned by those involved, but by their very nature they are celebratory and, although often the result of the most meticulous research by the artist, they lack immediacy. They are also quite well known, and another of our concerns has been to seek out the less familiar, and in some cases the never previously published, so while we do use some finished paintings, we have preferred the artist's own sketchbooks where available; they reveal not only the lengths the painters went to get details correct, but often cover occurrences that are not otherwise represented, or where the art world has lost track of the finished work.

In the search for original and, if possible, eyewitness depictions, we have also dipped into some of the logs, journals and contemporary manuscripts. Naval officers, in particular, were encouraged to observe closely, and part of the training process involved making sketches of everything from coastal features to life on board. To a lesser extent, this was true of army officers, who were often fine mapmakers – especially those in the technical branches like the engineers and the artillery (today most people in Britain are unaware of why the best official mapping of the country is called the Ordnance Survey).

However, the series was specifically inspired by the Prints and Drawings collection of the National Maritime Museum at Greenwich, on the outskirts of London. Reckoned to comprise 66,000 images, it is a surprisingly under-used resource, despite the fact that an ongoing copying programme has made three-quarters of it available on microfilm. While this forms the core of the series, we have also had recourse to the Admiralty Collection of ship draughts – itself running to about 100,000 plans – as well as some reference to the charts collection in the Navigation Department and logs and personal journals kept by the Manuscripts Department. This last is a very substantial holding with no easy mode of access to any illustrations it may contain, so although some work has been done in this area, it must be said that there is probably far more to discover if only time were available for the task.

The series is intended first and foremost to illustrate the great events of maritime history, and we have made little attempt to pass artistic judgement on any of the images, which were chosen for content rather than style. The pictures are grouped, as far as practical, to show how events were presented at the time. Since this is not primarily a work of art history, for the technical credits we have relied on the Maritime Museum's extant indexing, the product of a massive and long-running documentation programme by many hands with some inevitable inconsistencies, depending on the state of knowledge at the time each item was catalogued. We have reproduced what information there is, only correcting obviously wrong attributions and dates, and quoting the negative number or unique reference number of each illustration for anyone wishing to obtain copies of these from the museum or archive concerned.

Following *Fleet Battle and Blockade* and *Nelson against Napoleon* in chronology, *The Campaign of Trafalgar* is the third of five titles covering the whole of the period of the great French wars from 1793 to 1815, including America's 'Quasi-War' with France and the conflict with the Barbary states. The series follows the order of the original events, except that the War of 1812 fills a single volume of its own, and each otherwise covers its period completely. However, the thematic spreads are cumulative in their coverage, because we are keen to illustrate many general aspects of the weapons and warfare of the period which stand outside the chronological structure. Therefore, we devised a single programme of such topics and simply positioned each at an appropriate point in the series. The best example is provided by the many features on individual ship types and their roles, which will add up to a complete analysis of the function of the Navy's order of battle by the end of this five-volume set. Similarly, *Fleet Battle and Blockade* looked at the life of commissioned officers, while later volumes will do the same for seamen; and there will be ongoing picture essays on themes like the perils of the sea, and on individual ports and harbours. This, we believe, avoids predictability and gives every volume variety and additional interest.

Acknowledgements

The project would have been impossible without the co-operation of those at the National Maritime Museum's publications division, initially David Spence and latterly Pieter van der Merwe, who negotiated and set up a workable joint venture. I received generous and friendly advice from Clive Powell on logs and journals and from Brian Thynne on charts, while the staff of the library were endlessly patient with demands for myriads of photocopies and frequent requests to put right snarl-ups in the microfilm readers. The volunteer 'Friends' of the museum showed similar forbearance in the Picture Research Room.

With the minimum of fuss and bureaucracy Jane Costantini organised the numerous visits to the outstation where the original prints and drawings are stored, and Gale Dundas deserves particular praise for the spirit of co-operation that suffuses her outpost of empire: large numbers of heavy boxes were cheerfully hauled out and reshelved without a hint of complaint, and any queries were pursued with persistence and real enthusiasm.

However, our greatest thanks must be reserved, as always, for Chris Gray, Head of Picture Research, and his assistant David Taylor, who organised and executed the massive programme of photography that was demanded within our very unreasonable timescale. As the series has progressed we have all learnt by experience, but although the process is now smoother it still requires special attention, and we could not ask for better treatment than we receive from Chris and David.

For this volume my international debts are less extensive, but I would thank the staff of the Peabody Essex Museum of Salem, Massachusetts and, especially, Sigrid Trumpy of the Beverley R Robinson Collection at Annapolis who organised a particularly important image at very short notice.

Robert Gardiner
London, September 1997

INTRODUCTION 1803 – 1805

THE BATTLE of Trafalgar on 21 October 1805 is usually regarded by historians as the culmination of a campaign which commenced when Villeneuve broke out of Toulon with the French Mediterranean fleet in March 1805 and sailed for Martinique, successfully drawing Nelson and his Mediterranean force to the West Indies, only to return to European waters with the intention of combining with the French fleet in the Atlantic ports to escort an invasion force across the Channel. The past accounts of this campaign had a simple unity and focused in particular on the role of Nelson. However, the campaign had much earlier origins, and was in many ways the climax of a threat to invade Britain, and of a counter strategy aimed at confining or destroying the French fleet, that was shaped and evolved during the course of the French Revolutionary War.

The French Revolution in 1789, the execution of Louis XVI in 1792 and the attempt to extend Jacobinism from France to her neighbours remained, even in 1805, the main source of British fear. The domination of continental Europe by French armies between 1793 and 1802 reinforced that fear, for the very success of Gallic arms, coupled with the threat of invasion, made subjection to French tyranny a very real nightmare. Even as Napoleon, little more than a Corsican refugee in 1793, rose in power through the French army, that 'jacobin horde' invaded the Low Countries and pushed down into Italy. The rise of Napoleon to be First Consul in 1799, then to become Emperor of the French in May 1804, focused that fear firmly on the ascendant figure of the most accomplished military dictator Western Europe had yet experienced.

That this Emperor was not invincible was not lost on the British people. He had, after all, been forced to abandon his Army of Egypt following the debacle at Acre at the same time as the French had been forced out of southern Italy. Nevertheless, the repeated French defeats of the Austrians, most decisively at Marengo in 1800, and the trouncing of other allied armies, like the British-subsidised Russians at Zurich in 1799, demonstrated a military consistency which before 1801 the British army was not ready to contest. By comparison, British attempts to engage French troops, primarily as distractions for continental allies, in Flanders in 1793, in Quiberon Bay in 1795, and at the Helder in 1799, were side-shows of limited ambition and consequence.

The French Revolutionary War had proved that France would not easily be defeated on land. The coalitions of continental powers, painfully and expensively knitted together by Britain, had been knocked apart by French armies. The First Coalition had survived from 1793 until 1797, but the Second had endured only from December 1798 until the Austrians were defeated in June 1799. Austria, Russia and Portugal had formed the regular partners with Britain, but almost all the other states of Europe – including Holland until overrun, Spain until 1796, the Vatican and the Two Sicilies until invaded, and Turkey after 1798 – had subscribed and lapsed in membership as French power had either threatened or defeated them.

If hostilities before 1801 proved France was master on land, they had also demonstrated she was unable to control the seas. Combined with the destruction of French ships at Toulon in 1793, the Battle of the Glorious First of June 1794 and the Battle of the Nile in August 1798 had done much to reduce French morale, to sap France's resources in terms of ships and seamen, and to raise British confidence. And this confidence was justified. Although in 1796 the Bourbon monarchy of Spain had fallen under French influence, the battle off Cape St Vincent early in 1797 had severely dented Spanish pride. Although France had extended her influence into the Netherlands, the Battle of Camperdown in 1797 had crippled the Dutch navy. And although the Russian tsar succumbed to French influence in 1800 and, with Sweden, Denmark and Prussia, formed the Armed Neutrality of the North to defend their Baltic trade with France at the cost of the supply of naval stores to Britain, the Danish seagoing navy had been virtually destroyed at Copenhagen in 1801 by the fleet commanded by Sir Hyde Parker and Nelson.

For Britain, the twin means to defeat France were clearly access to financial resources unequalled by any of her continental enemies or allies, and the strength and confidence of her navy. For the management of Britain's war effort, the monarchy placed its confidence in a government led by William Pitt. His experience in working the mechanisms of finance and diplomacy was unparalleled. With the exception of the three years between March 1801 and May 1804, when Henry Addington held power, Pitt presided at the Cabinet as First Lord of the Treasury and Chancellor of the Exchequer from the end of 1783 until January 1806. Pitt's father, the Earl of Chatham, had made his name as architect of Britain's previous most successful war between 1756 and 1763. His son inherited the legacy. It was his confidence in the vital importance of British naval power that permitted the Royal Navy to enter the Revolutionary War in an unprecedented state of preparedness. It was his appreciation of the potentialities of long-term funded debt that permitted war to be waged on a scale, and at an expense, that daunted other contemporaries.

There was thus good reason why Pitt should have been at the head of the British government when the Royal Navy inflicted its greatest ever defeat on the French and Spanish navies at Trafalgar. Significant too was the presence of Sir Charles Middleton, Lord Barham, at the Admiralty. Middleton had presided at the Navy Board between 1778 and 1790 and appreciated the wartime strains on ships expected to be almost perpetually at sea, and the peacetime necessity to repair and rebuild a fleet while the dockyards were not preoccupied refitting. Pitt and Middleton had worked together between 1785 and 1790; and their fruitful collaboration might have been more bountiful in 1794-95, when Middleton returned to office at the Admiralty as a Sea Lord, had he not resigned in a fit of pique which had more to do with his own pride than the interests of the navy. He, among others at that time, nevertheless had time to establish as a persisting system the logistical organisation of the British blockade of the French naval ports.

This blockade strategy recalled that established by Anson during the Seven Years War. Since termed a 'blue water policy', this strategy made the British fleet the main weapon by which Britain waged war. Her fleet, maintained to rival in strength the combined naval forces of her main enemies, France and Spain, permitted Britain to keep those enemy fleets blockaded in their ports, while also preventing them receiving naval stores by sea or providing escorts to their trade. Hence France was deliberately cut off from her colonies, from whence she received a large proportion of her re-export trade, and was prevented from sending succour to those colonies attacked by British amphibious forces. The colonial conquests of the Revolutionary War – Tobago, Martinique, St Lucia, Guadeloupe – were a product of this grand strategy, even though all were given up either immediately or subsequently at the Peace of Amiens.

By strangling enemy trade, this strategy also had the effect of diminishing French merchant shipping and her pool of seamen. Britain's own seamen were not wholly reliable, as the Spithead and Nore mutinies of 1797 demonstrated, but the concessions made in consequence of the former and the punishments as a result of the latter struck a balance which British seamen seemed prepared to accept. The victory at Camperdown appeared to confirm this, while those of the Nile and Copenhagen reinforced the growing confidence in the British navy.

In 1801 this was all the more necessary, for that summer Napoleon revived French schemes for the invasion of Britain. Those attempted against Ireland in 1796-97 had not been successful, but they had indicated the potential of a major landing; after all, in December 1796 had not 15,000 French troops

got into Bantry Bay? These attempts gave France invasion experience, but they also revealed that Ireland would always remain a stepping stone unless the Catholic majority could be pacified and reconciled to Britain. The Irish insurrection of 1798 demonstrated a policy of appeasement was necessary, and the Act of Union politically unifying Ireland with the rest of Britain in 1800 pursued that course. However, it also had the effect of relegating Pitt to the Opposition benches from February 1801 after George III objected to allowing Catholics either to sit in Parliament or to hold high State office, a concession he regarded as a breach of his coronation oath.

The threat of invasion mounted in 1801 thus coincided with a new ministry led by Henry Addington. His first task was to negotiate the preliminaries of peace, signed at Amiens in February 1802. To the frustration and anger of many in British politics, by the terms of this agreement Britain returned to France, Spain and Holland all conquests except Spanish Trinidad and Dutch Ceylon. At the same time Addington accepted France's annexation of Savoy, control of the Cisalpine Republic, and a French military presence in the United Provinces (Netherlands). Also, because Addington refrained from negotiating renewal of commercial agreements, Napoleon was left free to close French ports and colonies to British trade whenever he wished. The Treaty thus favoured France far more than it did Britain, especially as the latter gained no guarantee that France would honour its undertakings to Austria in March 1801 to recognise the Dutch, the Swiss, and the Ligurian Republic.

To the credit of Addington and his colleagues, they did no more than recognise the Treaty as a truce. When Napoleon assumed the presidency of the Cisalpine Republic, declined to withdraw troops from Holland, revealed the nominal independence of the Swiss cantons was no more than a facade for French control, and blocked British trade from parts of Europe under his control, Addington demanded immediate French withdrawal from Holland and pointedly maintained Britain's occupation of Malta while requesting a ten-year lease. For Napoleon Malta was a stepping stone to the East which still tempted him; for Britain it was a central Mediterranean base which blocked Napoleon's eastern ambitions and from which

relief forces might be put into southern Italy. By mid April 1803 the British demand became an ultimatum. On 18 May the British government declared war.

In London the resumption of war had been foreseen for some months; indeed on 8 March George III had submitted his official discontent with France in a message to Parliament, and orders went to the dockyards to fit ships for sea 'without a moment's loss of time' by the night post of 10 March. Though only 32 line of battle ships had been in commission on 1 January, by 1 May there were 52, and by 1 June, 60. By the end of the year the British navy had 75 ships of the line and 320 other vessels, including 114 frigates, in sea commission. Britain's readiness for sea permitted her on 17 May, even before the declaration of war, to despatch ten sail of the line under Admiral the Honourable Sir William Cornwallis to cruise off Ushant to watch Brest. Another smaller squadron subsequently reinforced Cornwallis, cruising south of Brest. Other squadrons took station in the Irish Channel and North Sea, off Rochefort and Lorient.

By contrast, Napoleon had not expected war to commence before September and in May had only 47 ships of the line afloat, with another 19 either building or ordered. Moreover, those afloat were widely dispersed. Brest contained 21 battleships that were serviceable or nearly so; Toulon 12; while 9 were on course for France from St Domingo and eventually got into Rochefort, Ferrol and Cadiz. Dispersal to this extent, inferior strength and lack of preparation for sea precluded any immediate possibility of effective fleet operations. Orders were to complete new ships of the line as quickly as possible. Meanwhile, Napoleon contented himself with arresting all British visitors to France, sending troops to occupy Hanover (ruled by George III as Elector), and resuming plans for an amphibious assault on the south coast of England.

The Peace of Amiens had given Napoleon time for these plans to mature. In March 1803 the Minister of Marine, Denis Decrès, had been obliged to begin planning work on 50 *chaloupe canonnières* and 100 *bateaux canonniers*, shallow-draught landing craft. Orders for the former were placed on 18 May, the very day Britain declared war. On 24 May further contracts were placed for 1050 vessels, the first 310 to be delivered by 23 December that year. On 29 May, under pressure from Napoleon, this completion date was brought forward to 23 September. On 5 July he issued orders for the purchase and construction of a total of 2410 more vessels. At the same time Napoleon began massing troops around the French Channel coasts with their main headquarters at Boulogne.

Against this renewed threat of invasion Britain stood alone. Addington proved more active in preparations for war than his reputation and his critics suggested. His Army Reserve Acts of 1802 and 1803 raised an additional 30,000 men, more than half of whom accepted the option of transferring to the regular army; and his Volunteers Act raised an astounding 300,000 men in England and 70,000 in Ireland, who took many months to train and arm, but who in 1804 became useful units for regular support at defensive points in Britain. Nor was this all: his 'property tax' levied at the rate of one shilling in the pound on incomes over £150 had the advantage of being collected at source, which in this respect was an improvement over Pitt's income tax of 1798 that depended on payers to state their incomes. This financial innovation permitted the yield of the tax to be forecast with extraordinary precision, and his budgets of 1803 and 1804 built a firm foundation for war finance over the subsequent twelve years. Otherwise, he had too little time for diplomatic moves to bring allies into the war against France, for by the spring of 1804 his position was being undermined as Pitt moved into opposition with Fox and Grenville to attack his handling of the war.

Ironically, Addington's weakest point proved to be that which he had intended to be his strongest: the management of the Navy under Lord St Vincent. His naval administration had begun with promise. A long-standing combination of all categories of artificer in the dockyards demanding higher basic rates of pay had been appeased with 'an extra ration' in April 1801, then punished with the discharge of 340 committee men and agitators. In May economic reform had been imposed on the yards, entailing the abolition of 'chips' taken by workmen as well as the fees taken by clerks. With the signature of peace, he had sold off surplus hemp, and discharged another 1100 men, mainly old or injured, and obtained the

Commission of Enquiry into Irregularities, Frauds and Abuses in the Naval Departments and business of the Prize Agency. The latter was against Addington's will for, being retrospective, it was liable to bring forth skeletons and arouse opposition which, over the next three years it did.

However, it was not the Commission of Naval Enquiry that initially turned St Vincent from a political asset into a liability: it was his attitude to the Navy Board and to contractors. As a sea officer, he had prejudices against both. While peace lasted, these prejudices were a stimulus to economy, but when war resumed in May 1803 his conflict with the Navy Board and his refusal to employ contractors more than *he* thought necessary was a potential source of inefficiency and a target for attack. His conflict with the Navy Board was aggravated by his support for Samuel Bentham, Inspector General of Naval Works, who goaded the Navy Board with innovatory schemes for the management of timber and training of apprentices, insisting all the while on the superiority of judgement based on individual responsibility over that formed by board or collective responsibility.

St Vincent's opposition to contractors was founded on the belief that they were profiteers, who preyed on seamen and the public service. The belief was reinforced by the steeply rising price of timber, along with the growing size of the National Debt, and the apparent attempt of timber merchants to exact more money by the claim that the supply of mature oak timber in southern Britain was virtually exhausted. The Navy Board was prepared to believe the claim, but St Vincent was not, eventually sending out the Surveyor of the Navy and the dockyards' own purveyors to purchase the navy's supply at country sales, but where they only obtained one-tenth of the quantity of oak the dockyards consumed in one year.

His prejudice against building contractors was based on the belief that ships built by contract were constructed in a hurry and of green timber and therefore decayed faster than those built in the Royal Dockyards. At the same time, he was led to believe by Joseph Tucker, Master Shipwright at Plymouth, who had been appointed from East India Company Service, that all the ships necessary could be constructed in the Royal yards if shipwrights were

'The Earl of St Vincent, First Lord of the Admiralty', crayon manner engraving by Richard Cooper after an original by Sir William Beechey, no date. St Vincent's time at the Admiralty was controversial in the extreme.
NMM ref PAD8512

'shoaled' or classed and paid by ability. The shipwrights themselves and the Navy Board opposed the scheme, which only achieved a trial with fir frigates as St Vincent left the Admiralty. Support for it, however, led St Vincent to resist placing orders for ships of the line with merchant builders, and gave Pitt early in 1804 the point of vulnerability in Addington's administration to attack. At that time, when Pitt decided to undermine Addington, he pointed to the vacant merchant building slips along the Thames and asserted the principle that in time of war Ministers should use every possible resource to build ships that were wanted at sea.

At this time, there were few doubts that naval defences against immediate invasion were adequate. Here St Vincent's reputation reinforced his claim to his fellow peers: 'I do not say, my Lords, that the French will not come. I only say they will not come by sea.' Apart from the ships stationed on the French coasts to block up their ports, and the defensive squadron based in the Downs, the British coast and estuaries were filled with flotillas of gunboats and small craft intended to attack the landing craft massing around Boulogne should they attempt to cross the Channel. Nevertheless, when in April 1804 Pitt questioned his adequacy as a war leader, Addington was forced to resign, taking St Vincent with him.

Pitt replaced St Vincent with Henry Dundas, Viscount Melville, who promptly reversed the former's policies with regard to the purchase of timber and the construction of ships of the line by contractors, and placed orders for both. Mobilisation continued, if now at a slower pace, as ships were brought forward that needed more work before they were sent to sea, and with a greater emphasis on smaller vessels needed for defence. By the end of 1804 ships of the line in commission at sea had been increased to 83, and the number of smaller vessels to 425. Then in February 1805 the Commission of Naval Enquiry reported on the office of the Treasurer of the Navy, which had been filled by Melville between 1784 and 1800 and revealed that, contrary to the Act of 1782 prohibiting the Paymaster of the Navy from mixing public money with his own in his private accounts, Melville had permitted his subordinate to do so, even though in 1798 the Bank of England had protested to Pitt about the practice. There was some suggestion that Melville had privately taken loans from his Paymaster and he was charged in the House of Commons with malversation, an allegation that was carried by one vote in April 1805. Impeached on this charge, he was later acquitted. However, on 2 May he was forced to resign the Admiralty, his distinguished parliamentary career terminated.

To replace him, Pitt turned to Sir Charles Middleton. He was seventy-nine and disliked politics but, when offered a peerage as Baron Barham, he accepted with alacrity. In January 1805 Barham had already taken office as chairman of the Commission for Revising and Digesting the Civil Affairs of the Navy, a second naval commission established by Pitt to displace St Vincent's inquiry. Barham did not make any serious alterations in Admiralty policy; Melville had worked from guidance provided by Barham and now the latter simply took personal control. In consequence, his administration was generally characterised by continuity, with the principal fleet commanders remaining undisturbed: Admiral Cornwallis in the Channel, Admiral Lord Keith in the North Sea, Vice-Admiral Horatio Viscount Nelson in the Mediterranean, Sir John Duck-

worth at Jamaica, with Rear Admirals Sir Edward Pellew and Sir Thomas Troubridge sharing joint command in the East Indies. Only in the Leeward Islands did Barham make a change, relieving Commodore Sir Samuel Hood by the appointment of Rear-Admiral Sir Alexander Cochrane.

Barham's main additional responsibility was the administration of a blockade that now encompassed Spanish as well as French ports. Since the Treaty of San Ildefonso in 1796, Spain had been obliged when called upon to furnish France with 15 ships of the line and a supply of troops. In 1803 Napoleon demanded either this assistance or that Spain declare war on Britain herself. Initially Spain agreed to the former, but her war preparations called forth warnings and an ultimatum from Britain, which were followed early in October 1804 by the deliberate attack of four British frigates on four Spanish vessels approaching Cadiz carrying specie worth over £1 million. Spain thus declared war on Britain on 12 December 1804, a declaration received in London on 7 January 1805. Napoleon thus had the advantage of including in his calculations for invasion the force of the whole Spanish fleet.

At the beginning of 1805 the latter consisted of 31 ships of the line ready or fitting for sea at Ferrol, Cadiz and Carthagena. The fleet made a significant addition to Napoleon's strength, for the Spanish navy was re-emerging as a power to be reckoned with in Europe. During the eighteenth century she had built 227 ships of the line, had regained her Florida territories from Britain during her successful participation in the American War of Independence, and with the Malaspina voyages in 1789-94 had embarked on a programme of naval exploration in the Pacific with the intention of strengthening her empire. Although having suffered what the British regarded as a defeat at the Battle off Cape St Vincent in 1797, her navy was still buoyant with confidence, the best of her officers and seamen second to none in ability and enterprise.

The French fleet at the beginning of 1805 consisted of 56 French ships of the line ready for sea with another 15 at various stages of preparation. The combined Franco-Spanish force of 102 ships ready for sea was a real threat to the British fleet which at that same time amounted to 83 ships of the line in sea com-

mission with another 11 prepared for harbour service. Although in 1805 the British dockyards subsequently repaired and commissioned more than 20 of the line, including old worn-out vessels, the campaign of Trafalgar was to be fought between two naval forces of almost equal strength. The question remained, however, whether Napoleon, with his new parity in sea strength, could regain command of the English Channel for long enough to impose

his will on Britain by invasion. Could British naval hegemony, once imposed, be thrown off?

The campaign of Trafalgar was to be as much a test of morale and will as of strategy and naval force, and in the end to be decided by international forces quite unconnected with the sea. Although no more than a single phase in more than two decades of war at sea, it was the decisive one, revealing Britain's strengths, not just as a maritime power, but as a partici- pant of the first consequence in a European war on a world scale that was not to be sur- passed until the twentieth century.

The public relations exercise is not a modern concept. On 17 November 1804 Plymouth Dockyard staged a spectacular demonstration of its efficiency when it launched a First Rate and two frigates, and undocked a reconstructed Second Rate, all within a single tide. The Master Shipwright was a great supporter of St Vincent's views — indeed, he advocated the widespread introduction of shoaled gangs, which had been used to expedite the building of the frigates — so this effort was probably directed towards impressing the new Admiralty Board of Lord Melville. Unsurprisingly, this print was dedicated to St Vincent. 'This Plate representing the Launching of His Majesty's Ship Hibernia of 120 Guns, Circe & Pallas Frigates of 32 Guns each and the Undocking the St George of 98 Guns having undergone a complete repair on the 17th of November, 1804', coloured aquatint engraved by Bluck after an original by Robert Parker, no date. NMM neg X336

1

America's Barbary Wars

WHILE THE Peace of Amiens provided the great powers with a short-lived truce, it was not the end of all naval warfare in European waters. The newly established United States Navy, fresh from a most creditable showing in the so-called 'Quasi-War' with France, found itself in a formally declared conflict with the north African state of Tripoli.

This was the latest round in a struggle with the Barbary States that had been under way since American Independence, when the burgeoning merchant marine

2

of the US had lost the protection of the Royal Navy. The Muslim principalities of the southern Mediterranean littoral were virtually autonomous outposts of the Ottoman Empire, who carried on a desultory campaign against Christian shipping under the ever-thinner excuse of *Jihad* or holy war. Most of the smaller countries, including the new United States, paid tribute to keep the peace when threatened, but this form of extortion did not really constitute 'piracy' in any legal sense, contemporary or modern, and their actions were no more high-handed than those of any European navy in times of war. In fact, the great powers tolerated them because the Barbary States could not intimidate those with big navies but acted as deterrents to the carrying trade of their smaller rivals who were the usual prey of these so-called 'corsairs' (1). In the case of Britain, the Royal Navy had an especial interest in preserving their independence, in that the ports of north Africa were an important, and at times, sole source of water and supplies for blockading squadrons in the western Mediterranean.

The American merchant marine was the second largest in the world, but there were times after 1793 when no merchantman flying the Stars and Stripes was safe east of Gibraltar. Treaties and tribute were the short term response, but the threat of war with Algiers led to the establishment of the United States Navy in 1794. Diplomacy settled disputes with Tripoli in 1796 and Tunis in 1799, but the new navy was finally committed to action when Tripoli declared war in May of 1801. Even

then, the first squadrons sent out under Commodores Richard Dale and Richard Morris operated under circumscribed orders, and it was not until Edward Preble's force arrived in September 1803 (2) that a more aggressive strategy was adopted.

Flying his broad pendant in the *Constitution*, 44 guns, Preble sent the frigate *Philadelphia* ahead to Tripoli while he resolved a threatening situation with Morocco. William Bainbridge (3), the captain of the *Philadelphia*, was a man with an insult to avenge: as commander of the *George Washington* in 1800 he had suffered the humiliation of being ordered by the Dey of Algiers to turn his frigate into a transport for the Dey's tribute to the Sultan at Constantinople, a voyage perforce executed under the flag of Algiers. Perhaps thirsting for revenge, Bainbridge chased a Tripolitan vessel close inshore and ran the *Philadelphia* on to an uncharted rock barely five miles off Tripoli itself. Heroic efforts were made to back the ship off, guns and stores were jettisoned, and eventually the fore mast was cut away, but when the ship was surrounded by Tripolitan gunboats on which no return fire could be trained, Bainbridge surrendered *Philadelphia* and her 300-man crew (4).

This was a body blow, not merely to the strength and morale of Preble's blockading force, but to the international prestige of the infant navy. A 44-gun frigate was also a massive addition to the power of a Barbary navy, for the Tripolitans refloated the ship and carried her into the harbour. The destruction of the ship became a prior-

3

4

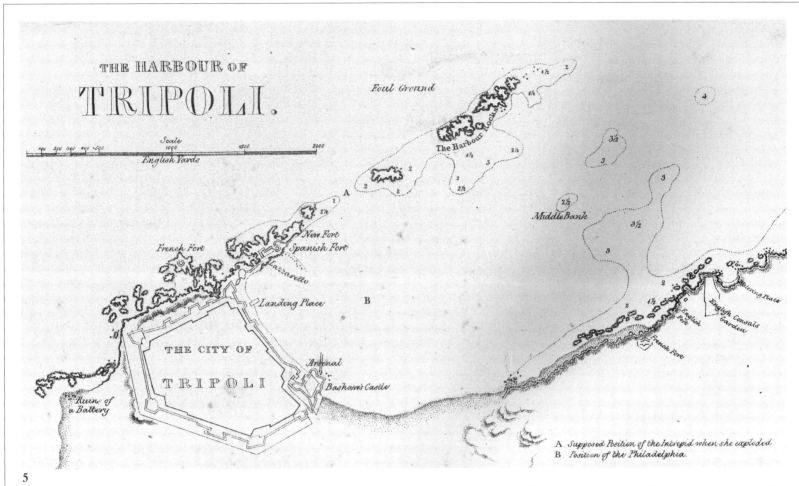

THE HARBOUR OF **TRIPOLI.**

A. *Supposed Position of the Intrepid when she exploded*
B. *Position of the Philadelphia.*

5

6

ity for Preble, and eventually he agreed to a plan, submitted by Lieutenant Stephen Decatur of his flagship, to enter the harbour in a captured local craft, appropriately renamed *Intrepid*, and set fire to the frigate. This was a tall order, since the prize was moored within half-gun-shot of the Bashaw's castle (5), but on the night of 16 February 1804 the raid was carried out with spectacular success. Piloted by an Arabic-speaking Sicilian, the *Intrepid* decoyed herself alongside the frigate on the excuse of having lost her anchors, and Decatur stormed the deck at the head of his 70 volunteers. Overcoming the small anchor watch, Decatur set fire to the frigate with great efficiency, and the *Intrepid* escaped without the loss of a single man (6). The exploit won the admiration of the maritime world – indeed, Nelson, with his usual generosity, described it as 'the most bold and daring act of the age' – and established the US Navy as a force to be reckoned with.

Borrowing six gunboats and two bomb vessels from the Kingdom of the Two Sicilies, Preble carried out a number of bombardments of Tripoli in the summer of 1804, but they were not as decisive as he would have wished (7). *Intrepid* was once more brought to the fore, and converted into an explosion vessel with a view to destroying the walls of the Bashaw's castle. On the night of 4 September, under the command of Lieutenant Richard Somers, the ketch sailed into the harbour, but blew up before getting into position, taking the whole crew with her (8). The actual circumstances are unknown to this day, but a popular story was that Somers had deliberately destroyed the ship when over-

7

whelmed by Tripolitan boarders.

Preble was superseded in the fall, and the war drifted to a close in June 1805, partly due to the effects of the blockade, but also to the capture of Jerna, the second

port of Tripoli, by an American land expedition. Very little was really resolved, but the US Navy could console itself with some fine individual performances and a growing self-confidence.

8

1. 'Ondra Algerina con Vento largo', anonymous watercolour, 1780. Although historically the Barabary corsairs were associated with oared craft – the notorious galleys where Christian slaves were consigned – by 1800 such types were largely replaced by conventional small warships that western navies would call corvettes or frigates; Tripoli is reported to have had only one galley in 1803. *NMM ref PAF8253*

2. Tetuan, Morocco, the usual British watering place for Gibraltar-based ships. HM ships *Caesar*, 80 guns and *Superb*, 74 at anchor, US frigate *Philadelphia*, 44 arriving. From *Naval Chronicle X* (1803), Plate CXXXII.

3. 'William Bainbridge 1774-1838, Commodore US Navy', lithograph printed by Michelin, no date. *NMM ref PAD3484*

4. 'Stranding and capture of the Philadelphia', etching after an original by Captain Hoff and Joseph F Sabin, no date. *NMM neg X2030*

5. 'The Harbour of Tripoli. Shewing position of Intrepid and Philadelphia', etching published by R Bentley, no date. *NMM ref PAD5681*

6. 'Burning of the Frigate Philadelphia in the Harbour of Tripoli, 16th Feb 1804 by 70 Gallant Tars of Columbia commanded by Lieut Decatur', anonymous coloured aquatint, no date. *NMM neg 372*

7. 'The attack made on Tripoli on the 3rd August 1804 by the American Squadron under Commodore Edward Preble . . .', engraving by John B Guerrazzi, published Leghorn 1805. *Beverley R Robinson Collection ref 51.007.398*

8. 'Blowing up of the Fire Ship Intrepid commanded by Capt Somers in the Harbour of Tripoli on the night of the 4th Sepr 1804. Intrepid boarded by Tripolines . . . surrounded by 5 gun boats . . . prefer Death . . . to slavery . . . (Somers) blew the whole into the Air', anonymous coloured engraving, no date. *NMM ref PAF4757*

Part I

THE COLONIAL WAR RENEWED

DURING THE Revolutionary War French imports had been seriously damaged by the British campaign against her West Indian islands; domestic taxes and exactions from invaded European states had nevertheless been sufficient to keep French armies in the field. During the early stages of the Napoleonic War, France was able to benefit from her peacetime resurgence of trade, but after May 1803, as the British blockade began to bite, her colonial trade, a vital source of re-exports and a major source of government revenue, again began to deteriorate. Napoleon, first and foremost a military leader, responded to this economic problem by building a campaign of colonial warfare into his grand strategy for the invasion of Britain. Only after that failed did he realise that he, as well as his principal antagonist across the Channel, had to engage in economic warfare. Until the Battle of Trafalgar, therefore, Napoleon trusted for the defence and seizure of colonies, and the welfare of French trade, to his own grand strategy. French colonies, merchants and shippers had to survive as best they might, while the First Consul and Emperor imposed his will on the French people.

By contrast, in Britain, where the Government was dependent on a measure of goodwill towards the war in the House of Commons, the close connection between public support and the welfare of trade and colonies was fully appreciated. In Britain long-term loans had come to form the main means of war finance, but those loans had to be serviced partly from high customs and excise revenues. The unpopularity of the Peace of Amiens owed partly from disappointment at the poor return in colonial gains from nine years of high taxation and wartime dislocation.

To appease this opinion, when war resumed in May 1803 the defence of British colonies and attack on those of France again formed a main component in the British war effort. It was a strategy facilitated by Britain's early mobilisa-

tion and declaration of war. Not only did this permit the rapid resumption of the blockade of French ports but the despatch of naval forces already in the West Indies to attack once again those French islands given up by Britain at the end of the Revolutionary War.

As early as 21 June 1803 Commodore Hood, with two 74s, some smaller vessels and a force of troops, anchored off St Lucia and took the town of Castries by the end of the day. Having refused to surrender, the principal fortress of the island was stormed at daylight next morning, whereupon, three days later, a detachment of the troops sailed for Tobago. They landed on 31 June and received the surrender of its commanding officer next morning. By the end of September 1803, the Dutch colonies of Demerara, Essequibo and Berbice had also come under British control, captures in the Demerara River including the Dutch corvette *Hippomenes.*

With news of the recommencement of hostilities, British ships had also sailed for St Domingue (the French half of the island later known as Haiti), where French troops were still resisting the black, former slave, insurgents under General Dessalines, the Haitian leader. An expeditionary force sent by Bonaparte during the peace had been all but destroyed by disease and a resourceful enemy. The British force was able to drive off the remaining French ships so that by the end of October only Cape François and St Nicholas Mole remained in French hands.

French forces on Cape François thus became besieged from the sea by the British squadron under Captain Loring as well as from the land by the black insurgents. By mid November the French garrison was reduced to a starving state. Their commanding officer, General Rochambeau, accordingly attempted negotiate from the British free passage for his troops to France in the French ships lying in the harbour. This was rejected. However, this object was secured from General Dessalines, the

insurgent leader, who allowed the French to embark by 30 November, but then threatened to bombard the vessels.

Nevertheless, the British ships remained on station and the French only sailed after negotiating an honourable surrender once they had reached the open sea. To this the 40-gun *Surveillante* and a number of smaller vessels conformed, but in emerging from the harbour the *Clorinde*, another 40-gun frigate, grounded on rocks under the guns of Fort St Joseph with over 700 French troops, their wives, servants and children on board. She lost her rudder and British boats went to her assistance, but could remove few of the 900 people on board before night fell. Acting Lieutenant Josiah Willoughby, however, got on board and persuaded the French general to surrender to him so that, as prisoners of the British, they might be protected from attack by the forces of General Dessalines. That night, furthermore, Willoughby got the *Clorinde* off the rocks and took her prize.

The British squadron then turned its attention to St Nicholas Mole where it attempted to induce General Noailles to surrender. This he refused with the claim that he had five months' provisions. At that, Loring's squadron sailed for Jamaica; but that very night Noailles sailed with his men in seven small vessels for Cuba, leaving St Domingue free of European forces apart from some isolated pockets of French troops holding out in refuges on the Spanish part of the island.

These opening moves in the Napoleonic War were followed early in 1804 by an attempt to make Dutch Curaçao repeat its capitulation of 1800. At that time the Dutch preferred to surrender to the British rather than the French who had a garrison six or seven times that of the Dutch in the other half of the island. However, following the resumption of war in 1803 they had no such inducement. Indeed in mid 1803 they had simply taken captive Captain Robert Tucker who, in his 18-gun sloop, demanded the surrender of Curaçao. On 31 January 1804 terms submitted by Captain John Bligh, supported by two 74s, two frigates and a schooner, were also rejected. He then attempted a landing. While the two frigates blocked the narrow entrance to the harbour of St Ann, where Fort Piscadero was taken, over 600 men and guns were landed in a nearby cove, from where an advance battery was established to attack Fort République covering the town and harbour. However, its Dutch and French defenders made repeated sallies and kept up a fire which, along with dysentery, so weakened the attacking British force that on 25 February it had been obliged to re-embark.

An expedition against Dutch Surinam at the end of April 1804 was more successful. A squadron under Commodore Samuel Hood, conveying over 2000 troops, successfully took the fortifications at the mouth of the Surinam River and then made ready to attack Fort Nieuw Amsterdam. On 5 May, however, that fort capitulated, and with it the whole Dutch colony.

Across the Atlantic, in spite of French enterprise, fortunes similarly favoured British forces. Under the terms of the Peace of Amiens, Gorée in Africa had not been restored to France and in January 1804 its British garrison came under attack from a superior French force which had crossed from Cayenne on the northeast coast of South America. The town was surrendered on 18 January. However, the French held it only until 8 March, when Captain Edward Dickson in the *Inconstant*, 36, arrived with three transports and a storeship. On discovering what had happened, he prepared to land his troops, but the French garrison surrendered before he could do so.

In the East, British forces retained possession of Pondicherry in spite of the despatch of a small French force under General Decaen from Brest in 6 March 1803 expressly for the purpose of taking control of the settlement, ceded to France by the Treaty of Amiens. A French frigate, *Belle Poule,* arrived in advance of the French squadron on 16 June and summoned the officers of the different British factories to transfer title to the properties, but they, forewarned of the resuming hostilities, declined to surrender and remained of this mind until, on 5 July, Vice-Admiral Peter Rainier arrived off

Cuddalore, 20 miles to the southwest, with nine vessels including a 74, two 64s, a 50 and four frigates. His arrival was timely for six days later, Rear-Admiral Linois joined the *Belle Poule* in the *Marengo*, 74, with two more frigates. By then two of Rainier's vessels had been placed at anchor before Pondicherry; and on the arrival of the French others re-anchored closer to Pondicherry. However, hostilities were averted by the delivery on 12 July of despatches to Linois by a brig that had left France ten days after the *Marengo* and brought not only information of George III's intimation to his parliament of the intended resumption of hostilities but instructions for Linois to equip his ships to a war establishment immediately at Isle de France. Rainier had been invited to breakfast on the *Marengo* on 13 July, but during the preceding night Linois and his vessels quietly slipped away, leaving only a few boats moored where the ships had been.

Suspecting that a formal declaration of war had arrived, Rainier immediately sent the greater part of his force to guard Madras, for which he too sailed in July. The formal declaration reached there only in mid September. But, even so, Rainier had too few ships to place on all the stations he was expected to fill, and to keep a sufficient force in hand to oppose the French should they have arrived in force, as they did in 1794, let alone attack the main French base in the Indian Ocean on the Isle de France. It may be recalled that the East Indies Station at this time extended so far east as the coast of China. Only later in the Napoloeonic War, as ships could be spared from European waters, was the Royal Navy able to assert greater command in the Indian Ocean, indeed to place the Isle de France itself under observation.

Hence, unobserved, after re-equipping at Isle de France, on 8 October Linois sailed to reinforce the Isle de Réunion, or Bourbon, and Batavia, the capital of Dutch Java. At the British trading settlement of Sellabar, close to Bencoolen on the island of Sumatra, he burned merchant vessels and warehouses before anchoring at Batavia on 10 December. Linois was to spend the following months attempting to damage British trade, and seize British East Indiamen, which were not only expensive losses to Great Britain but lucrative prizes for the French admiral. In spite of the scale of the Indian Ocean, he was assisted by

the known sea routes East Indiamen sailed, governed by prevailing winds, key landfalls and trusted channels, and a known timetable.

However, Linois achieved a noteworthy lack of success. The best known incident was the failure in mid February 1804 to take a fleet of sixteen East Indiamen and eleven 'country' ships that sailed from Whampoa in January 1804 and passed through the Straits of Malacca in mid February. Linois' squadron then consisted of the *Marengo*, 74, two frigates, a 22-gun corvette and a brig, which he had stationed off Pulo Auro, close to the mouth of the Straits. Commanded by a Company Commodore, Nathaniel Dance, the East Indiamen formed a line of battle, shielding the country ships, and waited for the French to attack. Linois suspected the line to contain some warships, a belief encouraged by Dance who hoisted a blue naval ensign and pendant rather than the East India Company's gridiron flag. Having worked to windward of the convoy, Linois attempted to cut off the rear of the line of Indiamen, but was intercepted when the leading merchantmen tacked in succession towards the French. Fire was exchanged, but the offensive posturing of the Indiamen so disconcerted the French that, after 40 minutes, they sheered off and made sail to the northeast. The Indiamen even had the temerity to give chase.

Although Linois took many other British merchantmen, he had another significant failure in September 1804 in Vizagapatam Roads. The *Centurion*, 50, was anchored there waiting for two merchantmen to load when the *Marengo* and two French frigates approached. One of the merchant ships ran itself aground, while the other surrendered to the French, but the *Centurion* managed twice to drive off the attacking vessels before they departed.

The failures at Pulo Auro and Vizagapatam damaged the reputation of Linois. In justice to him, however, the small size of his force, combined with the shortage of naval stores at Isle de France to re-equip damaged ships made him naturally reluctant to risk heavy action purely for the purpose of seizing merchantmen. The war on British trade in the Indian Ocean was predominately conducted by privateers. The well-known captain Lemême returned there in 1803 in the *Fortune*, 12, with a crew of 160 and soon took fifteen prizes. He was only caught by the frigate *Concorde*, and died on the voyage back to Britain. However, others, notably Surcouf, Dutertre and Courson, took his place.

French privateers made their way in even greater numbers to the West Indies where Martinique and Guadeloupe provided supplies and where innumerable small islands offered shelter. Over half of the encounters between the Royal Navy and French privateers between 1803 and 1805 recorded by Laird Clowes took place in the West Indies; and even those in European waters were with privateers sailing for, or returning from, the Caribbean. The entry of Spain into the war in 1804 added to the islands and American mainland ports in which such vessels could take refuge, and increased the danger of the Florida Straits, close to Spanish territory, where convoys invariably became separated amid the fast-flowing currents, navigational hazards and ever-present risk of gales. Convoys were assembled at Jamaica and Antigua, but merchantmen attempting to reach these congregation points were natural prey to the intelligent privateer.

Closer to France, the Greek archipelago, always a haven for pirates, provided another relatively secure and profitable hunting ground for the *guerre de course*. To reduce British merchant losses, in August 1803 Nelson ordered two warships to cruise between Cape Matapan and the western end of Crete, with others stationed off the south coast of Italy and at the mouth of the Adriatic. In addition Nelson refused to recognise as neutral any port that sheltered French privateers, a tactic that ensured many ports were closed to them, and received the thanks of the merchant corporations of London.

Trade protection in the western Mediterranean was made more difficult between 1803 and 1805 on account of the war between the United States on the Barbary States of North Africa. The North African corsairs had long preyed on the shipping of minor powers passing their coasts, but the blockade of French ports and the presence of British warships in the Mediterranean since 1793 had seriously reduced the European prey available to them. On the other hand, the number of American merchantmen entering the Mediterranean in the late eighteenth century was increasing, and with no naval support on hand to protect them, they became a very tempting target. Tripoli found a pretext to declare war and other states became threatening. By 1803 losses of American trading vessels led the United States to send a naval squadron. After the embarrassing loss of the 44-gun *Philadelphia*, the nascent US Navy performed very well in politically trying circumstances, but hostilities continued until 1805 when, in June, a treaty of peace was signed between the United States and the Regency of Tripoli.

British trade was protected by a sophisticated system of convoys operated by the Royal Navy. Building on the co-operation of Lloyd's and the Admiralty, the Convoy Act of 1798 made escorted sailings compulsory for all ships engaged in foreign trade, with the exception of East Indiamen, Hudson's Bay Company ships, vessels bound for Irish ports, and any ships fast and well-armed enough to sail independently as a 'runner'. Small coastal convoys protected

The expansion of British shipping, one of the principal sinews of the war effort, had its problems. One of the most pressing was the intense crowding in the Thames, London being by far the busiest seaport in the country. This caused expensive delays and damage, and encouraged pilfering, leading shipowners to construct a number of enclosed wet docks, massive engineering feats that were celebrated in public prints like this one. 'An Elevated View of the New Dock at Wapping', coloured aquatint and engraving by William Daniell (1769-1837) after his own original, published by the artist, 1 January 1803.   NMM neg B8431

ships travelling around the British coast; while the large out-going foreign trade convoys were assembled at the Nore and at Spithead and strictly controlled. As the war went on, it became customary for the Admiralty to consult the Committee of Lloyd's as to convoy regulations, ports of assembly and sailing dates.

Implicit in the relationship was the reduction of risk. In 1804, for example, Lloyd's was able to protest against the practice of despatching convoys with only a single escort, a danger made evident in the loss in March that year of the sloop *Wolverine*, 13 guns. In charge of a convoy on passage to Newfoundland, she had engaged the larger of two French privateers, the *Blonde* of 30 guns, but had been taken, and then sank as a consequence of her damage. Six of her convoy escaped but two were captured.

Escorts were usually only intended to counter small cruisers, the assumption being that larger squadrons would be confined to port by the blockade. Occasionally, this could go wrong, as for example in February 1805 when two French frigates, *Hortense* and *Incorruptible*, escaped from Toulon when Nelson had relaxed the blockade of that port while searching the eastern Mediterranean for the French squadron under Vice-Admiral Ville-

neuve. The French frigates met a British convoy defended only by the sloop *Arrow* and the bomb *Acheron* off Cape Caxine. Both were lost in the ensuing action, but the majority of the convoy escaped.

Marine insurance rates were deeply affected by the security of escort arrangements. For its part, Lloyd's ensured that naval reports of merchantmen not conforming to convoy regulations were promptly reported to the associations of merchant shippers in each of the principal port towns. The posts of the Master and his Mates thus came closely to depend on merchantmen complying with the demands of the navy. The success of the system and the confidence felt by insurance underwriters was revealed in 1805 when Villeneuve's fleet arrived in the West Indies. Insurance rates for the homeward voyage rose from an 8½ per cent to 15 or 16 per cent, but no more. These high-risk West Indian rates may be compared to those of 2½ to 3½ per cent for voyages to Ireland, and 1½ per cent for coastal voyages.

To keep these rates low, Lloyd's ensured the Admiralty took every possible measure to counter potential enemy threats and provided the Admiralty with all the intelligence it gleaned from returning merchantmen. It was an intelligence service that was greatly and rapidly expanded following the appointment of John Bennett to the secretaryship of the Committee of Lloyd's in 1804. The following year the Lloyd's-Admiralty pact produced the system of coastal signals which permitted the Admiralty to receive early warning of the approach of enemy raiders.

Lloyd's demonstrated as much interest in the preservation of life as of capital. In 1802, for example, it began assisting in the establishment of a series of lifeboats around the British coast. To encourage the Navy, Lloyd's also raised subscriptions for the relief of the wounded and the dependants of those killed in action. This policy culminated at a meeting on 20 July 1803 in the establishment of Lloyd's Patriotic Fund. The fund was intended 'to animate our defenders by sea and land', and was for 'granting pecuniary rewards or honourable badges of distinction for successful exertions of valour or merit'.

The salutary effect of collaboration between Lloyd's and the Admiralty in Britain was demonstrated by the capacity of British trade

not only to survive the resumption of war in 1803 but to recover and to continue growing. This recovery was especially important for West Indian trade which registered a marked decline in 1803-5 compared to the earlier years of peace. Whereas in 1801 imports from the islands had been worth £8,436,000, and exports to the islands £4,386,000; in 1803 the former were cut to £6,132,000 and the latter to £2,380,000, and neither were restored to their former levels until 1806.

It was a decline that made overseas trade from other sources all the more important, and was partly made up by the maintenance of high-value imports, especially those shipped by the East India Company. Tea imported by that company exhibited the phenomena of actually declining in price throughout the war years to reach in 1800 its lowest ever price since 1726 and during the years before Trafalgar it revealed only a very slight increase in price. The import of that commodity was encouraged by both the growth of population and of consumption per head: by 1800 on average every person in Great Britain consumed each year 2½ pounds of tea.

These high-value trades were not the only ones vital to the British economy. The Baltic, Newfoundland and Mediterranean trades, and above all the unglamorous but critically important coastal trades, like that in coal, kept the British economy functioning. The war itself was of course a stimulus to much shipping, for many vessels served as transports and carried contract cargoes for the supply of British forces overseas. The health of the shipping industry was reflected in the numbers of British merchant shipping registered in Britain. On 30 September 1802 there were 17,207 ships recorded; in all 1,901,000 tons. Three years later there were 19,027 vessels registered, totalling 2,093,000 tons.

This growth of the shipping industry was to continue for the greater part of the new century. The health of the British economy, dependent as it was on the shipping industry and on the navy that protected it, gave the greater part of the population of Britain a stake in its survival. It was as much for this stake, as from fear of French republicanism or Napoleon's dictatorship, that brought British people on to the side of the government in the defence of the country in 1803-5

THE CAPE OF GOOD HOPE;

from a Drawing taken on Board the

HENRY ADDINGTON by M.ʳ JOHN WOOD DEANE

previous to its being given up to the Dutch in Feb.ʸ

1803.

ENGLISH SHIPS	DUTCH SHIPS
N.º 1 H.M.S. *Lancaster*	8 *Pluto*
2 .... *Hindostan*	9 *Batave*
3 .... *Tremendous*	
4 .... *Le Braave*	
5 .... *Jupiter*	
6 .... *Diomede*	
7 H.E.I.S. *Henry Addington*	

1

East Indies and Africa 1803-1804

TWO PROVISIONS of the Treaty of Amiens were to affect the East Indies station in the renewed war. The first was the return to the Dutch of the important way-station of the Cape of Good Hope, carried out with due ceremony in February 1803 (1). The second was to have been a similar restitution of Pondicherry on India's east coast to France, but General Decaen, the designated French governor-general for India, did not arrive until 11 July, by which time the British in India, conscious of rumours of war in Europe, had already decided not to surrender the settlement. The French squadron under Rear-Admiral Linois in the *Marengo* (see following section) was forced to beat a strategic retreat, and thereafter Decaen and Linois conducted the French war effort in the East from the Isle de France (Mauritius).

2

Their opponent as commander-in-chief of the East Indies station was Vice-Admiral Peter Rainier (2), an experienced but rather tired man who had spent eight years in the post. Contemporary rumours abounded of the eccentricities of this rotund, bespectacled, physically unimpressive but not incompetent man: it was said that he was so fond of mangoes that their seasonal ripeness determined the positioning of his squadron, and his will certainly contained a curious bequest that left 10 per cent of his substantial fortune (mostly prize money) to help pay off the national debt. His command presented some real difficulties: how to protect British possessions

and trade, including the immensely valuable Indiamen over a huge area, whilst being prepared to cope with enemy squadrons known to be at large. He was at the end of a very long and slow line of communication back to the Admiralty, and never had adequate information. Ships sent out to him months before in response to a long-obsolete alarm would arrive in Indian waters and before they found him be sent off at the request of East India Company officials on wild-goose chases after Linois' squadron, or reports of French privateer activity. It would be months before these reinforcements actually became available to the admiral who needed their reinforcement, a source of considerable complaint on his part. Keeping his ships maintained and efficient was a constant worry. It must be remembered that there were Dutch ships of the line at large in his area as well as the powerful *Marengo* and her squadron. Fortunately for him the Dutch at Batavia pursued a strategy of masterly inactivity and only minimal co-operation with the French, whilst one Dutch admiral took his ships back to Europe out of annoyance at being superseded by a junior (he was sentenced to death, but reprieved).

Though the main French base at the Isle de France (Mauritius) was from time to time blockaded it was much too far away from any British base and Rainier had far too few ships to make this measure at all effective. Its inhabitants could no longer engage in trade and fell back on privateering to some considerable effect, though it

3

1. 'The Cape of Good Hope, From a Drawing taken on Board the Henry Addington . . . previous to its being given up to the Dutch in Feby 1803', coloured aquatint engraved by T Busby after an original by John Wood Deane, published by the artist, 1 June 1805. The British East Indies squadron, numbered 1 to 6 in the drawing, comprised: *Lancaster*, *Hindostan*, *Tremendous*, *Braave*, *Jupiter* and *Diomede*; the East Indiaman *Henry Addington* was an onlooker (7), and the Dutch ships were *Pluto* and *Batave* (8,9).
NMM neg 5406

2. 'Peter Rainier Esqr Admiral of the Blue from an original picture in the possession of the Honble Basil Cochrane', mezzotint published by C Turner, 1 August 1824.
NMM ref PAD3114

3. 'H.M.S. Director 1784 off St Helena', watercolour by George Lummny, no date. The ship was a 64-gun Third Rate, a type much used as escorts to important convoys.
NMM neg X229

4. 'Island of Goree, on the West Coast of Africa', aquatint and etching by Thomas Medland after an original by Nicholas Pocock, published by Joyce Gold, 31 March 1806.
NMM ref PA19429

was more the smaller ships of the 'country' (local) trade that suffered than the large East Indiamen which could usually look after themselves with considerable success against all except the largest and most powerful raiders. They were encouraged by Decaen, by now running the Island with great energy. The eventual answer was to capture the island, but this would require resources that Rainier had not got; he continued to react, rather than act, primarily because of his lack of resources in ships and men.

In 1805 Rainier came to the end of his stint in the East Indies, and was replaced by not one, but two flag officers, the area being divide between them. The fact that both Pellew and Troubridge were active and distinguished men made matters worse, and a major dispute was rumbling on between them by the end of that year.

The return of the Cape of Good Hope to the Dutch complicated the convoy arrangements. Returning East Indiamen had been met only at St Helena (3), but until the Cape was retaken in 1806 provision had to be made for long-range escort. Elsewhere in Africa the only significant events of the maritime war during this period involved Gorée, which had not been restored to France under the Treaty, but was captured on 18 January 1804 by a French force under Lieutenant Mahé, which had crossed the Atlantic from Cayenne in a number of small local vessels. However, the victors held the settlement for a short time only. On the morning of 7 March, the frigate *Inconstant*, accompanied by transports (4), arrived off the place, and, seeing the tricolour flying, sent a boat ashore under Lieutenant Pickford to find out what had happened. Not receiving any news, Captain Dickson manned and armed three boats, which cut out a vessel lying in the road, though the batteries sank a boat. From the prize the strength of the garrison was discovered. The *Inconstant* prepared for a landing, but when the morning dawned the British flag over the French showed that Pickford had persuaded the garrison to surrender.

4

1

Cruise of the Marengo

2

A PROVISION of the Treaty of Amiens was the restitution to France of Pondicherry on the Coromandel coast of India. In the previous war France and her native allies had been defeated, and French influence all but eradicated from the subcontinent. However, Napoleon saw in the treaty an opportunity to restore French fortunes in the east, but in order not to alarm the British unduly, the expedition he sent to take possession of Pondicherry was neither large nor commanded by a well-known officer.

As Captain-General of the French East Indies, he appointed Decaen, an ambitious and abrasive young army officer, but the naval side of the undertaking was under the separate command of Rear-Admiral Durand

3

4

5

heavily armed than the older British 74s to be found on the East Indies station; the Large Class 74s and 80-gun two-deckers—by analogy, the battlecruisers of their time—were few in number and confined to the main fleets, leaving *Marengo* superior to any single ship she was likely to encounter.

Happily for posterity, a detailed log of the exploits of this squadron survives in a remarkable private journal kept by one Duclos-Legris, who served in the *Marengo* as coxswain of one of her boats. A literate account from the lower deck is rare enough, but the journal is also illustrated with accomplished amateur sketches in indian ink (and a few with added watercolour) covering most of the notable incidents, as well as a few ships Duclos-Legris had served in earlier. Comprising seventy-seven in all, the sketches are too numerous to be reproduced in their entirety, but a selection of the more interesting illustrate this section.

The expedition set sail from Brest on 6 March 1803 (1), and after calling at the Cape sailed directly for India. When the squadron arrived at Pondicherry on 11 July (2), they found a confused and threatening situation, with rumours of war having broken out afresh in Europe. The *Belle Poule*, which had been sent on ahead, was lying under the guns of the *Trident*, 64 and sloop *Rattlesnake*, while the British authorities were clearly prevaricating about the return of the settlement. Furthermore, the British commander on the station, Admiral Peter Rainier, was in the offing with a more powerful squadron. While Decaen was protesting about the delay in returning the settlement to France, the brig *Belier* arrived with news of British preparations for war, rendering Linois' force liable to a pre-emptive strike. However, he contrived a dramatic night-time escape, by abandoning the troops already ashore, cutting his cables and leaving boats containing lights riding at his anchor buoys.

Definitive news of the declaration of war arrived in September by which time the expedition had retired to Isle de France (Mauritius), the centre of French power in the Indian Ocean. Linois sailed on his first war cruise on 8 October, heading for the Dutch East Indies, where he could expect supplies and possibly reinforcements. En route he raided the isolated British station of Bencoolen, near the Straits of Sunda, where two prizes were taken and five other merchantmen were fired by their crews; landing parties then set fire to the warehouses (3). After a very grudging reception by the Dutch at Batavia, Linois sailed early in 1804 on a mission to intercept the homecoming China trade. Virtually undefended, the convoy was a prize so valuable that its capture should have formed the high spot of his career, but in fact ended in the humiliating fiasco known to the British as 'Dance's Action' (see following section).

Linois. Unique among French admirals of the period, Linois could claim a victory over a superior British squadron, on the strength of his repulse of Saumarez off Algesiras, when he was able to capture a grounded British 74. Aristocratic, reserved and unenterprising, he was almost the diametrical opposite of Decaen: as Northcote Parkinson expressed it, 'Decaen had ability without reputation, and Linois had reputation without ability.' This divided responsibility, and clash of personalities, was to dog the French war effort in the Indies for the next three years.

Linois' squadron comprised one large and powerful 74, the *Marengo*, two heavy frigates, *Belle Poule* and *L'Atalante*, the smaller *Semillante*, and two transports, carrying a total of about 1350 troops. War had broken out by the time the expedition arrived so the troops could not be deployed to advantage, but the ships embarked on a campaign of commerce destruction as famous in its day as that of the *Emden* in the First World War or the *Graf Spee* in the Second. In fact, *Marengo* was a close technical parallel for a 'pocket battleship', being faster and more

6

7

Having lost a convoy worth an estimated £8 million in the money of the time, Linois found his treatment at Batavia even cooler on his return (4). A Dutch squadron flatly refused to co-operate, and although he was able to dispose of two prize ships taken earlier, he was forced to return to the Isle de France having achieved little, leaving only his two big frigates cruising against commerce. His action with the China fleet soon became public knowledge, and the resulting controversy eventually destroyed what small reputation he had achieved.

8

9

All illustrations are from the manuscript journal of Ducros-Legris, NMM ref LOG/F/2. There are seventy-seven full-page illustrations; those reproduced and their folio numbers are as follows:

1. Fol 2 The departure of the squadron, 6 March 1803. *NMM neg D9058-A*

2. Fol 6 Arrival at Pondicherry, 11 July 1803. *NMM neg D9058-B*

10

However, his very presence in the Indian Ocean reaped a dividend. The uncertainty of where he would strike next forced the British forces on to the defensive, as his steam-powered successors were to do a century or more later. In theory the earlier threat was more difficult to counter, given the greater endurance of the sailing ship, which was not tied to the need for frequently topped-up coal or oil. But in practice, stores and provisions were still a limitation, especially with an ill-provided base like Isle de France. As a result, Linois was always on the lookout for sources of supply, and before properly embarking on his second offensive cruise, he spent two weeks in July 1804 taking on victuals in St Augustine Bay, Madagascar – Ducros-Legris shows a whole bullock being brought aboard the *Marengo* (5).

The British anticipated a return to the Dutch East Indies, but Linois took his squadron into the Bay of Bengal shipping lanes, where he was able to pick up a number of unprotected merchantmen, including two rice ships captured on 19 August (6). As the British forces under Rainier responded to information on this incursion, Linois switched his attention to the opposite coast and was lucky to miss the hunting squadron by a few miles. He was less fortunate at Vizagapatam, where the Indiaman he was pursuing turned out to be protected by the 50-gun *Centurion*. In normal circumstances *Marengo* would have made short work of such an opponent, but the British ship made good use of shoal water – the action was not fought at the close range shown by Duclos-Legris (7) – and although the Indiaman was taken and a country ship driven ashore, Linois had to break off the action. This only enhanced his reputation for pusillanimity, but in fairness he ran the risk of all commerce-raiders that he might suffer damage that would be irreparable with the meagre facilities to hand.

For the British, the one certain factor was Linois' base, and a small squadron was sent to the Isle de France, but it was only strong enough to blockade one of its two main ports at any one time. Therefore in October when he returned, the ever-cautious Linois was able to ascertain that the squadron was off Port Louis and divert in time to Grand Port. Entry to this harbour was very tricky—as the British were to discover to their cost in 1810—and the *Marengo* grounded on the 31st, tearing off her rudder and part of the false keel (8).

The ship remained inactive during the winter and, refitted and repaired, sailed again on 22 May 1805, by which time the British East Indies squadron had a new and more energetic commander in Rear-Admiral Sir Edward Pellew. Nevertheless, off Point de Galle (Ceylon) he was able to take a major prize in the form of the Indiaman *Brunswick*, which had missed the previous year's homegoing convoy through damage (9). The *Brunswick*'s captain, Grant, had the enforced opportunity to observe Linois and his ship over the next few months and was not much impressed by either. Of the *Marengo* he reported:

She sails uncommonly fast; but her ship's company, though strong in number, there being 800 men now on board, does not possess 100 effective seamen. . . . There does not appear to be the least order or discipline amongst their people; all are equal, and each man seems equally conscious of his own superiority; and such is the sad state and condition of the *Marengo*

that I may with safety affirm, she floats upon the sea as a hulk of insubordination, filthiness and folly . . .

Linois confessed to Grant that he felt it 'impolitic' to risk action with an equal force, since he had no way of replacing a damaged lower mast in his flagship, so rerigging the *Belle Poule* after she lost her mizzen in a gale (10) must have strained his resources to the limit.

This nervousness for his top-hamper manifested itself once again when Linois ran into another fat convoy of Indiamen, bound for Madras under the escort of the *Blenheim*, 74, commanded by no less an officer than Sir Thomas Troubridge, most prominent of Nelson's 'band of brothers'. This time the French squadron closed in enough to discover that there was a real escort, but a short skirmish confirmed Linois' preference for discretion over valour. With the *Belle Poule* free to attack the merchantmen, Troubridge could not abandon the convoy to pursue the *Marengo*, so Linois made his escape, heading not for the Isle de France but for the Cape. He was to lose both his prize and the frigate *L'Atalante* to bad weather, but by the end of the year Linois had sailed out of the Indian Ocean—and beyond the scope of this chapter.

The final voyage home and *Marengo*'s epic fight with the *London* will be covered in the next volume.

3. Fol 13 Burning merchantmen after the raid on at Bencoolen, 3 December 1803.
NMM neg D9058-C

4. Fol 22 Entering Batavia, 25 February 1804.
NMM neg D9058-D

5. Fol 27 Reprovisioning at Madagascar, 6-18 July 1804.
NMM neg D9058-E

6. Fol 30 Boarding the two rice ships taken on 19 August 1804.
NMM neg D9058-F

7. Fol 33 Battle with *Centurion* off Vizagapatam, 18 September 1804; the Indiaman *Princess Charlotte* was taken, and the country ship *Barnaby* ran herself ashore.
NMM neg D9058-G

8. Fol 40 *Marengo* aground off Grand Port, 31 October 1804.
NMM neg D9058-H

9. Fol 45 Port de Galles, with the prize *Brunswick*, 11 July 1805.
NMM neg D9058-I

10. Fol 46 *Belle Poule* losing her mizzen.
NMM neg D9058-J

11. Fol 47 Attack on Troubridge's convoy, 7 August 1805.
NMM neg D9058-K

11

1

Dance's Action

IN JANUARY 1804 the Honourable East India Company had a problem. Assembled at the Chinese port of Whampoa were sixteen Indiamen, amongst the largest merchant ships of their day, heavily laden with the produce of a year's trading, and ready to sail for England. The ships and their cargoes were valued at around £8 million, a sum so great as to render the safety of the annual China convoy a matter of national importance: to put it into perspective, HMS *Victory* had cost £63,176 at the time of her launch, and about another £40,000 by the time she was ready for sea. In time of war the convoy could expect a naval escort, but this had not arrived, and the Indiamen could not wait indefinitely:

the hazards of wind and weather meant that they must sail by early February at the latest.

The Indiamen were impressive ships, amongst the largest and finest of their day, measuring around 1200 tons, armed with around 30 to 36 guns apiece, and closely resembling 64- or even 74-gun ships of the line. The resemblance was, however, purely superficial. The crews seldom numbered much more than from a 100 to a 150 men, of whom perhaps not more than 60 were British, the rest being Chinese or Lascars. By naval standards, this was woefully inadequate to both fight and manoeuvre the ship, which was in any case so weighted down with cargo as to be inevitably slow and cumbersome.

2

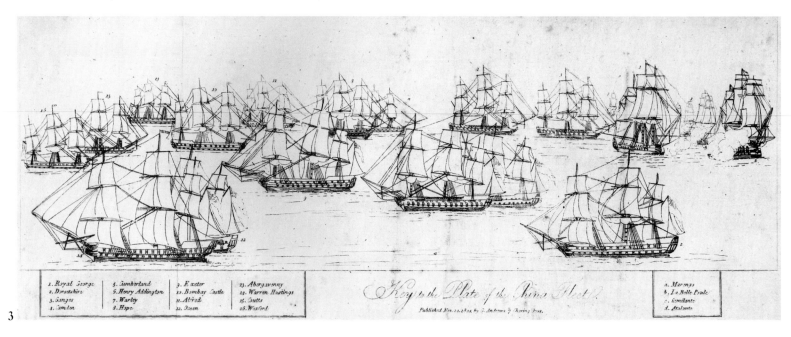

1. Royal George	5. Cumberland	9. Exeter	13. Abergavenny	a. Marengo
2. Dorsetshire	6. Henry Addington	10. Bombay Castle	14. Warren Hastings	b. La Belle Poule
3. Ganges	7. Warley	11. Alfred	15. Cutts	c. Semilante
4. Camden	8. Hope	12. Ocean	16. Wexford	d. Atalante

Key to the Plate of the China Fleet.

Published Nov. 21.1804 by G. Andrews & Faring Fort.

3

4

The guns themselves, whilst technically 18pdrs, were only cannonades, a cheap and nasty cross between the carronade and the long gun, lightweight and short-barrelled, with neither range, accuracy nor weight of metal to match a warship, effective as they might be in deterring the indigenous pirates of the eastern seas.

The fighting reputation of the Indiamen generally was not high. Only a month earlier, on 21 December 1803, a French privateer with only 12 guns to her name had not hesitated to attack what her crew assumed to be two Indiamen (unluckily for her they were in fact two 74-gun warships, *Albion* and *Sceptre*, the convoy's missing escorts). And as the ships presently in China had sailed before the outbreak of hostilities, there had been no opportunity to supplement their crews or armament.

The local Select Committee pondered the problem, and consulted the captains. Captain Henry Meriton thought the combined force of the Indiamen 'respectable in *reality*, and from their numbers much more in *appearance*', an opinion that may have been influenced by an incident in 1800 when the captain of the French frigate *La Medée* surrendered to him by mistake. Captain James Farquharson, on the other hand, had 'far too contemptible an opinion of the East India ships in general to consider them capable of acting in concert so as to be of mutual assistance to each other when opposed by even *an inferior force*'. The risk had to be taken. The convoy was placed under the command of the senior captain, Nathaniel Dance (1), a man of long experience, having first sailed with the Company in 1759 at the age of eleven. He was brave, competent and well-liked (with no great talent for business – the diarist William Hickey remarked that Dance always seemed to be poorer rather than richer at the end of a voyage, although he failed to

connect this with his own habit of demanding free passage for his friends, and favours for the transport of private goods).

Dance had fallen ill whilst in India, and was still in very poor health, but he was resolute in the determination to fight if the convoy was attacked, and strongly supported in this by his fellow-captains, who included John Timins, a one-time naval lieutenant. He also had the assistance of part of the crew of HMS *Investigator*, which had been surveying the coast of Australia under the command of the explorer Matthew Flinders, including the very able Lt Robert Merrick Fowler, Lt Samuel Flinders, and the young John Franklin. Following the loss of their ship they joined Captain Meriton's *Bombay Castle* at Canton 'on account of the reduced state of that ship's company and for the express purpose of assistance in the event of falling in with an enemy'. Fowler and Franklin both transferred to Dance's flagship, the *Earl Camden*, Fowler as an adviser, Franklin to act as signal midshipman.

The China fleet, accompanied by a further eleven 'country' ships – smaller vessels trading between India and the Far East, and bound now for the Indian Ocean – headed for the Straits of Malacca. Dutch hostility closed the Straits of Sunda, Banca and Gaspar to them; while Malacca and Penang were in British possession ('at least they were so by the latest intelligence'). The danger point was Pulo Auro or Aor at the entrance to the Straits, where the French squadron known to have left Pondicherry in July could wait, with the northwest monsoon bringing a constant succession of vessels with all the news from China.

Sure enough, on 14 February, off Pulo Auro, the Indiamen sighted strange sails in the southwest, and there, waiting, were the hunters: Rear-Admiral Linois

1. 'Sir Nathaniel Dance, Knt. Commander of the Earl Camden, in the service of the Honble East India Company, and Commodore of the China Fleet, in the year 1804', engraving by James Fittler after an original by George Dance, published by Joyce Gold, 30 November 1804. *NMM ref PAD3390*

2. 'To the Honble . . . East India Company. This Print of the Action between the China Fleet . . . and a Squadron of French Ships of War . . . Linois in the China Sea, on the 15th Feby 18004 representing the Commencing of the Attack lead on by Capt. I. F. Timmins in the Royal George is . . . dedicated by . . . George Andrews', coloured aquatint engraved by William Barnard after an original by F Sartorius, published by George Andrews, 24 November 1804. *NMM ref PAH8007*

3. 'Key to the plate of the China Fleet', etching published by George Andrews, 24 November 1804. *NMM ref PAH8008*

4. 'The Fleet of the East India Company homeward bound from China under the command of Sir Nathaniel Dance engaging and repulsing a French Squadron . . . near the Straits of Malacca Feby on the XV February 1804', coloured aquatint engraved by William Daniell after his own original, published by the artist, 20 September 1804. *NMM ref PAI6125*

5

5. 'The Homeward Bound Fleet of Indiamen from China under the command of Captain Dance engaging and repulsing a squadron of French Men of War near the Straits of Malacca Feby 15th 1804 . . .', coloured aquatint engraved by William Daniell (1769-1837) after his own original, published by the artist, 10 December 1804.
NMM neg C763

6. 'Repulse of Linois by the China Fleet. This view comprising Portraits of the several Ships in the Fleet on that memorable day, making Sail in pursuit of the retreating Enemy', coloured aquatint produced and published by Robert Dodd, January 1805 [?].
NMM ref PAH8006

with his squadron, the powerful 74-gun *Marengo*, *Belle Poule* (40), *Semillante* (36), *Berceau* (22), and *Aventurier*, a 16-gun Batavian brig. Dance sent Lt Fowler to station the country ships safely to leeward, and formed line of battle. On the *Ganges*, Captain Moffat's crew had to dismantle sixteen butts of water before they could get at the guns, but there was plenty of time – the French worked their way to windward, watched, and waited. Linois had been disconcerted by the militant bearing of the merchantmen, but was now expecting them to make a run for it as soon as darkness fell, after which he could pick them off at leisure. Fowler came back with a number of volunteers from the country ships, and Dance signalled the Indiamen to hold their line, show no lights, and keep their crews in readiness. Linois later wrote irritably that three of the ships kept their lights up all night: he was rapidly becoming convinced that the Indiamen must be stronger than they seemed.

6

In the morning the *Earl Camden*, *Royal George* and *Ganges* hoisted blue ensigns and pendants in naval fashion. When the French continued to hover indecisively, the convoy began to head once more for the mouth of the Straits. At this, Linois moved to attack the rearward ships. Dance immediately signalled the Indiamen to tack in succession, bear down in line ahead, and engage the enemy (2, 3). The leading Indiaman was the largest of them, the *Royal George*, commanded by John Timins. Undeterred by fire opening up from the entire French line, he headed straight for the *Marengo*. The *Ganges* followed, her first shots, fired with more enthusiasm than accuracy, raking the *Royal George*. The *Earl Camden* was next into action, followed by the *Warley*, the *Alfred* and then the *Hope*, so anxious to join in the fight that in trying to crowd past the *Warley* she ran foul of her (4). It was not quite the disciplined line of battle later depicted by artists (5), but to Linois it looked as if the entire fleet was attempting to surround him. His nerve broke, and after a fight that had lasted barely forty minutes, the French ships sheered off and fled to the northwest before the disappointed *Hope* could fire her first broadside.

For two hours there followed the almost incredible spectacle of merchantmen giving chase to a naval squadron (6). They had, fortunately, no chance of catching it, although the *Hope* had a try at cutting off the *Aventurier*. At 4pm Dance called off the pursuit and turned back for the Straits. The *Hope* had the small satisfaction of sending her surgeon to assist the *Royal George*; but although battered the ship was seaworthy, and only one man, a seaman named Hugh Watt, died.

The Indiamen duly reached England with their teas, silks and porcelain intact, and about 80 Chinese plants rare or unknown in England, in a plant cabin specially designed by Sir Joseph Banks, for the royal gardens. Their crews were welcomed as heroes for, whilst the British public were accustomed to naval victories, never before had a 'parcel of half-armed merchantmen' put an admiral to rout. The East India Company presented Dance with 2000 guineas and an annual pension of £500, the members of the Bombay Insurance Company subscribed 45,500 rupees, the Lloyd's Patriotic Fund departed from its usual rule to present him with a sword of honour, and the King knighted him. Timins, Fowler, and all concerned were similarly showered with rewards and honours, and the family of Hugh Watt pensioned. The Society of East India Company Commanders commissioned paintings of Dance and of the battle; and Dance in his turn was able to fulfil a pledge made some years earlier, of the gift of a hogshead of claret and a pipe of madeira, due to the Society whenever he 'should be able to leave off the sea in possession of money sufficient for the comforts of life'. He never went to sea again.

West Indies 1803-1804

ON THE morning of 21 June 1803, just over a month after Britain's declaration of war, Commodore Samuel Hood (1), flying his broad pendant in the *Centaur*, 74, and accompanied by the *Courageux*, 74 and several troop transports, anchored in Choc Bay, St Lucia. By late afternoon the capital, Castries, had surrendered and early next morning the fortress of Morne Fortunée was stormed by the soldiers under Lt-General Grinfield, with 130 casualties, 20 of them fatal. St Lucia having been taken so relatively easily, on the 25th the *Centaur*, with some small craft and transports in convoy, set off for Tobago, arriving there on the 31st. The French colony capitulated next day. By September three Dutch colonies, Demerara (2), Berbice and Essequibo had also fallen, without any loss to the British – one warship, the Dutch corvette *Hippomenes*, was captured at Demerara and taken into service.

The slave uprising in Haiti, with some co-operation from the Royal Navy, had left the French in possession of only St Nicholas Mole and Cape François (3), the latter under siege from the landward, and blockaded at sea by a squadron under Commodore John Loring. The French commandant, General Rochambeau, agreed evacuation terms with Dessalines, the leader of the besieging forces, that the French should quit Cape François by 30 November and return to France with such ships as were in harbour. This was not conceded by Loring, and the ships were still there on the due date. Seeing the blacks' artillery preparing red-hot shot, Loring allowed the ships to sail, but on condition they surrender to him, after being allowed the courtesy of discharging a formal broadside – the threat from Dessaline's soldiers of reprisal and atrocity against the French forces and their dependants were they to remain in Cape François was only too evident. The frigate *Surveillante* (4) was thus captured, but the *Clorinde*, with 900 people on board, grounded while leaving the harbour and lost her rudder. Seeing the artillery preparing to open fire on the helpless ship, Acting Lt Josiah Willoughby of his own initiative boarded the stranded ship, persuaded the French to forego the formalities and hoist British colours, then landed to persuade Dessalines of the folly of firing on the English flag, finally returning to salve the *Clorinde*, which was added to the Royal Navy.

The Dutch Antilles island of Curaçoa had surrendered to just a frigate in 1800, but the colony's mood was more resolute since its restoration at the peace. HM Schooner *Gipsy*, commanded by Lieutenant (Acting) Michael Fitton was sent from Jamaica in June 1803 to warn British shipping at St Anne, Curaçoa's harbour, of the declara-

1

2

3

tion of war. He found there the sloop *Surinam*, repairing but not apparently ready for sea. The *Gipsy* returned to Jamaica: *Surinam*'s commander hurriedly made plans of the harbour and covering batteries. When these were intercepted by the Dutch, he and his ship were seized.

A more powerful expedition was mounted in December, commanded by Captain John Bligh and comprising the *Theseus* and *Hercule*, both 74s, and the frigates *Blanche* and *Pique*, with Fitton's *Gipsy*, to either accept or compel the island's surrender but 'not to hazard more than the object is worth'. The *Vanguard*, which would have been a valuable and perhaps in the event decisive additional force, did not keep a rendezvous.

Arriving off Curaçoa (5) on 30 January, the *Gipsy* entered the narrow defended harbour of St Anne to deliver surrender terms. These were rejected, and a landing party of 600 men was put ashore, while the *Theseus* subdued a battery covering the landing place. With great labour, some guns from *Theseus* and *Gipsy* were carried to a spot commanding St Anne and from

there and a captured Dutch position, a bombardment began, the new battery commanded by Lt Willoughby, saviour of the *Clorinde*. However, answering fire from Dutch batteries, their frigate *Haatslaar* and two privateers in the harbour, continual skirmishing and not least an outbreak of dysentery so weakened the British force— there was even some desertion of a few of *Hercule*'s marines, half of whom were Polish soldiers captured at St Domingue and allowed to enlist—that the affair had to be abandoned at the end of February. Only the junior officers Fitton and Willoughby had really distinguished themselves in the business.

The brief campaign to capture Surinam (6) was more successful. Commodore Samuel Hood's force, the 74-gun *Centaur*, *Pandour* and *Serapis* (44s armed *en flûte*), *Alligator* (28 armed *en flûte*), the sloops *Hippomenes* and *Drake* and the schooner *Unique*, with 2000 troops under Major-General Sir Charles Green in transports, rendezvoused off the Surinam River with the frigate *Emerald* and the brig sloop *Guachapin* on 25 April. Five days later,

4

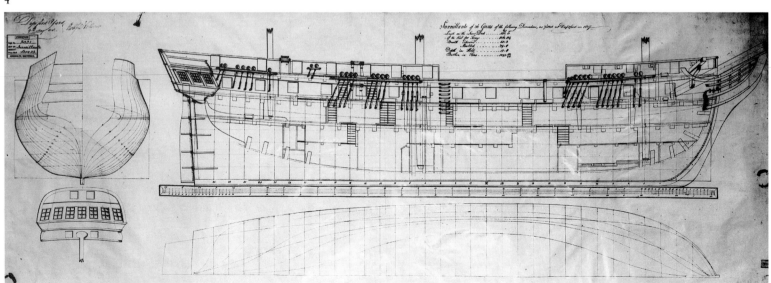

5

700 troops were landed at Warapee Creek, directed by Commander Conway Shipley of the *Hippomenes* and Commander Kenneth M'Kenzie of the *Guachapin*— M'Kenzie's sloop had been unable to make headway against the strong coastal currents, and he and the majority of his crew had come the last 150 miles in boats. In the course of the next few days, despite the difficulty of movement in the swampy jungle terrain, outlying batteries were taken, and further landings made, soldiers and seamen combining well. As final preparations were made for the assault on the colonies main strongpoint, Fort Nieuw Amsterdam, on 5 May the Dutch forces offered terms of capitulation.

The frigate *Prosperine*, a sloop and some gunboats, together with several merchantmen, were taken, and all for the very small loss to the Royal Navy of 5 killed and 8 wounded. The army's loss was also fairly insignificant, only 3 killed, while over 2000 Dutch prisoners and 282 guns were surrendered.

1. 'Sir Samuel Hood, K.B., K.S.F.', mezzotint engraved by Charles Turner after an original by John Dowman, published by George Andrews, 13 November 1806. The portrait shows him after the loss of his right arm in the action of 25 September 1806 off Rochefort.
NMM ref PAD4690

2. 'View of Georgetown, taken from the Entrance of the River Demerara', coloured lithograph engraved by Day and Heghe after an original by W S Hedges, no date.
NMM neg D3460

3. 'Vue de Cap François, Isle St Dominique, prise du Chemin de l'embarcadère de la petit Anse', etching by Nicolas Ponce after an original by Ferdinand de la Brumiere, no date.
NMM ref PA10401

4. Lines and profile of the *Surveillante* as fitted at Deptford in 1807.
NMM neg DR2031

5. 'View of the Town and Harbour of Amsterdam, with Fort George in the Island of Curaçoa, by officers of HMS Sans Pareil', grey wash by Lt Fores and Lt Rea, no date (but apparently after the capture of the island by the British in 1800 or 1807).
NMM ref PA10387

6. 'Paramaribo a la Riviere de Surinam Dedie . . . a sa majeste le Roi des Pais-Bas, Grand Duc de Luxembourg', coloured aquatint engraved by F Dieterich after an original by Pierre Beranger, published by E Masskamp, 15 February 1817.
NMM ref PA10420

6

1

HM sloop of war Diamond Rock

SINCE THE nineteenth century the shore establishments of the Royal Navy have been given names, prefixed by 'HMS' and preserving wherever practical the regimen of a ship. Accordingly, they are jocularly known as 'stone frigates'; but one of their predecessors had a far more literal claim to the description, for in 1804 the Navy seized, fortified and commissioned as a warship the 600ft pinnacle known as Diamond Rock. The strategic importance of this previously uninhabited islet was its position, which due to prevailing winds and currents, dominated the approach to Fort-de-France (or Port Royal as it was called by the British), the capital of Martinique and itself the centre of French power in the Caribbean.

On the renewal of war in 1803 the Leeward Islands squadron under Commodore Samuel Hood found its peacetime numbers too stretched to properly blockade Martinique, and the more enterprising neutrals – usually Americans – ignored the declaration of blockade and unless physically turned back would steal into Fort-de-

2

France through the Fours Passage between the Diamond and the main island. A battery on the Rock would prevent this blockade-running, and with a 40-mile visibility from the summit a valuable signal station could be set up to keep an eye on French activity in their main military and naval base and pass information direct to the British headquarters at St Lucia.

Hood reconnoitred the Rock in his flagship, the 74-gun *Centaur*, and although the obstacles would have looked literally insurmountable to a lesser man, he decided to attempt it. Heavy swells and narrow rock ledges made landings difficult but on 7 January 1804 the first party was put ashore. The island was either sheer cliffs or overhanging caverns for most of its lower circumference, but Hood was lucky in having a First Lieutenant, James Maurice, who was an amateur mountaineer. Maurice, who was to become the Rock's 'governor' with the acting rank of Commander, soon found and marked out a route to the summit; with the aid of pitons and handropes, the climb presented no problems to the agile seamen of a man-of-war.

Thereafter the work progressed steadily with building supplies and skilled specialists – smiths, masons and military engineers – brought in from St Lucia to aid the ships'

crews from the squadron. They constructed a floating landing stage, started work on the gun platforms and built a 3000-gallon cistern for drinking water, since there was no spring and virtually no rain fell on the island. In the middle of January an unusual arrival was a German-born artist, Johannes (often anglicised to John) Eckstein, who received Hood's permission to record for posterity one of the most astounding achievements of the age of sail. He missed the early stages, but his portfolio of aquatints published in 1805 includes all the most spectacular accomplishments and provides a firsthand picture of the curiosities of life on the Rock. He also wrote a series of long letters, whose publication did much to engender public interest and which are still a principal source of information on social aspects of the occupation.

The island's first defences were established at low level on the northeast corner, with two 2-ton 24pdr guns laboriously manhandled ashore, via some tricky boatwork, from the flagship's upper deck battery (1). Mounted about 150yds apart, with a shielded 'covered way' between, they were known as the Queen's and Centaur's batteries, the former threatening the Fours Passage and the latter pointing to the east (2). The Queen's was also the 'quarterdeck', and it was there on

1. 'Picturesque Views of the Diamond Rock . . .Sailors hauling the heavy Cannon, on the foot of the Rock, in a surf', coloured aquatint and etching engraved and published by Joseph Constantine Stadler after an original by John Eckstein, no date. *NMM neg 2057*

2. 'Picturesque Views of the Diamond Rock . . . The Centaur Battery', coloured aquatint and etching engraved and published by Joseph Constantine Stadler after an original by John Eckstein, 1 January 1805. *NMM neg 2056*

3. 'Picturesque Views of the Diamond Rock . . . South East View of the Diamond Rock, with the Cannon being hauled up from the Centaur by the Cable', coloured aquatint and etching, engraved and published by Joseph Constantine Stadler after an original by John Eckstein, 1 January 1805. *NMM neg 2062*

3

4

3 February, with seamen and marines drawn up with due ceremony, that Maurice read his commission; his pendant was run up and *Diamond Rock* entered the Navy List, a 'sloop of war' by dint of his rank of Commander. Curiously, the far-off Admiralty decreed that their latest 'ship' should be called *Fort Diamond* and her sloop-tender

the *Diamond Rock*, but locally the reverse was the case, and this usage has been passed down to history.

The Rock was only partly armed by mid February and the greatest achievement was still to come. Hood had sent to Antigua for two long 18pdrs, which he wanted to mount on the pinnacle of the rock, a position which would give them an extreme range of about two miles but with a reasonable chance of hitting the target at half that. Thanks to outstanding seamanship – not to mention a firm grasp of mechanics – the two guns, their carriages and associated equipment and stores were swayed up to the summit of the southwestern cliff by jackstay direct from the *Centaur* (3), from where they were man-handled to the gun platform (4). Anchoring in the deep water and sharp reefs off the Diamond was always difficult, and *Centaur* twice parted her cables during the week or so it took to complete this stage of the operation.

Fifteen tons of water and provisions for 120 men for four months were also landed, and much of this was hauled to safety from behind the Queen's battery by another jackstay lift. This device used a half-cask, in which a man could ride, as a container and the seamen quickly dubbed this rig 'the Mail Coach' (5). Similar imagination was applied to other aspects of domestic life

5

−the area in which the Governor's tent was pitched became Portland Place− and within a few months the sailor's typical ingenuity had made a barren rock perfectly homely (6). As Eckstein wrote to a friend, 'I am astonished at the efforts of a single ship's crew' and swore, 'I shall never more take my hat off for anything less than a British Seaman!'

Diamond Rock, her tender and boats, allowed Hood to declare Fort-de-France blockaded *de facto* as well as *de jure*, and in her 18 months of existence the stone sloop significantly tightened the British grip on shipping movements around the island. Villaret-Joyeuse, the Governor of Martinique, made one abortive attempt to take the Diamond, but its existence so irritated Napoleon that the first priority for the West Indian expedition of Missiessy was the removal of 'the symbol of British insolence from the doorstep of Martinique'. In fact, this was not to be achieved until Villeneuve threw overwhelming force at the Rock in May 1805 (see pages 120-121), when Maurice (7) was forced to surrender from lack of water after an earth tremor had emptied the cistern.

It did his career no harm, however; but he did become regarded as a specialist in stationary commands, going on to govern Guadeloupe in 1808-9 and Anholt in 1810-

6

12. This last, another commissioned island, provide his finest hour, when on 27 March 1811, he repulsed a major Danish attack, driving off the invaders in a fashion that he might have achieved on Diamond Rock had his water and powder held out.

7

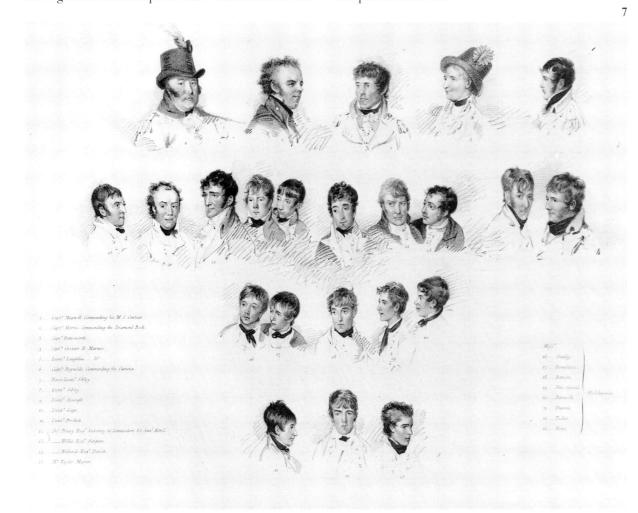

4. 'Picturesque Views of the Diamond Rock . . . General View of the Diamond Rock from the N.E. side with the Queen's Battery', coloured aquatint and etching, engraved and published by Joseph Constantine Stadler after an original by John Eckstein, 1 January 1805. Although described as the Queen's Battery (which was at low level), the engraving seems to represent the Diamond Battery near the summit. *NMM neg 2061*

5. 'Picturesque Views of the Diamond Rock . . . The passage upon the Rock, with the Mail-Coach', coloured aquatint and etching engraved and published by Joseph Constantine Stadler after an original by John Eckstein, no date. *NMM neg 2054*

6. 'Picturesque Views of the Diamond Rock . . . A Lodgement under the Rock on the South-west Side', coloured aquatint and etching, engraved and published by Joseph Constantine Stadler after an original by John Eckstein, 1 January 1805. *NMM neg 2060*

7. 'Picturesque Views of the Diamond Rock . . . Portraits of the Officers of his Majesty's ship Centaur', stipple engraving by W Reynolds after an original by John Eckstein, published by Joseph Constantine Stadler, 1 January 1805. Maurice is second from left in the top row. *NMM neg 2066*

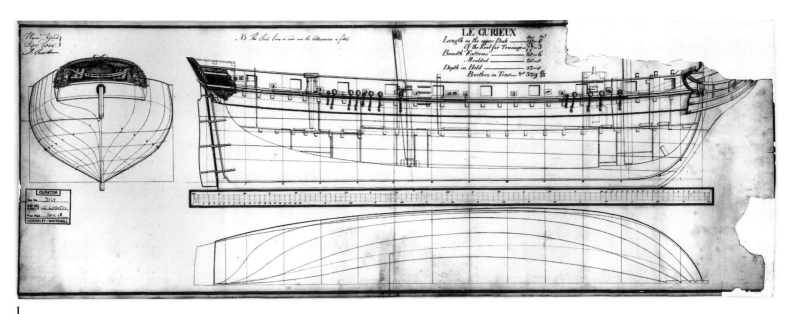

1

Poacher turned gamekeeper

MOST OF the damage to British trade in the West Indies was perpetrated by relatively small vessels of 20 guns or less, and of these the majority were privateers. Captured commerce raiders were often turned into trade protection vessels, but privateers rarely met the Royal Navy's standards in terms of construction (they were too lightly built), fitting (they were not equipped for extensive cruising), or seaworthiness (being often low, wet and over-sparred). A better bet was a purpose-built brig or corvette, but there were few of these available in 1804. In fact, the only warship at Martinique was the *Curieux*, a new and well manned brig of 329 tons armed with sixteen 6pdrs. Built in 1800 at that centre of privateering, St Malo, the brig was a sharp design by the naval *constructeur* Pestel (1). She was said to be a particular favourite of the governor, Admiral Villaret-Joyeuse, and 'the best manned and disciplined sloop in the French service'—although both sentiments were expressed by the British after her capture so the proverbial pinch of salt needs adding.

Early in 1804 Commodore Hood decided that the *Curieux*, then lying in the harbour of Fort-de-France, was a potential threat to the Diamond Rock operation (see previous pages). Accordingly, during the night of 3/4 February he sent in four boats from his flagship, the 74-gun *Centaur*, carrying sixty seamen and twelve marines under the command of Lieutenant Carthew Reynolds. Although the brig herself was well prepared, with loaded guns, boarding netting triced up and a substantial watch on deck, the harbour itself had no guard boat. As a result, the brig was surprised and boarded over the quarters (2), and although the French put up a spirited resistance, she was soon taken and sailed out of the harbour under the fire of three forts and batteries.

Even by the standards of the Royal Navy it was a well executed cutting-out operation, with only six wounded on the British side (although Lieutenant Reynolds was to die of his wounds six months later). Virtually all the French officers were wounded, a midshipman being killed and the captain knocked overboard, while thirty of the crew were seriously wounded, some mortally. Both sides exaggerated the numbers involved, the French making their 72 assailants into 225, but whereas the British put the brig's crew at 100 one of her surviving officers claimed she had only 70 'fighting men'.

As often the case with prizes, command of the *Curieux* was earmarked for the senior officer of the attacking force, but on Reynolds' death it went to his second, George Bettesworth, who was promoted Master and Commander. She became a very effective cruiser on the station, but possibly her finest hour was the capture of the notorious privateer *Dame Ernouf* a year later (3). A twelve-hour chase finally brought the privateer to bay, and a 40-minute gunnery duel followed; both were armed with sixteen 6pdrs, but having a crew nearly twice that of the *Curieux*, the privateer attempted to board. When this was thwarted by the *Curieux* lashing the privateer's jibboom to her fore shrouds, *Dame Ernouf* was raked into surrender.

Curieux continued to play a part in the naval history of the West Indies station, being chosen by Nelson during his pre-Trafalgar pursuit of Villeneuve to carry home his dispatches in June 1805 (see pages 122-123). Crossing the Atlantic *Curieux* spotted the Combined Fleet, and by hurrying the information to the Admiralty played no small part in the dispositions that led to Nelson's last battle. She went back to the Caribbean and her career was eventually ended when she was wrecked on 3 November 1809.

1. Lines and profile of the *Curieux* brig as fitted at Plymouth, September 1805. *NMM ref 7149/48*

2. 'Cutting out the *Curieux* at Martinique, 3 February 1804', oil painting by Francis Sartorius (*c*1775-1831), signed and dated 1804. *NMM ref BHC0537*

3. 'HMS *Curieux* captures the *Dame Ernouf*, 8 February 1805', oil painting by Francis Sartorius (*c*1775-1831), signed and dated 1806. *NMM ref BHC0538*

1

Privateering actions

I N FRANCE, perhaps resulting from a shortage of
conventional naval heroes, there has always been a
tendency to idolise the nation's privateers. Whereas
the Royal Navy names its warships after Nelson,
Rodney, Howe or any number of victors in fleet engagements, the *Marine Nationale* usually has a *Jean Bart, Duguay-
Trouin* or *Surcouf* in its line-up. Celebrations of privateering successes were common subjects for contemporary
French printmakers, and indeed the older generation of
naval historians, who turned the capture of large and
valuable merchantmen into morale-boosting examples
of France's maritime prowess. Needless to say, the British
attitude was diametrically opposite, favouring stories
about plucky merchant ships beating off their assailants
(1), or better still the capture of some particularly trou-
blesome privateer by a nominally inferior warship.

2

This kind of contemporary rhetoric and propaganda
tends to obscure the essential nature of privateering.
First and foremost it was a business, by which investors
hoped to reap a profit from captured ships and their cargoes; it was no part of the privateer's function to take on
warships, which even if of lesser firepower possessed the
significant advantage of better discipline and training in
the arts of war. Merchant ships were their legitimate tar-
gets, very few of which were equipped in any way to
offer effective resistance.

The glory days of French privateering had been under
Louis XIV, when the Sun King's navy had joined forces
with private enterprise to make the *guerre de course* a serious national strategy. What Mahan called 'this profound
delusion' had been downgraded by 1793, but there were
still personalities to stir French patriotism, chief among
them being Robert Surcouf. Directly descended from
his great seventeenth-century namesake, as well as
Duguay-Trouin, he was almost predestined for a career
as what romantics called a corsair. He leapt to promi-
nence in 1796 with the daring capture of an East
Indiaman with a boarding party of only 18 men.
Approaching in the pilot brig *Cartier*, taken earlier, he
was able to surprise the 800-ton HEICS *Triton* lying in
Balasor roads with officers and passengers at dinner (2).
To reinforce the British view that privateers were little
better than pirates, Surcouf had no letter of marque
licensing his activities, and the colonial government of
the Isle de France lawfully claimed all his prizes—
although he eventually got his money by appealing to
Napoleon.

East Indiamen were the largest, and often most valu-
ably freighted, of all merchantmen, so were prime tar-
gets. Conversely, they were the best armed and were
expected to be able to frighten off the average privateer,
if not to actually capture them (3). Surcouf was far from
average, possessing daring, leadership and a willingness
to subject his men to naval-style discipline, but the loss
of the *Triton* was a dangerous precedent, as reported by
the captain of the country ship *Jane* when she was captured as a result of being deserted by two Indiamen:
Surcouf told him 'they were two Tritons, alluding to the
easy capture which he made of that ship, and said the
commanders deserved to be shot. This was the universal
opinion of the French officers. I fear their conduct will
be attended with bad consequences to the Honourable
Company's ships, as it has given the Frenchmen a very
contemptible opinion of them, and will subject them to
many attacks, which a spirited behaviour would have
freed them from.'

In the *Confiance* Surcouf went on to take another, the
Kent, in April 1800, but he was not the only successful
captain in this line. Jacques Perroud of the *Bellone* took

the *Lord Nelson* (4) in the following war, and proved a scourge of Indian Ocean trade until captured by the sloop *Rattlesnake* and the 74-gun *Powerful* on 9 July 1806. Several other privateers were captured around this time but Pellew, the East Indies commander, said 'I reflect with much pleasure on the capture of *La Bellone* in particular, as from her superior sailing, as her uncommon success in the present and preceding war against the commerce, in the Indian and European seas.' The east was a happy hunting ground for French privateers, for besides Surcouf and Perroud signal successes were scored in these waters by Mallerousse, Jean Dutertre and François Lemême, this last taking fifteen prizes in his 12-gun *Fortune* in 1803 alone, until his career was curtailed by the frigate *Concorde*.

For any one of these stars of the profession, there were many trying to grind out a living in command of small vessels in inshore waters—and not always finding the pickings easy (5). Recent research has attempted to evaluate how profitable privateering really was, and there is some suggestion that it was more a negative response to restrictions on conventional trade in times of war rather than a positive espousal of the opportunity for profit. St Malo, Surcouf's home port and a major centre of the *guerre de course*, offers some statistics, which may be indicative: between 1793 and 1801 annual registrations of privateers varied between 5 and 31, taking an average of only about 1.5 prizes per registration while suffering losses

3

between 30 and 100 per cent of their numbers in any one year; for 1803-14 the respective figures are between 4 and 25 registrations making less than 1 prize each while losing up to 70 per cent of their number.

A well documented case is that of Surcouf himself, who after 1803 turned *armateur*, as the privateering entrepreneurs were termed. In all, his eleven ships made fifteen cruises (in two of which no captures were made), one ship was laid up without ever taking a prize, five made losses and only three made a profit; but one, *Marsouin*, made enough to make the whole venture worthwhile. This amounted to a net profit of about

4

5

200,000 *livres* over the period 1803-14, but to put this in context the cost of one his best-equipped privateer, *Napoleon*, amounted to 346,000 *livres*.

Privateering, then, was something of a lottery, with a few rich prizes grabbing attention while many investments were lost altogether. Besides the business risk, it was also a physically dangerous activity. The Royal Navy made a priority of hunting down commerce-raiders, and even well defended harbours need not offer the expected protection — two were taken out of the Spanish port of Muros in one copybook attack, for example (6). During the course of the war 700 privateers were captured and over 20,000 of their men ended up languishing in British gaols and hulks: playing the lottery does not usually have such a positive down side.

---

1. 'The snow Jenny of London . . . on a Voyage from Oporto, being attacked on the 29th Novr 1804 by a French Privateer . . . the Jenny struck the privateer on the quarter . . . tore her mainsail & carried away her boom . . . thus disabled . . . Jenny proceeded . . . lost sight of her', aquatint and etching by W J White and J Jeakes after an original by William Anderson, published by John P Thompson, 11 May 1805.
NMM ref PAH8014

2. 'Abordage du Triton par le Corsaire le Hasard. France Maritime', etching by Pardinel after an original by I Garneray, no date.
NMM neg X164

3. 'The Capture of the La Venus French privateer after a close engagement with the Union Extra East Indiaman . . . with the Ships Sir William Pulteney & Eliza Ann, the Privateer mounting 16 Guns, 12 large Swivells & 73 men, the Union 18 Guns 80 men Lascars . . . 22nd August 1804', coloured aquatint and etching engraved and published by J Ryland, no date.
NMM neg B9275

4. 'Prise de Abordage Du Vaisseau Anglais Le Lord Nelson par le Bellona', coloured lithograph engraved by Sabatier and Lemercier after an original by

A Mayer, published by François De La Rue, no date. The action took place on 14 August 1803 and, typical of the exaggeration of the time, the Indiaman is credited with 50 guns (18pdrs) to the privateer's 32 (8pdrs); the caption ignores the mercantile status of the *Lord Nelson*, 'vaisseau' being the usual technical term for a ship of the line.
NMM neg B9279

5. 'The Cambrian of Boston, Willm Marshall Master, beating off a French cutter privateer, on 23 October 1804', engraving by W Barnard after an original by Joseph Cartwright, 1804.
NMM neg B4022

6. 'To the Right Honble Viscount Nelson . . . The Magnanimous Attack on El Muros Fort and Town, by His Majesty's Ship La Loire . . . which were taken on the 4th of June 1804', aquatint engraved by Chesham after an original by Thomas Buttersworth (1768-1842), published by George Andrews, 6 November 1805. The *Loire* had already been active against privateers, and on this occasion the 490-ton *Confiance* and the brig *Bélier* were cut out.
NMM neg C654

6

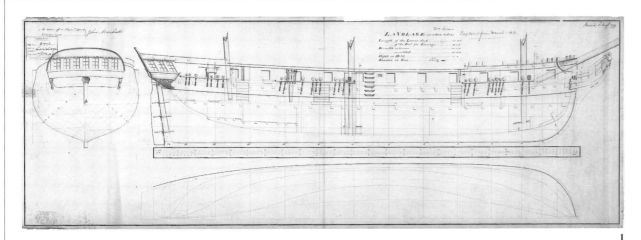

1

Privateering vessels

IN THE mind of an eighteenth-century seaman, the term 'privateer' conjured no image of a particular ship-type. Since a privateer was defined solely by its employment, this is not surprising, and indeed a wide range of craft were used as private warships. Historians have even argued about whether, in general, privateers were purpose-built or simple conversions of the most suitable vessels available. Clearly there are many recorded examples of both, but in all the eighteenth-century wars there was a noticeable delay before the privateering effort gets into its stride, which suggests that a significant proportion of vessels were being built for the task. This is reinforced by analysing the draughts of those taken into the Royal Navy, which admittedly are probably the most overtly warlike.

Although it is true that privateers came in all shapes and sizes, there were certain consistent operating conditions that tended to favour the same design emphases. Most importantly, the *guerre de course* was always the strategy of the weaker naval power, so privateers expected to hunt in waters dominated by the enemy. Secondly, for all the propaganda surrounding successful captains, privateering was a business, expected to return a profit for the investors—this could be maximised by running down and capturing the most merchantmen while suffering the least loss to gear and equipment. Heroic actions were not the point, and engagements with warships were to be avoided at all costs.

These factors put sailing qualities—both speed and weatherliness—at the top of the *armateur*'s shopping list when ordering a privateer. This can be seen in some of the sharp hull forms, like that of *Volage* (1), which was by no means extreme; but low topsides were another common feature, the flush-decked corvette being a popular layout among the larger ships (2). This may seem at odds with the other principal requirement of a privateer, which was to accommodate large complements for use

as prize crews, since the small holds of sharp-built vessels would not stow provisions for a long cruise; however, the calculation was that the prize crews—and perhaps even the privateer herself—could be fed from the captures. In practice, the main drawback of low, fine-lined hulls was poor seakeeping, but presumably the prospect of profit diverted attention from the hours of wet and uncomfortable cruising.

Small ships were more prone to this disadvantage, so a desire to combine speed and seakeeping may have been the reasoning behind some of the larger privateers. Otherwise, there is not much commercial logic to big ships. Not only did they represent a very substantial capital cost, but the risk involved in potential loss was commensurate, and they needed to be disproportionately successful in prize-taking to repay the investment. The merchantmen they sought were lightly armed and poorly manned, so they needed only enough firepower

2

1. Lines and profile draught of the *Volage*, 22, as captured 1798. She was a 522-ton flush corvette built in 1797 and armed in British service with twenty-two 32pdr carronades. *NMM neg DR2776*

2. The 16-gun privateer *Triton*, a watercolour by Duclos-Legris who served in the ship as a seaman for a month in 1797. From the Duclos-Legris ms NMM LOG/F/2. *NMM neg D9058-N*

3. Lines and profile draught of the 18-gun brig *Fantome*, a 384-ton privateer captured in May 1810. Taken off at Deptford Yard, 12 June 1811. *NMM neg DR7151*

4. Sheer and profile of the lugger *Defender*, late the privateer *Bonne Marseilles* of 139 tons, as taken off at Sheerness Yard, 25 April 1810. She was captured in December 1809 by the brig sloop *Royalist*. *NMM neg DR3650*

5. 'Divers Corsaires français de la Méditerranée. Plate 3 in *Collection de Toutes les Especes de Batimens . . .* 1ère Livraison', engraving by J J Baugean after his own original, published by Jean, 1826. *NMM ref PAD7379*

3

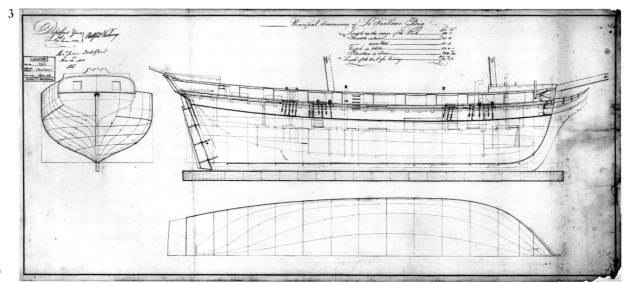

4

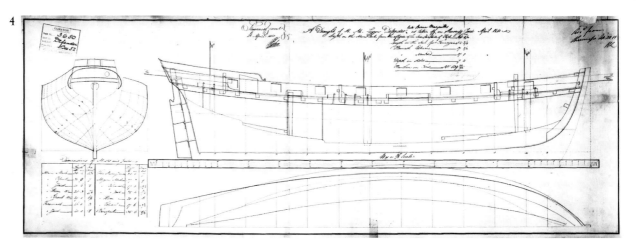

5

to persuade the target that resistance was futile, and even a small vessel with a dozen guns was sufficient to overawe most traders. Conversely, privateer crews lacked real discipline, training and, above all, the necessary motivation for sea battles, so would shrink from engaging even warships of significantly weaker nominal gunpower: what, then, was the point of building a ship with the broadside of a frigate?

Most of those investing in the *guerre de course* understood this, and the general size of privateers was remarkably small. St Malo, for which statistics survive, was a leading centre of the business, and the average burthen of registered ships in this port actually declined from 188 to 76 tons between 1688 and 1813. During the Napoleonic War 41 of 126 registrations were for ships of 100-200 tons, and this seems to have been about the norm for ships operating in the Channel approaches. Brigs were popular (3), since they were both handy and fast, and so many merchantmen were similarly rigged that corsair brigs drew no especial attention to themselves.

In the more confined waters of the Channel itself, privateers were often smaller, some being described by the outraged British as no more than 'rowboats': in fact, most were modifications of the prevailing local craft like the lug rigged *chasse-marée* (4), or big open boats like the pilot gigs and galleys. Barely distinguishable from harmless fishing vessels or coasters, they were a menace to unescorted shipping moving along the English coast to join convoys in the Downs or at Spithead. Much the same applied in the Mediterranean or on the coast of Spain and Portugal, where the danger often came in the form of one of many local craft types, turned into privateers by the simplest of modifications—a few extra men and some small arms—to add to their letter of marque (5).

Privateers could add to their chances of success by careful attention to their appearance. Ideally, they did not want to look too formidable or warship-like from a distance (so their prey took flight and prolonged the pursuit), but exactly the reverse close-up, to overawe the victim. An example of the former was the disguised gunports of the schooner *Marseilles* (6); while Surcouf's *Confiance* was painted black with straw coloured upper-works, deliberately designed to look lower and meaner.

Having established that the efficacy of privateering was dependent on large numbers of small craft, it has to be acknowledged that most of the publicity was generated by the few large and spectacularly successful. At the top of the spectrum, a handful of ships were the size of small frigates, the largest taken into the Royal Navy being the *Brave* of 775 tons, which served as the *Barbadoes*, 28 (7). A high proportion were built in the Biscay ports, probably with a view to blue-water cruising. Bordeaux was responsible for the 491-ton *Confiance* and the 605-ton *Vaillante*, both captured in 1805, while the infamous *Bourdelais*, although built in Nantes, operated out of Bordeaux; before her capture in 1799 this 624-ton ship was reputed to have taken 160 prizes, worth at contemporary value a phenomenal £1 million.

The newspapers of the time credited such vessels with almost supernatural powers: *Bourdelais* was supposedly pursued for over 24 hours by the big frigate *Revolutionnaire* which at times logged over 13kts. However, probably no

6

privateer enjoyed as exaggerated a reputation as Surcouf's famous *Revenant* ('ghost'), with her ghoulish figurehead and apparent ability to appear and disappear at will. This 18-gun 400-ton ship corvette was specially built for Indian Ocean cruising, and was so successful that within a year the local merchants were complaining to the Admiralty that never had British trade 'suffered such a series of single captures, in so short a period, as has been made by the *Revenant* privateer, on the coast of Coromandel'. However, under a different commander she was soon captured, and served as the British sloop *Victor* for a year until again recaptured by a French frigate in 1809, so her sailing qualities were not magical.

Enterprising but circumspect handling made for good privateering, and the success of most of these ships depended a much on the skill of the captain as the quality of their design.

6. 'A Notorious Privateer Marseilles ca. 1810', anonymous watercolour, no date. The schooner has side-hinged half-ports painted the same colour as the topsides, which not only hide their presence but also allow the guns to be fired in an emergency without opening them.
NMM neg X880

7. Lines and profile of the *Barbadoes*, 1816. By this time the vessel was rated as a sloop, but was earlier classed as a Sixth Rate.
NMM neg DR2524

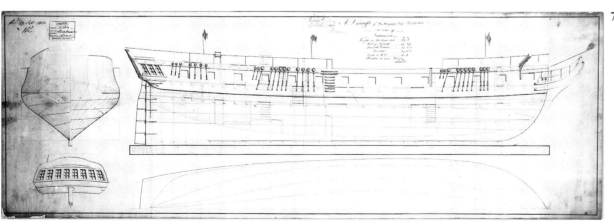

7

1

2

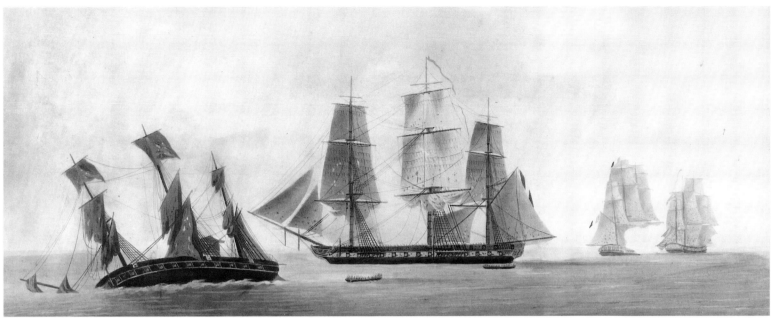

3

An epic of convoy defence

THE COMPLEX workings of seapower are nowhere better demonstrated than in the case of the February 1805 attack on the Mediterranean convoy, and the sequence of events leading up to this incident. Nelson preferred a distant blockade of Toulon to encourage the French fleet to emerge, increasing his chances of destroying it. For this he needed a large number of cruisers to keep a close watch on the harbour and report any sortie while others kept in touch with the French fleet. This left him short of escorts for convoys, but as long as he was bottling up the French fleet the trade needed only relatively small ships that could drive off the kind of minor warships and privateers that always eluded the main blockade. This interlocking nature of fleet strategy and trade protection is most clearly revealed when it goes wrong, as it did early in 1805.

In January Villeneuve's squadron escaped from Toulon during bad weather, and Nelson, fearing as always for Egypt or Naples, went east. An important homegoing convoy of over thirty ships from the Levant sailed from Malta at the same time with a scratch escort force of the Benthamite sloop *Arrow* (see *Nelson against Napoleon*, page 102) and the bomb vessel *Acheron*, a converted merchantman. On 3 February the convoy was sighted by two powerful French frigates – *Hortense*, 40 and *Incorruptible*, 38 – that had become separated from Villeneuve's fleet. Neither of the British ships carried a single long gun, and although *Arrow*'s close-range carronade armament was powerful, the light conditions made it unlikely that she would ever be allowed near

enough a well-handled frigate to do any real damage. Nevertheless, the duty of the British ships was clear, and one thinks of similar decisions made in later ages by captains of outgunned armed merchant cruisers like *Rawalapindi* or *Jervis Bay*.

Taking station between the convoy and its pursuers, *Arrow* and *Acheron* were not in range until the early hours of the 4th. The ensuing battle was one-sided, but not short since it took four hours for two 18pdr-armed frigates to subdue the two British ships (1). *Acheron* was badly damaged aloft early in the action and the brunt of the defence fell to the *Arrow*, whose broadside of fourteen 32pdrs was destructive if the range could be closed. She was finally pummelled into submission by *L'Incorruptible* (2), surrendering after sustaining 40 casualties from her complement of 132. *Acheron* then attempted to make off, but had no chance of escaping *Hortense* and hauled down her flag shortly afterwards. Both ships were defended to the utmost, *Arrow* sinking shortly after the battle (3), and *Acheron* being so badly damaged that she was fired by her captors the following morning. But they had achieved their aim: 31 of the 34 ships in the convoy escaped.

Not surprisingly, both commanders – Vincent of the *Arrow* and Farquhar of the *Acheron* – were promoted to post captains. The President of Farquhar's court martial, Sir Richard Bickerton, summed up the attitude of the Navy and the country as a whole when he said, 'I hope you will soon be called upon to serve in a ship that will enable you to meet *L'Hortense* upon more equal terms. The result of the contest may prove more lucrative to you, but it cannot be more honourable.'

1. 'To the Rt Honble Lord Viscount Nelson . . . This Print of the . . . gallant defence made by . . . Arrow . . . and . . . Acheron . . . against . . . L'Hortense and L'Incorruptible . . . 4th Feby 1805 off Cape Palos', coloured aquatint engraved by J Jeakes after an original by F Sartorius, published by George Andrews 21 October 1805. *NMM ref PAH8037*

2. 'Portrait of French naval vessel L'Incorruptible', black and watercolour pen and ink by Joseph Auge Antoine Roux, no date. *NMM neg A652*

3. "To the Rt Honble Lord Viscount Nelson . . . This Print representing the sinking of . . . Arrow . . . and the Acheron leading away L'Hortense . . . 4th Feby 1805 off Cape Palos', coloured aquatint engraved by J Jeakes after an original by F Sartorius, published by George Andrews 21 October 1805. *NMM ref PAH8038*

1

The convoy system

THE CHIEF tactic in the defence of trade, from the depredations of both warships and privateers, was convoy, a system of gathering shipping together under naval escort which had proved effective since early medieval times. In the vastness of the ocean a convoy was not much easier to locate than a single ship, and since commerce-raiders attracted to such a target were countered by the escort, it was a more cost-effective anti-raider tactic than offensive cruising.

However, by the 1790s convoys were only one element in a sophisticated strategy aimed at making British trade safe. They formed the base of a three-tier system: at the top, the main battlefleets were to checkmate the opposing naval forces by keeping them blockaded; next, independent cruisers and local squadrons patrolled the sea lanes and principal landfalls, and after 1805 a network of coastal signal stations passed information about enemy activity in the offing (1); convoys and their close escort, therefore, were only intended to deter individual raiders, or at most a small squadron. Naturally, the power of the escort depended on the value of the convoy

and the scale of the perceived risk, but generally speaking, in the wars of 1793-1815 substantial losses were only incurred when the system broke down. One may cite Villeneuve's capture of fifteen merchantmen during his brief escape to the West Indies in June 1805, or the unexpected attack on the Mediterranean convoy the previous February, but there was no equivalent of the great disaster to the Smyrna convoy in 1693, nor even to Córdoba's capture of the Levant trade in August 1780.

The pattern of convoys had been refined over the preceding century and the regular ebb and flow of trade was well understood—most movements were seasonal, for weather reasons (like ice in the Baltic, Caribbean hurricanes, or the monsoon winds of the Indian Ocean), or determined by the natural cycle of the harvest. Originally, merchants had been obliged to petition the Admiralty for individual convoys, but by this period there was regular liaison with committees of merchants in particular trades or ports to establish requirements; the resulting convoys were announced through Lloyd's List or bulletins in the Royal Exchange. A rendezvous

1. 'Fannet point and Signal station, Lough Swilly', Plate 481 from the *Naval Chronicle* 37 (1817), published by Joyce Gold.
NMM neg D9049

2. 'The Windham East India Man with the Fleet sailing from St Helena, under convoy of His Majesty's Ship Monmouth', coloured aquatint engraved and published by Charles Turner after an original by John Collins, 24 April 1809.
NMM neg 6169

3. 'Flag tables of order of sailing headed Distinguishing Vanes & Pendants to be used by the following ships under convoy of HMS Diomede', black pen and ink by Charles Copland, c1810. The names of the ships suggest an East Indies convoy.
NMM ref PAF2362

4. 'The Triton lying to', watercolour by Nicholas Pocock (1740-1821), 1808. The frigate is assembling her convoy, possibly in St Helens roads—although the rendezvous is often given as 'Spithead' the anchorage was actually in this sheltered stretch of water off the Isle of Wight.
NMM neg B5501

2

would be appointed with dates of sailing, and since the ports and rivers themselves were too crowded, in effect the assembly points were reduced to the Nore (for shipping destined for Canada, the Baltic and northern Europe), or Portsmouth (for all other trades); there were also calling points en route where other ships might join. Once at sea the courses steered emphasised safety over speed—for instance, the outward West Indies trade sailed via Cork, Madeira, and Barbados (even though the last was off course for Antigua or Jamaica ships, but avoiding the worst of the privateer menace); evasive routeing was also practised, so that in the Mediterranean convoys proceeded along the north African coast, as far from French bases as possible.

The escort did not necessarily cover the whole voyage: Hudson's Bay ships were only accompanied to and from the Orkneys, while East India ships were usually only seen safely out of Soundings, although returning ships were escorted back from St Helena (2). The escort was sometimes extended to the Cape, and more generally any escort might be reinforced for the most dangerous stretch of voyage, and patterns changed in response to strategic developments—such as the French occupation of the Ionian Isles—or tactical ones, such as the breakout of a French squadron.

Convoy was so important that it was governed by legislation, and by the 1798 Convoy Act it became compulsory for all ships, except those of the East India and Hudson's Bay companies, Irish-bound ships and fast and well-armed independents specifically licensed as 'runners'. As in Britain's twentieth-century wars, there were never enough escorts for frequent sailings, so convoys tended to be large and occasional. Merchants complained about the glut on the market caused by such arrangements, but were compensated by more favourable insurance rates.

The discipline of a convoy was laid down in printed sailing instructions issued by the escort commander to all masters of ships in convoy, giving signals and instructions for station keeping etc, and sometimes additional orders (3). Unless these had been received, a ship was not reckoned to have joined its convoy and any insurance claim on a policy 'to sail with convoy and return' would not be honoured. Most naval officers abhorred convoy duty—merchant ships were slow, undermanned, and often skippered by bloody-minded individualists—and keeping them together was always a most difficult task (4). Lloyd's, the merchant committees and the Admiralty co-operated to act against Masters who broke convoy, or conversely naval officers who behaved tyrannically or neglected their charges. There was little profit in such duty: few privateers were a match for a naval vessel, even a sloop, and they had no interest in battle in

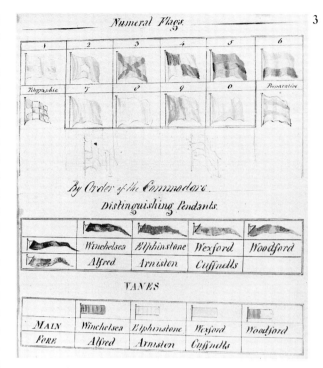

any case. Furthermore, the only glory was likely to be pyrrhic: if attacked by overwhelming force, the safety of the convoy was always paramount, and the escort was expected to sacrifice itself, a famous example being the *Arrow* and *Acheron*.

However unromantic and inglorious, convoy was a very successful tactic. It has been calculated that during the war of 1793-1801, merchant ship losses amounted to only 3.44 per cent of all sailings (2.75 if recaptures are deducted); this would be doubled as a percentage of round voyages, but losses from marine risk were at least as great. As a further measure of the effectiveness of trade protection, the British merchant marine grew from 16,000 ships of 1.5 million tons in 1792 to 24,500 vessels of 2.6 million tons in 1814. As Northcote Parkinson pointed out, it is a pity that no nineteenth-century study was made of the efficacy of convoy, for it would surely have been introduced promptly in 1914, avoiding much needless loss of merchantmen during the First World War.

1

1. 'La Frégate la Ville de Milan
Capitaine Reynaud enlève à l'abordage la Frégate anglais la Cléopâtre
dans le passage des Iles Bermudes',
tinted lithograph after an original by
P C Causse, published by Charpentier
pere, fils et Cie, no date.
NMM neg X2026

2. 'To Captain Z Mudge . . . of the . . .
Blanche . . . the gallant defence made
by that Ship in the Sombero Passage
on July 19th 1805 against a French
Squadron', coloured aquatint after an
original by F Sartorius, published by
George Andrews, 1 September 1806.
NMM ref PAH8041

3. 'The St Fiorenzo, Captn Henry
Lambert, having Recaptured the
Thetis Country Ship in the Indian
Seas tacking to engage La Psyché
French National Frigate Captn
Bergeret & L'Equivoque Privateer . . .',
coloured aquatint and etching by
J Hamble after an original by S C
Clarke, published by Edward Orme,
1 January 1806.
NMM neg A565

Frigate actions

NOT ONE of the three major frigate actions in the period following the breakdown of the Peace of Amiens gave much support to the idea of automatic British superiority in single-ship actions. All three happened in early 1805, two in the West, and one in the East Indies.

On the morning of 16 February 1805, off Bermuda, the *Cleopatra*, 32 sighted the *Ville de Milan*, 40. The *Ville de Milan* was on her way back from Martinique to France with despatches and (as was usual) had orders to avoid action. After a day's chase, the *Cleopatra* got within ¾ mile and tried the range with her bow chasers, the *Ville de Milan* replying with an accurate fire from her stern chasers. The *Cleopatra* was forced to steer for a point broad on the *Ville de Milan*'s quarter. When she had closed to within a cable's length, the *Ville de Milan* luffed up and fired two broadsides. In the close action which followed, the *Cleopatra* knocked away the *Ville de Milan*'s main topsail yard; but she herself suffered serious damage which greatly reduced her manoeuvrability. Overhauling the

Ville de Milan, the *Cleopatra* tried to rake her. Just then, a shot struck her wheel, making her ungovernable. At once the *Ville de Milan* drove her bows upon the *Cleopatra* and, her musketry clearing her opponents deck, she carried the *Cleopatra* by boarding (1). Immediately after the surrender, the *Cleopatra*'s bowsprit and main and fore masts went by the board, leaving only the mizzen standing, but during the night after the action the Frenchman's main and mizzen also went. Some days later, on 23 February 1815, both vessels were sighted by the *Leander* (50). Neither was in a condition to offer resistance, and both were soon captured.

On 19 July 1805 the *Blanche*, 36 was on her way from Jamaica to Barbados with despatches when she ran into a small French squadron to the north of Puerto Rico, consisting of the *Topaze*, 40 (Captain Baudin), the *Département des Landes*, 22, *Torche*, 18 and *Faune*, 16. The *Blanche* first mistook them for part of the homeward-bound West India fleet, but when they closed fast and made no reply to signals, Captain Mudge took alarm and endeavoured to escape. A few shots were put in by the *Département des Landes* and the *Torche*, but despite the implications of contemporary prints (2) in the ensuing action *Topaze* did most of the work. After half an hour, the *Blanche* attempted to cross the *Topaze*'s bows and rake her; but the *Topaze* luffed up sharply, passed under the *Blanche*'s stern and raked her instead, wounding her masts, holing her, shooting her sails and rigging to pieces and dismounting several of her guns, whilst suffering only slight damage herself. After 2¼ hours of action, the *Blanche* surrendered. She had lost more than her opponent and sank some hours after the action. It is difficult to escape the conclusion (reinforced by other episodes in his career) that Mudge was inept, his crew slack, and that neither measured up to Captain Baudin and his crew.

On 13 February 1805 the 18pdr 36-gun frigate *San Fiorenzo* was cruising off the coast of Malabar in search of the *Psyché*, 32, and sighted the French frigate with two of her prizes, one of which she was arming under the name of *Equivoque*. The British ship had to chase for nearly two days in light and baffling winds before she got within range of the *Psyché*, whereupon the two frigates hammered one another. The British ship had her rigging cut up badly but, firing into her opponent's hull, considerably reduced her gunpower. Both sides beat off the others' boarders, and continued to batter at each other. For a while they lay unable to hit each other, but the larger British ship managed to repair her rigging, and the *Psyché* only had two effective guns left, virtually no ammunition, and over half her crew casualties. Captain Bergeret surrendered after a skilful, brave and tenacious defence against the odds.

2

3

Ships of the Royal Navy: the 12pdr frigate

I N THE French navy the introduction of the 12pdr frigate had followed close on the heels of 8pdr ships, the prototype, *Hermione*, being launched in 1748. In Britain the 12pdr ship was adopted at the outbreak of the following war in 1756, with designs for 32-gun and 36-gun classes. Both carried main batteries of twenty-six 12pdrs, but the secondary armament was six and ten 6pdrs respectively. These ships were regarded as replacements for the old two-decked 44s, but because one deck of the new frigates was unarmed they were seen in some conservative circles as relatively expensive ships judged on a firepower-to-tonnage criterion. As a result, only three 12pdr 36s were ordered (the *Pallas* class), and the size of British 32s was held down to about 700 tons for

3

4

the whole thirty-year period in which they were built (1). For their time they were excellent ships, and many enjoyed long service careers; the very first 32, the *Southampton*, for example lasting from 1757 until wrecked in 1812 (2).

To the British Admiralty the most important criterion for cruising ships, perhaps even more than for battleships, was numbers. There were never enough frigates and the more theatrical admirals claimed they would die with 'want of frigates' engraved on their hearts, so the small-ship policy made strategic sense because it maximised the number of ships that could be built for any given budget. However, it made real sense only when Britain enjoyed naval supremacy, when the navy was not forced at the level of fleet, squadron or individual ship to act on the defensive. This was not the case during the American Revolutionary War, when Britain lost command of the seas to her French, Spanish, Dutch and American opponents. A new confidence in the French navy made 12pdr frigates as large as 900 tons and more very formidable opponents, threatening to completely outclass the small British equivalents.

This lead to some radical rethinking at the Admiralty, and the rapid introduction of three major innovations. The first, and arguably most important, was copper sheathing, tested on the 32-gun frigate *Alarm* in 1761 and subsequently extended to the whole cruising fleet. This had the effect of lengthening the amount of time ships

could spend at sea between dockings – in effect multiplying the number of ships available for duty at any one time – and also made ships faster and allowed them to retain their performance longer since it reduced frictional resistance and slowed the rate of fouling compared with earlier modes of sheathing (anti-fouling). The second innovation was the carronade, which

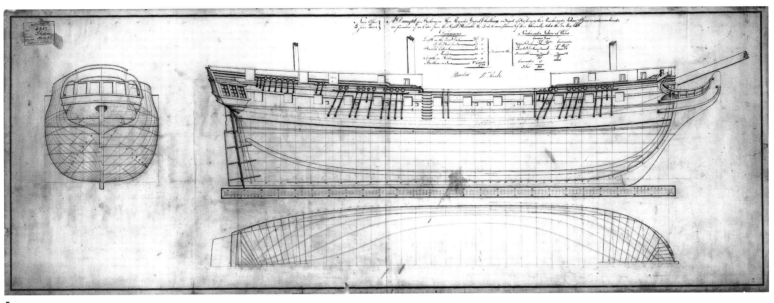

5

although short-ranged fired a heavy shot for its weight. This was ideal for frigates, with large areas of their upperworks unarmed, so there need be no (or at least minimal) loss of long guns. The augmented firepower provided by these new weapons went a long way to redressing the balance between British frigates and their far larger French and Spanish opponents. The third novelty was a quantum leap in firepower with the introduction of 18pdr-armed frigates in the late 1770s (see *Fleet Battle and Blockade*, pages 55-57).

Despite a rearguard action by the two-decked 44, the 18pdr frigate had proved itself by 1783 and thereafter no new 12pdr designs were ordered. There were a few tardy completions of the wartime building programmes, and 18pdr ships were still very rare, so 12pdr ships dominated the Navy List up to the end of the French Revolutionary War.

Year	No in Sea Service	No in Ordinary or Repairing
1793	21	23
1797	50	9
1799	45	13
1801	43	1
1804	22	11
1808	35	8
1810	32	3
1812	20	5
1814	11	0

The vast majority of ships added to the 12pdr classes were prizes, some of the ex-French and Spanish frigates being as large as British 18pdr ships (3). The French built few 12pdr frigates after the outbreak of war with Britain,

one of the last being the *Chiffonne* (4), launched at Nantes in 1795. There were a few new British-built 12pdr ships, but no new designs – the old *Richmond* class 32 of 1756 was revived in modified form by St Vincent's administration in 1804 for eight ships (one subsequently cancelled) of the *Thames* class (5), but the fir-built *Shannon* and *Maidstone*, and James Gambier's experimental *Triton* were designed for 18pdrs and reduced to 12s during construction. By the 1790s the 18pdr was the norm for frigate main batteries.

In terms of employment, the introduction of 18pdr frigates rendered their 12pdr-armed sisters second-class ships, but such was the shortage of big frigates in the 1790s that a few 12pdr ships found themselves operating in key roles. For example, among the 18pdr ships of Warren's crack squadron in the mid 1790s was Sir Richard Strachan's *Concorde*. She was a big ex-French 12pdr 36, and such ships remained popular on the strength of excellent sailing qualities, but they were usually regarded as too weakly-built for the rigours of close blockade. The 12pdr ships were not popular for fleet duties in general, especially when frigates came to be regarded as a means of harrying and if possible delaying fleeing battle squadrons, as with Strachan's destruction of Dumanoir after Trafalgar. Here his four frigates played a crucial part, but the 12pdr *Santa Margarita* was far more seriously damaged than the other, 18pdr, ships.

As the war progressed and more 18pdr ships entered service, there was a tendency to consign the 12pdr ships to more distant and minor stations. A number continued to serve in the North Sea – the traditional cinderella of British fleets – but increasingly they were to be found in the East and, particularly, the West Indies, where they still outgunned the average privateer that formed much of the threat to commerce.

Part II — THE INVASION THREAT

IN 1803 Napoleon based his plan on the experience he had so far accumulated of invasion projects. He had been placed in charge of the invasion attempt in 1798 but had then cancelled it on account of the greater attraction of the invasion of Egypt. That failure had taught him much: especially the need for long-term planning, for the proper co-ordination of the navy and the army, and for the logistical supply of both. In 1803 the idea of invading England was already taking practical shape by the time Britain declared war on France in May. French armies were not needed elsewhere, but speed of invasion was of the essence, for British strategy was to enlist continental allies and Britain had to be subjugated before those allies could become dangerous.

Men, horses, equipment and supplies would have to ferried across the Channel, and on such a scale that any landing would be self-sufficient until the main forces opposing the attack had been crushed and a bridgehead established so large as to include London and permit the French forces to live off the land as they had done elsewhere in Europe. The invasion attempt demanded the creation of special embarkation port facilities and landing craft. The first order for such craft had been placed in March 1803. Six days after the British declaration of war on 18 May, 'Citizen Forfait', Pierre-Alexandre Forfait, the former Minister of Marine, was appointed Inspector-General of the National Flotilla, later known as the Imperial Flotilla, to be responsible for it construction and management. He worked under Rear-Admiral Denis Decrès, who had replaced him at the Ministry in March 1801 when Decrès was only forty years old. An able and decisive naval officer who had caught Napoleon's attention, Decrès was egotistic and disparaging of Forfait's work.

The combination of the ambition, deference and goading of these three energetic men was expected to produce a flotilla capable of carrying an army, estimated in September 1803 at 114,000 troops and 7000 horses for cavalry and artillery. As building proceeded, moreover, the army capable of being transported was enlarged. By August 1805 the planned landing craft were sufficiently numerous to carry nearly 167,000 men across the Channel, though no more than 93,000 men were immediately available at the Channel ports, the closest other reinforcement being stationed at Paris.

Vessels of all sizes were ordered to be built not just in naval dockyards, but in hundreds of private shipyards on the rivers as well as on the sea coasts of France. Orders were placed as far east as the Rhine, and in Bruges, Ghent, Liège, Namur, Lyons, Compiègne, Strasbourg, Lille, Amiens, Versailles, Toulouse, Grenoble and Rouen; 300 'commercial vessels' were ordered to be purchased, capable of holding at least 90 to 100 men each. On 5 July 1803 construction orders included 50 *prames*, 300 *chaloupes canonnières*, 300 *bateaux canonniers*, 50 *caïques* (longboats), 10 *bombardes* (bomb vessels), 700 *péniches*, 1000 *chasses-marées* (coasting luggers), making a total of 2410 vessels.

Of these four types of landing craft, orders were placed for 1301 by the end of 1803. Yet, they proved poor bargains. The prototype *prames*, with very shallow hulls, held the wind badly and could not be relied upon to steer a straight course; the hulls of the *chaloupes* were generally too weak for their loads; and even moored in sheltered waters, choppy seas came over the gunwales of the *bateaux*. In bad weather in July 1804 Napoleon conducted a trial of some of the landing craft, when an estimated 400 soldiers and seamen were drowned. Nevertheless, by then he was committed to them; indeed the pace at which orders had been carried out meant that most were built of green timber and had soon to be repaired or rebuilt.

By May 1804 Forfait had 1273 vessels of all classes ready for the flotilla. He should have been assisted by the extension of construction to Dutch territories following the Convention between France and the Batavian Republic of 25 June 1803 when the Dutch were required to provide 100 *chaloupes canonnières* and 250 *bateaux canonniers* with 100 other transport vessels, half of them for horses, with all their crews, equipment and supplies. However, these were slow coming forward and even then were ill equipped, partly because the Dutch territories were already exhausted of war supplies.

As the invasion plan became known among the French people, would-be inventors from among them came forward with less conventional ideas. One suggestion was for a surprise attack via a Channel tunnel; another was for giant hot-air balloons each carrying 3000 men and 600,000-pound payload. Among the more practical projectors was the twenty-nine year old American Robert Fulton, who in 1797 had proposed to the French naval ministry a three-man, 21ft submarine or diver. At that time the French government were wary of advancing funds for a project they feared the British might quickly copy, so Fulton had raised the cash himself and built a prototype, the *Nautilus*, which was successfully tested in the River Seine in April 1800. In October 1800 and July 1801 it even placed mines called 'torpedoes' against ships in the harbours at Le Havre and Brest and blew them up. Nevertheless, funding was still not forthcoming to build more and better submarines. In September 1803 Fulton was interviewed by Decrès, and offered by letter to Napoleon to build sufficient submarines to blockade the River Thames and the approaches to the British naval dockyards. However, Fulton's proposal was turned down, and in 1804 he crossed the Channel to offer his invention to the British government.

By then, Napoleon had decided on the distribution of his force. Possibly as a reserve or second wave, Flushing was to hold 100 *chaloupes canonnières* and 200 *bateaux canonniers*, with the main invasion force further south. Its right wing of 300 vessels, enough to carry 30,000 men, was to sail from Ostend and Nieuport. Its

FRENCH INVASION of BUONAPARTE Landing in Great-Britain.

'French Invasion or Buonaparte landing in Great Britain', coloured etching published by H Humphrey, 10 June 1803. It is a long-established tradition for the British to lampoon their most serious enemies, and not everyone shared the optimism of this cartoon.   NMM neg B5143

centre was to be grouped in the ports of Dunkirk, Gravelines and Calais, which would hold 300 of the larger vessels. Its left wing was to be held in Ambleteuse, Boulogne and Étaples, where there would be 2380 vessels capable of transporting 100,000 men and 3000 horses.

Inevitably, few of the ports had wharfage and quays sufficient to embark men and horses in such numbers into invasion craft that had to be able to float at all stages of the tide to permit departure *en massse* when required. Napoleon himself took much interest in ensuring the ports were adapted to suit the craft he had ordered. At Boulogne, for example, he ordered the creation of a kilometre of new quays and the excavation of a large artificial basin on the south bank of the River Liane capable of containing 100 *chaloupes canonnières*. The course of the river itself was redirected and its flow controlled by the construction of a retaining dyke and locks. Forfait also proposed a 'floating fort' (which did not actually float, but being surrounded by water at high tide, appeared to) for Boulogne, and this became known as Fort

Rouge. The forts *de l'Heurt* and *de la Crèche*, were also built on outcropping rocky headlands on either side of the port to protect its flanks.

Such protection was indispensable, for the port of Boulogne suffered regular bombardment from British ships offshore. The works there were so disrupted during September 1803 that twenty batteries had to be established along the sea front between the two flanking forts. By the summer 1804 that port was protected by 180 guns, howitzers and mortars. However, they still did not deter British ships. Napoleon himself witnessed an attack on 45 brigs and 43 luggers before Boulogne by five British ships on 19 July 1804; about seven French vessels were sunk or wrecked, and over 400 seamen killed or drowned. To keep the British vessels at bay and to provide cover for French craft creeping along the coast, Napoleon created ten new batteries between Boulogne and Calais, a distance of 42 kilometres. They contained long-range mortars as well as 24pdr and 36pdr cannon and were manned by 'coastguard artillerymen'. To cover

the coast south of Boulogne, as far as Le Havre, six artillery flying columns were established, each of four guns and fifty horses.

While these preparations for invasion were going on, the British government were not neglectful of preparations for defeating them. St Vincent at the Admiralty in 1803 established a 'triple line of defence'. The first line, consisting primarily of frigates and gun-vessels, was deployed along the French and Dutch coasts, attempting to keep even fishing craft in port. Sir Sidney Smith commanded a squadron of five small vessels off Flushing until May 1804, but his was part of a command containing over 170 vessels of all classes, including 21 ships of the line and 29 frigates, which blockaded the whole coast of Holland and the Channel coast of France.

The second line was for the defence of the English coast and was drawn from a squadron of ships of the line and frigates, based in the Downs, specifically intended to contest the passage of an invasion force. Nelson had commanded that force in 1801 and it was now reinforced. Behind this line, in all the estuaries and inlets along the coasts of southern Britain, lay the gunboats of the Sea Fencibles: some 800 vessels, often former fishing vessels and river craft armed with cannon, and manned by volunteers numbering about 25,000 men by May 1804. They were organised in twenty-eight coastal divisions stretching from as far west as Swansea and Hartland Point to as far east as Great Yarmouth; there were in addition divisions as far north as Whitby, Berwick and the Firth of Forth.

The value of this third line was always contentious, and some argued that it was formed as much to absorb energetic volunteers as to provide a realistic opposition to landing craft. St Vincent, for example, maintained that the French craft could not approach a single ship of the line, or even a frigate, without inevitable destruction, so this last-ditch defence was unnecessary. By May 1804 Pitt had adopted the same reasoning. Although he had attacked Addington's administration for lack of preparation with regard to small craft, when he came to office he ordered forty-five new 12-gun brigs and thirteen 18-gun brig sloops for the Navy rather than attempting to enlarge the numbers of shallow-water craft manned by the volunteers.

This was partly because the scale of volunteer forces was becoming unwieldy. By the end of 1804 the rosters of volunteer regiments recorded over 300,000 men in England and over 70,000 in Ireland. They included both infantry and cavalry, known as yeomanry. In 1803 men between the ages of sixteen and sixty had inundated recruiting offices, too many to arm at once, and even when armed of doubtful quality against Napoleon's regular troops. Nevertheless, they were keen and colourful, good for local morale, and of many potential uses. They were stationed in towns, at route junctions and canals to relieve regular troops of sentry duties, and, equipped with farm carts, provided a transport service for 'camp kettles and necessaries'.

More reliable in case of invasion was the militia, raised by the Home Secretary working through the Lord Lieutenants of the counties. The Militia Act of 1802 was intended to raise 51,500 men between the ages of seventeen and forty-five, to be known as the Army of Reserve. It was bolstered by a supplementary Act the fol-

lowing year adding another 25,000 men to the force. Recruited through the incentive of £7-12-6d bounty, the militia men enrolled for five years service anywhere in Britain. By May 1804 45,492 men had come forward, but over 2000 had been discharged unfit, nearly 600 had died, and 5561 had deserted, while 7000 had been deemed too young or undersized and had been drafted to garrison battalions to grow up! The country had thus obtained only about 30,000 effectives. Nevertheless, officered on the whole by men who had seen service in the regular army, they were administered by the General Officers commanding the military districts in Britain and, when trained, revealed a discipline that promised close support for the regular troops. Furthermore, the facility that permitted militia to transfer to the regular army obtained for the latter some valuable recruits.

After the Peace of Amiens, these regular forces totalled 132,000 men of which 50,000 were stationed overseas, especially in the West Indies where they permitted the rapid reconquest of the French colonies of St Lucia, Tobago, Demerara and Essequibo after war resumed in 1803. With bounties as large as £60, the remaining 81,000 at home were increased to 116,000 by the beginning of 1805. The force might have been greater but for the desertion and the practice of permitting substitutions. Even so, combined with the militia and supported by the Volunteers, the regiments available for defence against invasion were thought to be quite enough to oppose any force Napoleon could land on a British coast.

Initially both militia and regulars were dispersed in large military camps at Beachy Head, Southbourne, Brighton, Bexhill, Hastings, Winchelsea and Rye. However, as the threat of invasion intensified, arrangements were made to concentrate these forces at immediate notice. When he became Minister for War in July 1805, Castlereagh instructed the Commander-in-Chief of the army, the Duke of York, to establish a striking force of 30,000-35,000 infantry and 8000-10,000 cavalry, stationed near Cork, Portsmouth and east Kent with designated transports, equipped and victualled nearby, capable of carrying 10,000 men in one lift anywhere a French army threatened.

All along the British southern coast batteries were established at strategic points and old forts were manned. Around London a breast-

work was built stretching from Blackheath to Battersea in the south, and from the River Lea to Highgate and Wisden Green in the north. Plans were made to flood Romney Marsh. Behind it, begun in 1803 and completed in 1806, was the Royal Military Canal: a waterway intended to act as barrier to a landing that crossed the marsh before it could be flooded. The earth dug out in its construction acted as a rampart overlooking the canal and sheltered a military road.

In addition, along the south coast seventy-four Martello towers were built between 1803 and 1805, providing not only lookout stations, but also defensive points to which local forces might rally. Thirty-foot high, with solid walls 6-9ft thick, they were built to withstand short sieges. With their flat, bomb-proof roofs, and one or two guns capable of being traversed to command a wide front, they were intended to hold up any forces that might land long enough to permit the arrival in strength of the British army.

Just in case of a landing, preparations were made for quick communication throughout the country. The naval bases, Chatham, Sheerness, Portsmouth and Plymouth were already linked to the Admiralty by shutter telegraph. For the general population, beacons were prepared to communicate the event of a landing throughout the country: faggots, wood and tar were prescribed for the fire by day; three or four barrels of tar were to be added at night.

In Whitehall, the focus of national tension within Britain, the propositions of Robert Fulton received a cautious welcome. In the summer of 1804 any means of destroying the gathering flotilla across the Channel were considered. His floating mines, known as torpedoes or carcasses, designed to blow up by time fuse against a ship's hull, or allowed to float against the hull with a current, were tried by Sir Home Popham at Boulogne but were diverted by strong tides, exploded prematurely, or failed to ignite. Nevertheless, in trials conditions, one blew up a brig at Walmer, and they were tried again off Boulogne by Sir Sidney Smith in November 1804. This time, however, the weather prevented the mines from being placed where they might do harm. Wind and rain also prevented Smith from using the newly introduced Congreve rockets effectively.

That summer Smith had employed himself at Dover building two prototype catamarans, and in September gained approval for their trial by the Navy. One was 48ft long, carried masts on the beams joining the two hulls, which could also be rowed with eight oars a side. The other was twice the size, yet both drew only 18ins of water. Mounted with guns and manned by Smith and twenty members of the Royal Artillery, they had successfully sailed and fired their guns in calm water.

In the event Smith's larger vessels were not used to attack the French flotilla. But the ideas of Smith and Fulton were combined that autumn in the development and use of 'cata-marans' that contained explosives: 21ft long, twin hulls were lead lined and took about forty barrels of gunpowder each, which were detonated by a clockwork timer. Equipped with a grappling iron, the catamaran had to be towed, then allowed to drift, against enemy shipping. Five were employed alongside fireships in an attack at Boulogne early in October 1804. However only one did damage, and that because it was chased by a *péniche*, which got foul of it, and was accordingly blown up with the loss of her commander and 13 men.

Yet even this mild achievement was counter-productive. A cry went up on both sides of the Channel against this resort to unchivalrous weapons. More practically, henceforward the French protected their flotilla craft by partially surrounding them with booms and chain cables. Above all, the trial failed to impress Lord Keith who was present and never a supporter of 'gimcrack' weaponry. Although the catamaran-torpedo was used again in December 1804, among the higher command of Britain's naval forces, attention turned to contesting the real naval threat posed by Napoleon. That December Spain entered the war in full alliance with France and Napoleon had their combined fleets with which to invade the Channel, and it was to this objective that he now turned his mind.

A chart of the Straits of Dover, showing the main French invasion ports from Ostend to Étaples, and the short distance to be crossed. The Downs anchorage off Deal was the centre of local British naval defences. From Naval Chronicle *XXXVI (1816), Plate CCCCLXXVI.   NMM neg D9041*

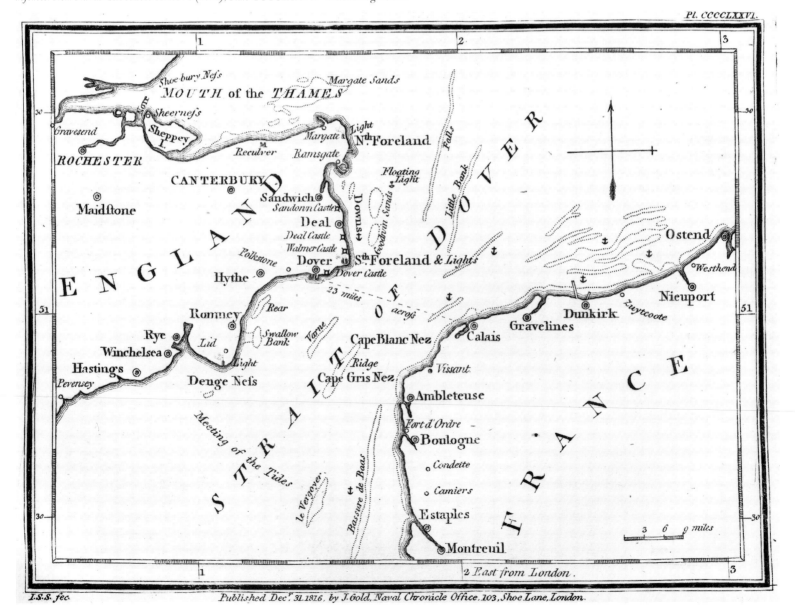

1

Invasion craft — the nightmare

OR THOSE who have lived through the Cold War overestimating the capacities of a feared and hated enemy has been an everyday experience, but apprehension about secret weapons of unknown characteristics must be as old as the Wooden Horse of Troy. For the British of the decade around 1800, more seriously menaced by invasion than at any time in their recent history, the nightmare was fed by a printselling industry that became an eager, if unwitting, extension of the French propaganda machine.

For a nation possessing a deep-seated faith in its navy, invasion by conventional means could not be much of a threat; but Britain was also in the throes of the industrial revolution and continuously presented with novel and ingenious inventions. For the French to succeed, therefore, they must have unconventional modes of transportation, and there was a willingness among the lay public, if not the military professionals, to believe in such weapons. Furthermore, the Revolution had overthrown accepted patterns of thought and *ancien regime* civilities, so there was no doubt that the French would have no scruples about employing 'methods of barbarism'.

From the late 1790s a series of bizarre devices were presented in the public prints, and although widely differ-

ent in actual design, all shared a few common features: they were gigantic, unconventional, and all claimed the authority of an original plan or eyewitness account, although they could not agree on the port in which they were supposedly building. The most common rumour concerned a huge raft, whose various incarnations had two features in common — a massive citadel appropriate for land fortification (one version had a very Norman-looking tower keep) and propulsion by windmill-driven paddle-wheels. The most restrained estimate claimed 'This Machine is 600 Feet long and 300 broad, mounts 500 Pieces of Cannon, 36 & 48 pounders, and is to convey 15,000 Troops &c for the Invasion of England' (1). At the other end of the scale, it had become 2100ft by 1500ft to carry 60,000 troops.

Perhaps the most imaginative is a ship-like interpretation of similar features which is even given a name, *La Terreur d'Albion* (2). This is an early exponent of psychological warfare, sporting examples of the terrifying revolutionary iconography — a statue of Liberty with the bloody red cap and, better, an iron skeleton waving the Grim Reaper's scythe — surmounting the machinery towers, for this vessel's paddles are turned by horses working inside these turrets.

1. 'A View of the French Raft, as seen Afloat at St Maloes, in February 1798', aquatint published by John Fairburn, 13 February 1798. *NMM neg C1431*

2. 'An accurate and Perspective View of the Raft called The Dread of Albion as building at Calais, January 1798', coloured etching published by Robert Laurie and James Whittle, 2 February 1798. *NMM neg A5503*

3. 'A Correct Plan and Elevation of the Famous French Raft constructed on purpose for the Invasion of England and intended to carry 30,000 men, ammunition, stores &c &c. Engraved from a Drawing made by an Officer at Brest and now in Possession of the Publisher', anonymous coloured etching, no date. *NMM ref PAD4060*

4. 'Divers Projets sur la descente en Angleterre', a contemporary French print showing a tunnel and a squadron of balloon-bombers. *Musée de la Marine, Paris ref 131199*

5. 'A Correct View of the French Flat-Bottom Boats, intended to convey their troops, for the Invasion of England, as seen afloat in Charante Bay in August 1803', published by John Fairburn, 17 August 1803. *NMM ref PAH7437*

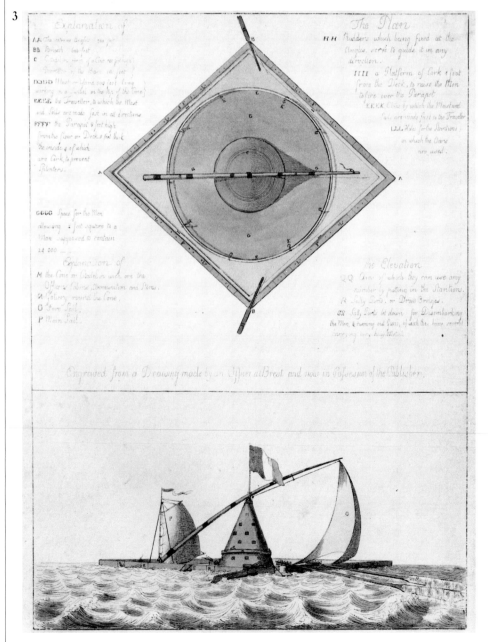

More conventionally propelled but of equally unlikely naval architecture was a lozenge-shaped raft with a conical citadel (3). This was to use sails and sweeps and, 700ft across, was again estimated to transport 30,000 men. The drawing is keyed, and some of the features are worked out in surprising detail – like the cork-lined parapets in which sallyports are cut, and the 500ft lateen yard which pivots on a swivel – but there is no attention to the practicalities, like the strengths of the materials available, or the impossibility of manoeuvring the craft with the power and rudder areas available.

So many features of these craft are comparable in the abstract – like the bombproof citadel (hides covered by iron 'scales' in one case) with a fighting gallery – but differing in terms of layout and appearance, that one suspects a common prototype; possibly verbal description rather than a drawing, whatever the prints may claim by way of origin. Furthermore, versions of these prints were published in the French-dominated Netherlands, so there is a strong possibility that it represents deliberately released 'misinformation'. It is known that the Ministry of Marine was inundated with proposals from visionary projectors relating to the invasion of England, and some of these designs may have started life as serious, if impractical, propositions, turned to France's advantage in the propaganda war in a way they could never have managed more conventionally.

Some of these notions are only ridiculous in terms of the technology of the time (4). A tunnel under the Channel has recently come to pass – and much of the British misgivings about it might be traced back to the security worries of times like 1804-5 – while aerial bombardment has become a horrible fact of twentieth-century warfare. The French had actually made some use of observation balloons in campaigns in the Low Countries, but filled with hydrogen rather than hot air that could only be produced by a laborious and time-consuming process; the leap of the imagination is to see them as bombers. However, the most interesting aspect of (4) is the aerial defence by man-carrying kites, an apparently risible idea but one which in reality attracted many experimenters in the early history of aviation.

The British public would have slept more easily if they could have seen what the French were actually building for the invasion, but even here the observers seem to have been looking through the wrong end of the telescope (5). The giant rowing boat supposedly seen in Charente Bay in 1803 was bigger than any of the standard type of landing craft then under construction. Although the *prame* was 120ft long, like the boat in the print, it carried a full ship rig; none of the invasion craft was 40ft broad, nor could they carry anything like 500 troops.

Many have assumed that when as First Lord of the Admiralty St Vincent told the House of Lords 'I do not say they cannot come; I merely say they cannot come by sea', he was making a cumbersome joke; but it may equally have been his answer to the wilder predictions about the proposed invasion.

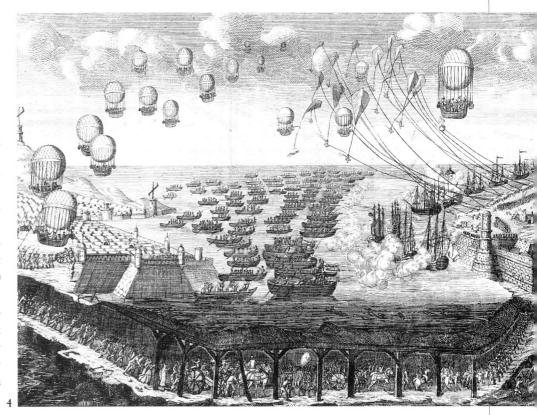

4

5

A Correct VIEW of the FRENCH FLAT-BOTTOM BOATS, intended to convey their TROOPS, for the INVASION of ENGLAND, as seen afloat in Charente Bay in August 1803.—Those flat-bottom Boats are about 120 feet long, and 40 broad, and will carry 500 Men each, they have on board 4 small Boats, calculated to carry out, or weigh, a kedge-anchor, with which they can heave the vessel a-head, on light, or contrary winds, when they are near the shore.

| References | 1.1. Draw-bridge for embarking and landing the Troops. | 3.3. Two Guns long 18 Pounders. | 5.5. Boats, carrying out a Anchor. | 7.7. Eighteen Sweeps on each side. |
| | 2.2. The Lee Boards. | 4.4.4. Three Gangways, for heaving the vessel a-head &c. | Publish'd Aug.t 17 1803, by John Fairburn, 146, Minories, London. | 6. A head view of one of the flat-bottom boats with a flying top-sail set. | 8. The Draw-bridge. | 9. A flat bottom boat embarking Troops. |

The National Flotilla

AS THE cautious accommodation of the Peace of Amiens drifted, in an atmosphere of mutual recrimination, back towards active hostility between Britain and France, Napoleon began gathering invasion forces once more, into an organisation called the National – and after his self-coronation as emperor – Imperial Flotilla. Almost none of the landing craft assembled for earlier invasion threats survived in usable shape, but the renewed effort was to be on an unprecedented scale in terms of planning, organisation and funding. An active commission began to collect fishing boats, coasters and small shallow-draught merchantmen from around the Atlantic coast of France and to convert and arm them to act as landing craft. The satellite state of the Netherlands promised enough landing craft to transport 35,000 men and 1500 horses whilst the Italian Republic offered funds to build two frigates and 12 *chaloupes cannonières*.

National enthusiasm in France produced yet more funds to build ships for the navy in general (Paris paid for a 120-gun ship, Lyons for one 100, Bordeaux and Marseilles for an 80 and a 70 respectively) and the invasion flotilla in particular. In June 1803 some 100 *chaloupes cannonières*, 300 *bateaux cannoniers* and 300 *péniches* were laid down in coastal ports from Dunkirk to Bayonne and also on the rivers flowing into the Atlantic and Channel. There were even invasion craft building on the Quai d'Orsay in Paris itself. The initial requisitions had brought in 88 large and 38 medium boats, 318 transports, 88 coasters, 140 vessels of between 50 and 100 tons and 350 fishing boats (including 'newfoundlanders' and whalers), which together, it was estimated, could carry 12,940 men and 5296 horses. The horses would be needed for general transport as well as cavalry and artillery, as it was known that the English would do their best to drive all draught animals from the invasion area at the first signs of a landing.

The French assigned some of their best men to the command of the invasion vessels. On 7 September 1803 Vice-Admiral Bruix was given command of the flotilla with Rear-Admirals Magon and Emeriau under him, and Captain Lafond as chief of staff. However, Bruix was even at this stage far from well, though his death in early 1805 may have been hastened by his dismissal from the command in the previous July (for refusing Napoleon's direct order to send vessels to sea in a rising gale). Napoleon took the keenest interest in developments, making frequent visits to the preparations (1).

By September 1804 the flotilla was complete in fourteen divisions of first class boats, each division of 18 *chaloupes cannonières* divided into two sections. There were nineteen divisions of the second class boats of 18 *bateaux cannoniers* each divided into two sections, which in their turn were subdivided into three squadrons of three vessels each. The sixteen divisions of *péniches*, 18 craft per division, were also subdivided into two sections and six squadrons. The number of horse transports in each of the fifteen divisions was also 18 (subdivided into two sections per division); whilst there were four divisions of artillery transports and seven of baggage transports. All this massive total of landing craft were shared out between Boulogne (2), Étaples and Wimereux, the specially enlarged invasion ports. It also meant a massive supply problem of guns, ammunition, hand weapons and other items for the flotilla, not to mention the question of manning. Although the soldiers were intended to help with the sailing or rowing of the vessels, and with manning the guns and assisting the defence of the vessels by musketry, sailors were essential and the demands of the French navy had already sadly diminished that particular human resource.

At the beginning of July 1805 the flotilla was poised to launch its attempt on England, in anticipation of the maturing of Napoleon's naval plans and the arrival of Villeneuve. The left wing, based at Étaples and commanded by Rear-Admiral Courand would transport the 23,000 men of Marshal Ney's corps. The actual carrying power in one 'lift' of the 402 landing craft based here was

1

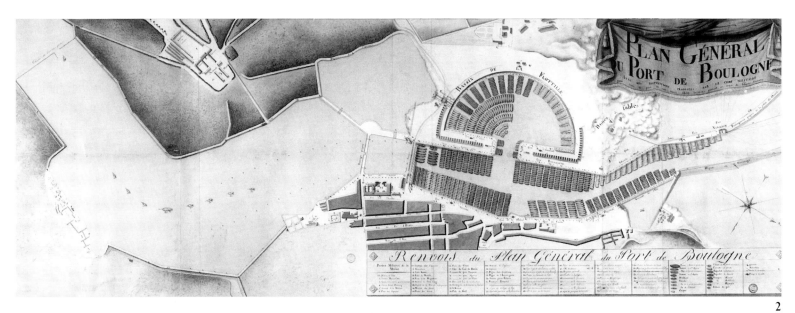

2

27,077 men and 1588 horses. The left and right wings of the central force, under Admiral Savary and Captain Leray would each transport a corps (both under Marshal Soult, 40,000 men all told). These would be in the approximately 1000 craft based at Boulogne itself, with a first-wave capacity of 68,956 men and 3266 horses (3). Captain Daugier would embark Lannes' 15,000 men of the right wing from Wimereux in 276 craft whose actual carrying capacity was 16,844 men and 767 horses. The fifth corps was the Batavian (Dutch) flotilla under Vice-Admiral Verhuell at Ambleteuse, and it would transport Davout's 20,000 troops (its capacity was 15,109 men and 675 horses in 175 vessels, but this was a 'second wave' for-

mation). The 6th corps, the reserve at Calais, would embark the cavalry and an Italian division under Prince Louis after the other corps had landed. The 203 craft at Calais (capacity 16,252 men, 2033 horses), 157 at Dunkirk (13,762 men, 280 horses) and 55 at Ostend (3070 men, 370 horses) consisted mostly of Dutch gunboats and transports. The first four corps, the ones which would effect the landing, were more specifically divided up into squadrons, each intended to carry a division of four regiments of line infantry, one of light infantry plus its cavalry, artillery and baggage. Nor should it be forgotten that extra troops (assembled at Brest) would be embarked in the fleet to take part in the invasion.

3

VUE DU PORT ET RADE DE BOULOGNE
Prise au moment du départ d'une partie de la Flottille, allant prendre ses lignes d'embossage

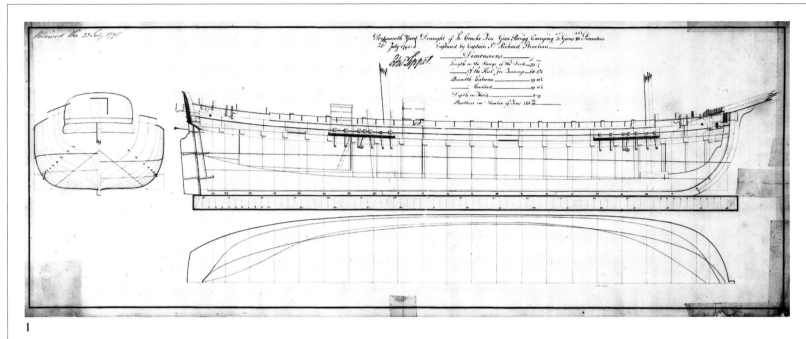

1

Invasion craft – the reality

IN STARK contrast to the fevered imaginings of the propagandists and printsellers, the actual craft built for the invasion of Britain were fairly conventional, even mundane, in design. Indeed, they were regarded as inadequate by the seamen who had to use them, and were held in derision by their enemies, suggesting a lack of proper consideration before the programme was put in hand. However, specialist landing craft had been under development since the invasion schemes of the 1790s, and after 1803 it was decided to standardise on several types which were then constructed in large numbers.

The initial inspiration had come from an Antwerper called Muskein who had experience of the Swedish

1. Lines and profile of the 'gun brig' (gunboat) *Crache Feu*, as taken off at Portsmouth Yard, 20 July 1795. By British measure she is 143 tons and is said to be armed with '3 guns 18 pounders'.
NMM neg DR6361

2. Lines and profile of the 'gun lugger' *L'Eclair*, taken off afloat at Portsmouth Yard, 2 July 1795. She measured 101 tons and also carried three 18pdrs.
NMM neg DR7003

3. Draught of the *péniche*. This and the other French drawings of the Flotilla craft were actually produced in 1862 for the *Atlas du Génie maritime*, but were based on original draughts of 1803.
Musée de la Marine, Paris ref 92983

4. Draught of *bateau cannonier*, Carlin type.
Musée de la Marine, Paris ref 92982

5. 'To George Montagu, Esqr Admiral of the Blue and Naval Commander in Chief at Portsmouth, this print representing the French Gun Vessels, Captured Jany 31 1804 by His Majesty's Ships Tribune and Hydra . . . inscribed by . . . Rd Livesay', coloured aquatint engraved by Joseph Constantine Stadler after an original by Richard and John Livesay, published by the artist and F Asperne, 21 February 1804. Note the stern port of the vessel to the right.
NMM neg X1905

6. Draught of *Prame*.
Musée de la Marine, Paris ref 92985

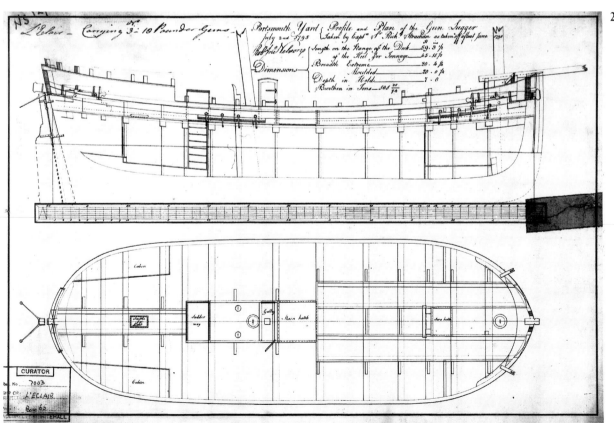

2

Inshore Fleet. This army co-operation force included a number of ingenious designs by the great naval architect Frederik af Chapman, but being optimised for the sheltered waters of the Swedish archipelago, these were not an entirely appropriate starting point for a cross-Channel flotilla. The British were familiar with the general characteristics of the French designs, having captured a few of the original craft, including the *Crache Feu*, a brig rigged *chaloupe canonnière* armed with one 18pdr aft and two 18 or 24pdrs forward on slide mountings (1). This was to become one of the standard designs built in numbers after 1803. With dimensions of 80ft by 20ft and a 6ft draught, they had a crew of 22 and could transport 130 men, plus a 6in or 8in howitzer. There were also more conventional, and more seaworthy types, like the 'gun lugger' *L'Eclair* captured with *Crache Feu* in 1795 (2), a 100-ton vessel with three 18pdr guns on slides.

Although purchased fishing and coastal craft continued to play a part in the invasion planning, after 1803 there was more standardisation, four types coming to predominate. The smallest was the *péniche* (3), a long and low lug rigged boat measuring approximately 64ft by 11ft, with a draught of 4ft. They carried a crew of 5, 66 men and two small howitzers or an 8in mortar, and although fast under sail they were not fit for open water in all but a flat calm.

Next in size was another lug rigged type, the *bateau canonnier*, which measured about 64ft by 14½ft and drew 5ft; capacity with 6 crew was 106 men, 2 horses, one 24pdr, 1 howitzer and 1 field piece. There were two very similar variants, one the original Muskein design and the presumably improved Carlin type illustrated here (4); both featured a stern ramp to land the field gun and horses.

The third craft was the *chaloupe canonnière*, which was very similar to the *Crache Feu*, and more of this type was to fall into British hands during the next few years (5). The flotilla was also to contain large numbers of what were called *caïques* but which were no more than warships' boats armed with a single 24pdr. For close escort the invasion force was to be accompanied by the final specialist type, the ship rigged *prame*, a powerfully armed (twelve 24pdrs) shoal-draught corvette measuring 117ft by 26½ft and drawing about 8½ft; each had a crew of 38 and carried 120 men (6). Judging by the flat bottom with three 'skids' or false keels, the *prames* were intended to beach with the first waves of the assault force to give covering fire.

Thus, like Second World War landing craft, there were a number of types for different roles. The numbers planned varied wildly according to Napoleon's changing ambitions, but one early scheme called for 18 *prames*, 331 *chaloupes*, 454 *bateaux*, 451 *péniches*, and 41 *caïques*, of which only 2 *prames*, 13 *chaloupes*, and 165 *bateaux* already existed,

but even this ambitious programme was to be more than doubled later. An idea of the investment involved can be gleaned from these contemporary estimates of the unit costs of each main type in francs: *prame* 70,000, *chaloupe canonnière* 32,000-42,000, *bateau canonnier* 18,000-23,000, and *péniche* 8000-9000.

Although they were clearly designed for their task, the overriding emphasis with all of these types was on beaching, so they were of shallow draught, if not actually flat-bottomed, which made them leewardly and unhandy under sail. Sliding keels would have been a big improvement, but there is no evidence they were ever considered, although by this date the French had cap-

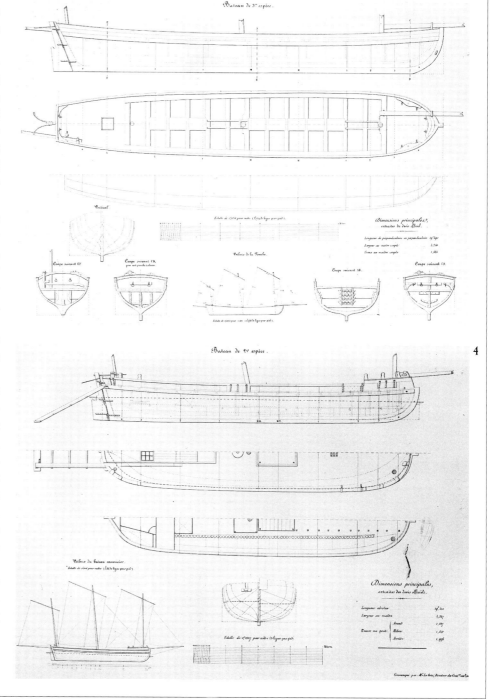

5

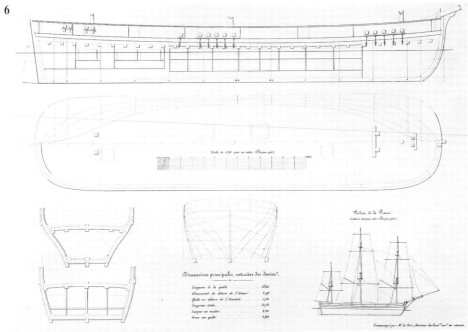

6

tured a number of British gunboats fitted with Schank's device. They were also of low freeboard to aid disembarking, but this made them particularly vulnerable to the kind of seas more common than not in the Channel. This lack of seakeeping restricted any potential invasion 'window' to the lightest possible conditions, further reducing the likelihood of a favourable opportunity to launch the expedition.

They were never subjected to the ultimate test of a full-blown invasion, but some idea of their performance can be glimpsed in the famous debacle of 20 July 1804, when Napoleon ordered an embarkation exercise despite the threat of a gale. Admiral Bruix was dismissed for refusing to carry out the order, and the demonstration went ahead; some twenty craft were wrecked, losses being put at between 200 and 400 dead.

While they were not as wildly visionary as some of the published ideas, in practical terms these invasion vessels were almost as unlikely.

The Downs Command

1

'THE FRONTIER of Britain is the coastline of the enemy' was an old adage, but during the first years of the nineteenth century it was almost literally observed by the frigates, sloops, brigs and other small craft of the Royal Navy and their crews. The number of these which were lost on the French coast proves the point.

Lord Keith (1), somewhat disgruntled at losing the Mediterranean command that he coveted to the much more junior Nelson, took over the crucial Downs command during the crisis years from 1803 to 1807 and performed to admiration. He was the classic example of a 'safe pair of hands' who could deal with politicians, prickly soldiers and headstrong subordinates, run an immense administrative organisation (he was responsible for convoys and trade defence in his area as well as anti-invasion preparations) and be capable of rapid, decisive action if needed. A man of great experience and authority, he was respected rather than loved, but although he lacked the charisma of a Nelson or Sidney

Smith he was equally incapable of the idiocies committed by these men. He was responsible for the coasts from Selsey Bill well beyond Portsmouth down-channel round to the North of Scotland, and the seas off those coasts, an immense command. He ran it from Cliff House near North Foreland in Kent—looking both out to the North Sea and the Channel, and overlooking that magnificent anchorage protected by the Goodwin Sands, the Downs, from which ships went down Channel, up or across the North Sea, or waited for tide and wind to be favourable for going up the Thames (2). From there, on a clear day, you can also see the French coast, where the invasion armies assembled.

In the event, Napoleon—like Hitler after him—chose the beaches of Kent and Sussex as his invasion area, but his opponents could not know this and were as concerned with East Anglia, sometimes even more so. However, the general principle of defence was clear enough. The First Lord, Melville, wrote to Keith on 6 June 1804: 'I always go on the principle that as we ought to have a threefold

2

3

naval protection, it is highly essential that we should have as many vessels armed as possible . . . I say a threefold protection; I mean that the enemy should be met first at the mouth of their own harbours and on their own coasts; secondly they should be annoyed every inch of their passage in crossing the sea, and lastly that they should be again met by every resistance that can be opposed to them on our own coast when they approach it.'

For a summary of the invasion coast we can turn to Keith's own words, in a briefing letter to the army commander, the Duke of York, dated 21 October 1803: '. . . All the coast from Weymouth to Dover can be invaded by vessels from Cherbourg, Havre de Grace [Le Havre] and Boulogne with winds from S.E. to S.W.; but it is to be observed that southerly winds must make a surf upon all that shore; that in bad weather it is impossible to

4

land; and that in good weather our squadrons will be off their ports. We have also an increasing naval force upon our own coast, and the armed boats and vessels, their crews being strengthened by the Sea Fencibles, will form a third line of defence for opposing attempts to land. Off Selsey Island in the Park there are two sloops of war. There is a considerable squadron off Havre, another off Dungeness and a third before Boulogne which will anchor off that place when the weather will admit of an enemy putting to sea in boats.'

Keith went on to enumerate the possible landing beaches, the most suitable seeming to be those of Sussex and southeast Kent. Parts of north Kent were also vulnerable, but substantial force of armed vessels were gathered at Margate and Sheerness, and Keith felt the Thames estuary well protected. On the Essex coast there were warships in each river entrance, and the intricate nature of the navigation would deter large vessels, but small boats would find it easier and Keith advocated arming the local craft to deal with them. He concluded with a seaman's appreciation of the enemy's problems in assembling their invasion shipping within the tidal constraints of their ports—'At Boulogne there is not above five hours of tide out of twelve to depart with and the troops must be seen embarking'—and explained the weather conditions which made the attempt most likely.

The forces Keith had to tackle the problems of his station consisted primarily of smaller ships. His few line of battle ships were mostly old Dutch prizes converted to floating batteries to defend estuaries, and to be manned mostly by local volunteers. The headquarters ships for the various area groups and flying squadrons into which his forces were divided were usually 50-gun two-deckers, neither ships of the line or frigates but ideal for this purpose. The main backing-up function for the smaller craft, however, would be performed by the large numbers of frigates (3) and smaller Sixth Rates available. The closest inshore work was performed by the specially-built gunbrigs with the (usually hired) cutters and luggers (4). In between came large numbers of sloops, mostly brig rigged (5)—the ship rigged sloops were mostly mercantile conversions used for convoy work and not thought much of. Finally there were usually four or so bomb vessels for shore bombardment.

Keith had many problems, not least some of his subordinate commanders, and the various schemes proffered for attacking the invasion flotilla with novel weapons. In 1805 he wrote: 'Sir Sidney [Smith] seemed to have only one wish, which is to get all the force on this coast put under his direction, to create an *éclat* in the papers: Mr F [Fulton] is full of coffers, carcasses and submarine boats which will not answer here: Mr Congreve, who is ingenious, is wholly wrapt up in rockets from

which I expect little success, for Mr Congreve has no idea of applying them professionally.' However, Smith was also a very useful player in the game of intelligence gathering (a major concern for Keith), though Keith had to rein him in from time to time. Other enterprising naval officers came under Keith—for example the ingenious Home Popham, whose direction of a 'carcass' attack caused much jealousy amongst other officers. But the real hero of the anti-invasion flotillas was the reliable, sensible and very effective Captain Owen, who impressed even the First Lord: as Melville wrote to Keith in October 1804, '. . . I have taken a very strong prepossession in his favour and would always conceive any business to be in safe hands that is entrusted to him.'

Each invasion port was closely 'marked', so however quickly Napoleon managed to get his men aboard they would be seen, and however many tides it took to get the flotilla out of the ports the predators would be waiting to pounce just outside the range of the shore batteries. Even had Villeneuve contrived to appear off Boulogne without a matching British fleet he would have been very hard pressed to defend the straggling mass of invasion craft from the efficiently-organised squadrons awaiting them. The clumsy, unseaworthy, poorly built and ineffectually armed craft, crammed with seasick soldiers would have been vulnerable to bad weather as well as the British vessels. It would have been a massacre.

1. 'Admiral Lord Keith. From an original picture in the possession of His Lordship', coloured engraving by William Greatbach after an original by John Jackson, no date.
NMM ref PAD3346

2. 'English men of war in the Downs', black and watercolour pen and ink by Thomas Yates, 1792.
NMM ref PAG9686

3. A frigate and two cutters close inshore, with a brig in the offing. Anonymous undated watercolour, but about 1800.
NMM ref PAH4080

4. 'A cutter and a lugger in a fresh breeze', grey wash by Robert Cleveley, no date.
NMM neg D2528

5. 'A Brig Sloop of War Reconnoitring the Bay of Boulogne', aquatint and etching by Robert Dodd (1748-1815) after his own original, no date.
NMM neg A4624

5

Anti-Flotilla operations: the Channel

1

THE ROYAL Navy was not passive in its preparations against invasion, but undertook a number of counter-attacks against the facilities and growing numbers of Flotilla craft in the Channel ports. A leading light in these operations was Captain Edward Owen (1), whose flagship was the frigate *Immortalite* (2). A brief log of the principal actions will give some idea of their intentions and achievements – nuisance raids in the main, but a few were more ambitious.

14 June 1803: Captain Owen near Cape Blanc Nez chased ashore two gun-vessels. *Cruiser* and *Jalouse* went in, silenced the batteries, after which both were brought off.

1 August: an armed lugger, forced close to the beach at Le Havre, was attacked by the *Hydra*'s boats. She was abandoned by her crew, who with some troops fired from the sand dunes, but failed to stop her being taken and salvaged.

14 September: Owen with the *Immortalite*, and the bombs *Perseus* and *Explosion*, bombarded Dieppe and then St Valery-en-Caux.

13/15 September: the frigate *Cerberus*, with Rear-Admiral Saumarez aboard and a force of smaller vessels, arrived off Granville, to cover the bombs *Sulphur* and *Terror*. Bombardments were carried out in the small-hours of the 14th and again on the 15th, though not with much effect. Though opposed by twenty-two gun-vessels, besides the batteries, they suffered no loss and very little damage. However, the *Cerberus* grounded on a shoal. Gunboats began to attack her but were driven off, and she was refloated.

27 September: a division of small craft, under Commander Jackson, bombarded Calais for several hours, inflicting some damage, but receiving none. The British vessels were then driven off by a northeasterly gale; and on the following day, taking advantage, many gunboats left Calais for Boulogne safely, although they were chased and fired at by the *Leda*, Captain Honeyman. On 29 September, twenty-five more followed. The *Leda* drove two ashore; but the rest reached their destination.

31 October: Honeyman, with the sloops *Lark* and *Harpy*, saw a gunbrig and six other craft coming out of Étaples and making for Boulogne. He ordered the *Lark* and *Harpy* to chase; but before they could get up with the enemy, the hired cutter *Admiral Mitchell*, already off Boulogne, intervened, although opposed by a battery as well as the vessels (3). She drove ashore the gunbrig and a sloop. She had a carronade dismounted, rigging damaged and several shot in her hull; but only five wounded (4).

20 February 1804: the hired cutter *Active* off Gravelines, sighted sixteen craft going from Ostend to Boulogne, with which she maintained a chasing fight for half an hour. A transport surrendered and the others sheltered under the batteries.

23 July and 1 August: *Melpomene*, with sloops, bombs, and small craft, bombarded Le Havre; but with little effect on French preparations.

19 July: after Napoleon had ordered an exercise, a strong wind and heavy sea endangered the French flotilla in Boulogne road, and forced the leewardmost vessels to work to windward, and others to run for Étaples. Captain Owen ordered the *Harpy*, and the brigs *Bloodhound* and *Archer* to run in and open fire upon the vessels attempting to stand off from the land. They were joined by the *Autumn*, and for several hours the enemy was attacked. By daylight on the 20th, only nineteen brigs and eight luggers remained in the road and the

2

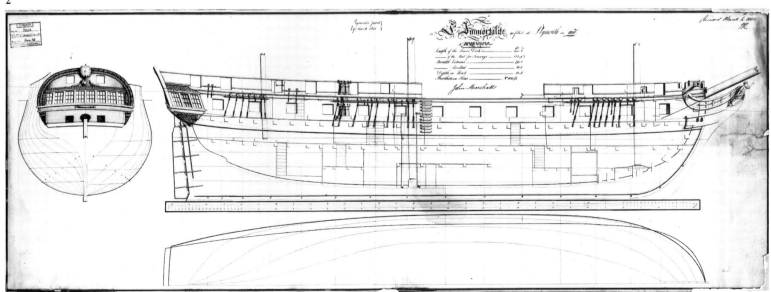

3

4

weather continuing bad, these soon began to slip, and to run for Étaples or St Valery-sur-Somme. The *Autumn* and her consorts were too far to leeward to intercept; but *Immortalite* and *Leda* stood in close to the town. It is uncertain how far the British fire was responsible, but the frigates could see that a brig, a lugger, and several large boats were stranded, that three other brigs and a lugger were total wrecks, and that a brig and two luggers, anchored close to the rocks, had signals of distress flying, and were in clear danger. Upwards of four hundred Frenchmen are known to have drowned under Napoleon's gaze on this occasion.

25 August: a division of gunboats, under Captain Julien Le Ray, was ordered out to attack the gunbrig *Bruiser*. She opened fire which attracted the *Immortalite*, who began to engage both the gun-vessels and the batteries. She soon found she was too close inshore, and withdrew. Early on the following morning the brigs *Bloodhound* and *Archer* got into distant action with some luggers which were rounding Cape Gris-Nez; and later in the day another division of gunboats, together with some mortar vessels, joined Captain Le Ray, who was manoeuvring offshore. The united force numbered sixty

brigs and over thirty luggers. The *Immortalite*, with the *Harpy*, 18, *Adder*, gunbrig, and the hired armed cutter *Constitution*, later joined by the *Bruiser*, came in to engage; whereupon the batteries opened, and most of the craft remaining in the roads weighed to help their friends. The *Constitution* was sunk by a 13-inch shell which, falling on her deck, passed through her bottom. Her crew were saved by the boats of the squadron. A shell also fell in the *Harpy*, but failed to burst. The *Immortalite* was twice struck in the hull; but the British casualties were only one killed and four wounded. The batteries protected the gunboats well though a couple of gunboats beached themselves to avoid sinking. Desultory firing was renewed on the 27th and 28th, with no serious damage on either side.

8 October: after lookouts in Jersey saw gun-vessels close under the Normandy coast, *Albacore* drove them under a battery. She lay off until the next morning, then stood in with the tide, anchored just outside the edge of the surf, and cannonaded until all five drove ashore with the waves breaking over them. She was not able to complete their destruction, for she dragged her anchor and hauled off.

1. 'Sir Edward Willm C R Owen, G.C.B., G.C.H., Admiral of the White', mezzotint engraved by G T Payne after an original by William Pickersgill, published by the artist, 1 November 1849. Owen had a long life and became a full Admiral, but in his young days he was one of the most active frigate captains.
NMM ref PAG9378

2. Sheer and profile draught of *Immortalité* as taken off at Plymouth 1 March 1800. This 36-gun 18pdr frigate had been taken from the French in 1798.
NMM neg DR7065/36

3. 'To the Rt Honble George Lord Keith . . . This Plate representing the Commencement of the Action of the Adm Mitchell Cutter . . . with a French Gun-Brig and Six Armed Sloops and Schooners near Boulogne, Octr 31 1803 Is . . . Inscribed by . . . R Livesay', coloured aquatint and etching by Joseph Constantine Stadler after an original by John Livesay, published by R Livesay and J Wilkinson, 12 March 1804.
NMM ref PAH8002

4. 'To the Rt Honble George Lord Keith . . . This Plate representing the Conclusion of the Action of the Adm Mitchell Cutter . . . with a French Gun-Brig and Six Armed Sloops and Schooners near Boulogne, Octr 31 1803 Is . . . Inscribed by . . . R Livesay', coloured aquatint and etching by Joseph Constantine Stadler after an original by John Livesay, published by R Livesay and J Wilkinson, 12 March 1804.
NMM ref PAH8003

Vincejo at Quiberon

1. 'John Wesley Wright Esqr Commander R.N.', stipple engraving by T Blood after an original by Gaelano Galleia, published by Joyce Gold, 31 July 1813. *NMM ref PAD3087*

2. 'First view of HM Sloop El Vincego J W Wright Esqr, commander, Taken in the Bay of Quiberon, on the 8th of May 1804', coloured aquatint and etching by I Clark after an original by C Hiller, published by the artist 1 July 1817. *NMM neg B6367*

3. 'Second view of HM Sloop El Vincego J W Wright Esqr, commander, taken in the Bay of Quiberon by Six Brigs & Eleven Gun Boats of the French, on the 8th of May 1804', coloured aquatint and etching by I Clark after an original by C Hiller, published by the artist 1 July 1817. *NMM neg B6368*

4. 'The Tower of the Temple, a principal revolutionary state-prison at Paris', engraving by Bailey, Plate 451 from *Naval Chronicle* XXXIV (1815), published by Joyce Gold. *NMM neg D9054*

THE SLOOP *Vincejo*, a Spanish prize taken in 1799, was an unconventional vessel, one of very few brigs with a quarterdeck and forecastle. Her mission, 'cloak and dagger' work involving inshore surveys and the landing of subversives and counter-revolutionaries, and the career of her commander John Wesley Wright (1), were equally unusual.

Early on 8 May 1804, Commander Wright had just returned from a nocturnal landing on the island of Houat in Quiberon Bay when in sight of Port Navalo, the breeze died to a calm. Wright had seemed to be under some premonition of disaster, repeating to himself a line of poetry – 'return victorious, or return no more' – but when French gunboats were seen approaching under oars, he snapped out of his reverie, and ordered the *Vincejo*'s boats to tow the brig; he brushed aside any suggestion that he make his escape in the cutter *Fox*, *Vincejo*'s consort.

As they pulled toward the open sea, the tide swept them inshore toward the Toughness rock, forcing Wright to anchor. The French flotilla, seventeen brigs and lugger, was powerfully armed with thirty-five long guns, 24pdrs and 18pdrs, totally outmatching and outranging the *Vincejo*'s sixteen 18pdr carronades. After an unequal contest lasting over two hours, the brig's rigging was cut to pieces and her hull all but shattered; with her armament out of action under the wreckage of spars and booms, Wright was forced to strike (3). French casualties from their force of 700-800 men are not known; of the *Vincejo*'s 51 officers and men, plus the very high proportion of 24 boys, 2 were killed and 12 – including Wright – wounded. The *Fox*, a handier vessel, escaped.

Wright knew that his previous history would place him in jeopardy if ever he were made a prisoner. Born in 1769, he was entered for the navy during the War of American Independence, and served in HMS *Brilliant* and at the siege of Gibraltar. Paid off in 1783, he was sent for training in a merchant's office, culminating in a five-year stint in St Petersburg. On his return to London, a polished, capable and cosmopolitan young man with a gift for languages, he was introduced to Sir Sidney Smith. Smith offered him the post of secretary, with Midshipman's rank, in HMS *Diamond*, and his life and career thereafter are inextricably linked with Smith, and the world of naval intelligence. After two years of operations in HMS *Diamond*, in April 1796 he was captured with Smith during a cutting out operation, and imprisoned with Sir Sidney in the Temple prison in Paris, until their dramatic (and highly improbable) escape in May 1798. He remained at Smith's side in his next appointment, HMS *Tigre*, and was active throughout the campaign at Acre and on the Egyptian coast, where he played a significant role in the defeat of Bonaparte's ambition of Eastern conquest. For his services – later described as 'peculiarly inimical' and 'exciting in the breast of Buonaparte a deadly malice' – he was promoted in 1802 to commander; in 1804 he took command of the odd little *Vincejo* ('one of the most inefficient vessels ever to hoist the English pendant').

2

3

After his capture, Wright was sent under escort to Paris, where he was again imprisoned in the Temple (4), by coincidence in his former cell—he found a set of improvised escape tools exactly as he left them hidden years before, though this time there was to be no way out. Implicated in a disastrously compromised plot to assassinate Bonaparte—the royalist agents General Pichegru and Georges Cadoudal had been put ashore in France by the *Vincejo*—Wright was subjected to interrogation and solitary confinement but refused to give any information, despite threats of execution. The French conspirators were, of course, doomed. Pichegru was strangled in his cell; Cadoudal, the Duc d'Enghien and others were shot.

Wright remained in solitary confinement, comforted only by a 'little amiable cat'. The British Government's approaches to have him exchanged were contemptuously dismissed. It may even be that by this time he was already dead: on 28 October 1805 a French newspaper reported 'Captain Wright, of the English navy, a prisoner in the Temple, who had debarked on the French coast Georges [Cadoudal] and his accomplices, has put an end to his existence in his prison, after having read in the *Moniteur* an account of the destruction of the Austrian army'. He had been found in bed with his throat cut. The news created outrage in England; the ostensible reason for Wright's suicide was just too absurd, and the circumstances too suspicious, for it to have been anything other than murder, probably to the order of the highest authority.

After 1815, Sir Sydney Smith tried personally to unravel the mystery of Wright's death, but without any clear result. The chief suspect was naturally Napoleon, but from his exile in St Helena he maintained a vehement denial of any involvement; however, it was never accepted that Wright killed himself, nor was Napoleon ever entirely absolved of blame.

4

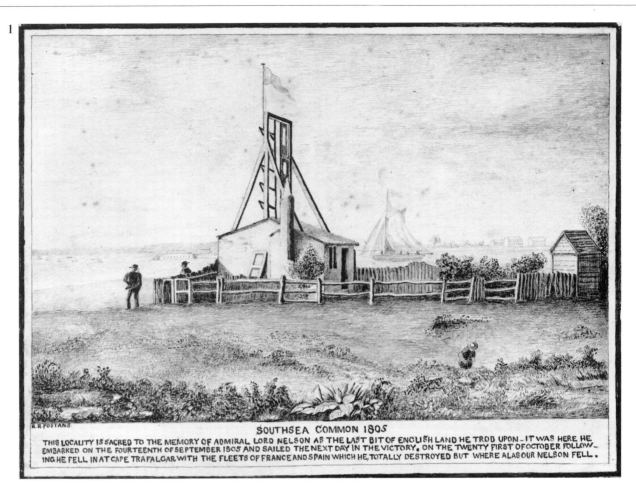

SOUTHSEA COMMON 1805

THIS LOCALITY IS SACRED TO THE MEMORY OF ADMIRAL LORD NELSON AS THE LAST BIT OF ENGLISH LAND HE TROD UPON — IT WAS HERE HE EMBARKED ON THE FOURTEENTH OF SEPTEMBER 1805 AND SAILED THE NEXT DAY IN THE VICTORY, ON THE TWENTY FIRST OF OCTOBER FOLLOW— ING HE FELL IN AT CAPE TRAFALGAR WITH THE FLEETS OF FRANCE AND SPAIN WHICH HE, TOTALLY DESTROYED BUT WHERE ALAS OUR NELSON FELL.

1. 'The Old Semaphore Southsea Common 1805 . . . sacred to the memory of Admiral Lord Nelson . . .', black and grey wash by Robert Baxter Postans, no date. *NMM neg B7603*

2. 'Martello Towers near Bexhill, Sussex', brown mezzotint engraved by W Say after an original by J M W Turner, published by the artist, June 1811. *NMM ref PAF5095*

3. Draught of the converted barge *Dover*, fitted with three carronades on slides, is probably typical of the kind of improvised gunboats operated by the Sea Fencibles. *NMM neg DR6420*

4. 'A View of the Frigates Stationed in the Hope under the Command of the Elder Brethren of Trinity House', coloured aquatint engraved by William Daniell after his own original, published by the artist 20 January 1804. *NMM ref PAH8005*

5. Walmer Castle, the headquarters of the Warden of the Cinque Ports, where William Pitt spent the years 1801-1804 when out of office drilling the Volunteers. Plate CCXXIII from the *Naval Chronicle* XVII (1807), published by Joyce Gold. *NMM ref D9047*

Invasion defences

IT IS odd that the secondary defences against Napoleonic invasion are far better known than the primary one. Books have been written about the Martello towers, the Royal Military Canal, the telegraph, not to mention the militia, the volunteers, and the regular soldiers who stood ready to cope with the after-effects of a successful landing. The real counter was the Navy's flotillas, which in all probability would have smashed any such attempt as it emerged from the protection of its shore batteries into mid Channel, as already prefigured in a number of minor engagements (see pages 72-73).

In fact the defences against invasion were multi-layered and varied. Working from the rear forward, some attempt was made to fortify London, whilst the fortifications around the Medway towns and Colchester were greatly strengthened. These places were heavily garrisoned and were to be the main redoubts to be held against an invading army, depending on which side of the Thames estuary it landed. We now know that Napoleon (like Hitler after him) was going for the shortest sea passage and intended to land in Kent and Sussex, but contemporaries had not the advantage of hindsight

and were very scared of a landing from the Dutch ports on the Essex shore. Admiral Keith was particularly aware of this possibility, though confident that the shifting sands off that shore would limit the possibilities available. The front-line port of Dover also had its defences strengthened, both to prevent it being seized by the enemy and so that it could act as the base for a counterattack. News of the invasion would be spread by beacons and church bells, whilst details would be transmitted by the Admiralty's shutter 'telegraph' whose stations were on high ground between London and the dockyards at Chatham and Portsmouth (1), with the former line carrying on down to Keith's HQ at the Downs. As this happened the country behind the beaches would be 'driven' with all horses and draught cattle being taken away inland to deprive the enemy of transport. The Royal Military Canal was built across the landward side of Romney Marsh to serve the dual purpose of carrying reinforcements and munitions as well as providing a water barrier. Should things go badly the Government was quite prepared to carry on the struggle from the rest of the country, even if London fell — the ordnance depot at Weedon in Northamptonshire was turned into a sort of national redoubt, which would shelter the royal family and the executive, while acting a centre for the collection of armaments. It is almost impossible to speculate on the possibilities of partisan warfare, of which the British country folk had no experience, which could have been both a weakness and a strength.

There were a good number of troops available for defence, there being few overseas distractions for the British army at this time (save for the perpetual worry of nearby Ireland). The regular army was slowly, if not very obviously, regaining its stature as a very effectively trained force after its recent victory against the French in Egypt. Great things were being prepared by John Moore at the Shorncliffe Camp with the new Light Division. The militia, restricted to home defence, but well organised and drilled appears to have been a fairly reliable force. The varied units of Volunteers, Fencibles and the like were a much more doubtful quantity. Their ability to stand against Napoleon's veterans was very much in question, but they did provide numbers and could not be a totally negligible quality.

The British defences of the seashores themselves would probably have been reasonably effective. The extensive batteries prepared behind all the obvious beaches (fewer than might be apparent because of offshore obstacles such as sands and currents) should have caused heavy casualties, particularly if rapidly reinforced by field artillery and infantry (who would often have been carried to the scene of action in carts, etc). The batteries were backed up by the rapid construction of the circular strongpoints known as Martello towers (2).

2

These were copied from an original which had proved itself against the Royal Navy in Corsica. The guns mounted on turntables at the top of these towers were initially intended to be manned by the Sea Fencibles. However, as one naval officer wrote, it was foolish for the men of this maritime local defence force to be 'ordered to man batteries at the same time as they are ordered to go afloat, which being two duties to perform which at the same time it is impracticable to execute'.

The Sea Fencibles had been initially set up in 1798 and were revived in 1803 at the insistence of both Keith and the Duke of York (the C-in-C of the army). They were

3

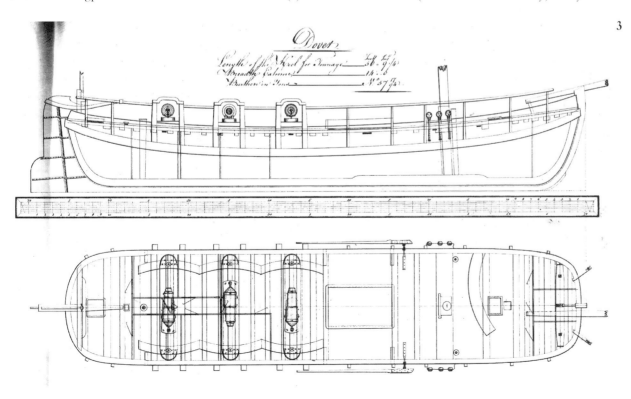

4

intended for coastal defence and served under naval officers. Approximately 5000 of them were available in late 1803 on the invasion coast, and perhaps 300 or more fishing and other local boats available to them. There were three main duties which these men would be called upon to do if the invasion came: they might man fortifications; they would help man warships committed against the invasion force (this also applied to other requisitioned vessels, though one officer commented that his men, mostly smugglers, loathed having to be on board customs vessels!); finally they might man their own local boats, which would be given armament (3). The dockyard craft of Portsmouth and Chatham, of which there were many, hoys, barges, and large rowing boats used as tugs, would also be armed and used.

As part of the Fencible movement the Elder Bretheren of Trinity House manned and paid for a force of ten old frigates to be moored across the lower Thames. The ships were moored so as to ride with the tide, a 'gate' being left in the channel for normal ship movements (4), but on receiving news of impending invasion they were to be warped head-to-stern across the river and the gap closed. The crews were organised as the Royal Trinity House Volunteer Artillery with Pitt as the honorary Colonel of the unit. He must have been a busy man while out of office, since he was simultaneously Warden of the Cinque Ports, and Colonel of its volunteer regiment, which he commanded from Walmer Castle (5).

It is true that there was a certain air of improvisation about many of these expedients, even of amateurishness, but it is perhaps as well for the men of the *Grand Armée* that they never had to embark for Britain in earnest. Having looked at the preparations made for their reception one tends to agree with Lord St Vincent that they could not have come by sea. Even if some had survived the crossing they would have been unlikely to get far ashore.

5

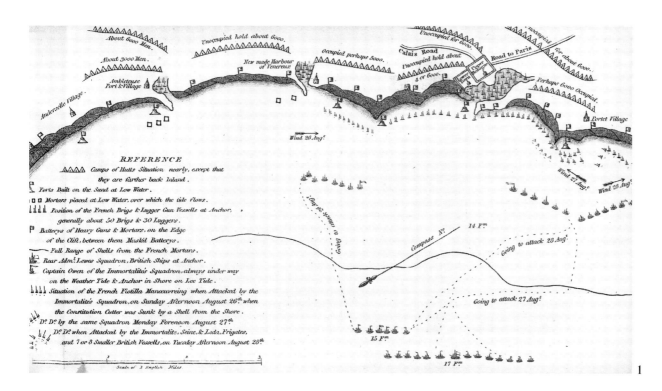

1

Torpedoes and rockets: the attacks on Boulogne

DESPITE THE best efforts of the Royal Navy's inshore squadrons using conventional means, the French continued to concentrate invasion craft at Boulogne with great success. There remained the, admittedly difficult, option of attacking it in its lair, and the early assaults were also conventional in method and limited in achievement. The attack during the last days of August 1804 demonstrated the problems, in that the British forces had to operate inside the range of defending mortars (1) if they wanted to destroy the line of Flotilla craft drawn up outside the port (2). On this occasion Napoleon himself went afloat to encourage his men, and in his usual bombastic style claimed to have 'withstood' the fire of a British frigate (3), although none was close enough inshore to have threatened him. While such bombardment was not very effective, it was less costly in human lives than the kind of desperate hand-to-hand combat employed during Nelson's cutting-out raids of August 1801 (4).

The British government's growing frustration with conventional means forced the sea officers to listen to inventors and desperadoes of varying degrees of madness. In 1803 an American, Mumford, assisted by a smuggler, Etches, proposed sinking stone-filled blockships in the channel out of Boulogne harbour. The burden of anti-Flotilla operations was increasingly falling on Captain Edward Owen, who expressed strong scepticism about the value of such an achievement and even more about its chances of success: 'Those opinions are more

and more confirmed, with the further conviction that Mr Mumford has not the knowledge necessary . . . It seems [the enemy's] object . . .[is] to have foundations to build their batteries as far out as possible in the river. . . To lay these vessels where they do not interrupt the

2

3

navigation is making for them another foundation of which they would not fail to take advantage for erecting another battery, and the more solid the masonry the more to their advantage . . .' The 1918 attempts to block Ostend and Zeebrugge lend retrospective support to Owen's doubts about the ideas of 'sapient blockheads'

4

(so described by his forthright lieutenant, Abraham Crawford). Clockwork-controlled bombing attacks from small balloons were also proposed—which is less far-fetched than might at first appear, since the Austrians did it against Venice forty years later.

Napoleon had ordered the strengthening of Boulogne's defences, which by the end of 1804 were truly formidable (5), so there was even greater incentive to try something different. Eventually the government came to espouse Fulton's 'catamaran' torpedoes and, later, Congreve's rockets. The American inventor received some support from the Royal Navy's long-standing mavericks, Sidney Smith and Home Popham, but most of the fleet was less enthusiastic.

Catamarans were first tried in October 1804, when about one hundred and fifty craft, moored in double line, outside Boulogne Pier, gave the opportunity for using fireships and catamarans. Early on 1 October, Lord Keith, in the *Monarch*, 74, with three 64s, two 50s, and a number of frigates, sloops, bombs, brigs, and cutters, anchored about five miles from the Flotilla. Rear-Admiral Lacrosse, in the *prame Ville de Mayence*, expected, and was fully prepared for an attack, his boats rowing guard, and his shore batteries alert. After nightfall on the 2nd the fireships *Amity, Devonshire, Peggy,* and *Providence,* towed by armed launches, set out to attack, with a strong tide and breeze. The French opened fire as they approached, and sent forward some gunboats to dispute the passage with British launches, when some fighting ensued. The launches then released the fireships to drift. The French failed to sink them. The *Providence* blew up between two of the enemy's gunboats; the *Peggy* exploded after having passed through the French line; the *Devonshire* did not do so until later. *Amity* blew up innocuously, the other three wounded seven Frenchmen but did no real damage.

At the same time four or five catamarans were employed, the last exploding early in the morning. A clever feature of the deployment of these devices was the order that the pins whose withdrawal started the fuses should be returned by the operators to prove that they had actually armed the devices. As usual nobody seems to have bothered to tell the people who had to do the job. John Allison wrote:

> I proceeded with two casks in the *Leopard*'s long cutter, one in the bow, the other in the stern sheets, stood inshore and made the round battery to the southward. I dropped down until I could plainly see the flotilla, and driving directly for them by the tide, at the distance of about half a cable, I took the pin out of the machine on the aftermost cask. William Bailey, boatswain, laid hold of it after it was out. I put my ear

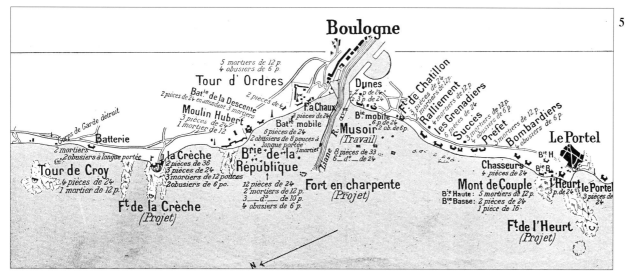

1. A plan of the 25-28 August 1804 attacks on Boulogne, Plate CLXIX from the *Naval Chronicle* 13 (1805). *NMM neg D9044*

2. 'A SE View of the town and Harbour of Boulogne with the Encampments on the heights, Shewing also the situation of the French and English Squadrons as taken at anchor by E D Lewis, HMS *Tartarus* off Boulogne', watercolour, no date. Although undated, it clearly relates to the August 1804 attack and not 1801 as erroneously assumed in *Nelson against Napoleon*. *NMM neg A929*

3. 'Napoleon essuyant le feu d'une fregate anglaise', wood engraving by Edeschamps after an original by Karl Cirardet, printed by H Plon, no date. *NMM ref PAI8480*

4. 'Combat naval devant Boulogne . . . nuit de 15 au 16 Aout 1801', engraving by Chavaut after an original by Crepin. *Musée de la Marine, Paris ref 79675*

5. Defences of Boulogne 1804, from original maps in the French Archives de Guerre, published in E Desbrière, *Projets et Tentatives de Débarquement aux Iles Britanniques*, Vol 3 (Paris 1902)

6. 'Calais. Fort Rouge', coloured aquatint after an original by Clarkson Stanfield, 1827. *NMM ref PAH2262*

to the machinery and heard it going, then ordered it to be thrown overboard and told Mr Gilbert, Mid., with Wm Rogers (whom I had stationed forward) to take the pin out of the cask in the bow. They answered it was out. I then ordered the cask to be thrown overboard. Mr Gilbert reported to me that he heard the machinery going. I think they must have heard the splashing of the casks from the shore, as they commenced firing musketry immediately, the balls coming over the boats. This was the first firing that took place. As I was intended for another service, viz to go with the armed boats; and having only had time to have the machinery explained (which I perfectly understood) I received no instructions to preserve the pins, nor did I think it necessary.

Only one caused damage: while chasing British boats *péniche* No 267 ran foul of one and was blown up with fourteen killed. There were no British casualties, but comparatively little return for the effort invested.

Fulton had already worked for some years in France, and in any case the French captured enough examples of his devices to know what they were up against. Thereafter, they effectually protected their flotilla by partially surrounding it with a very elaborately constructed arrangement of booms and chain cables.

On 8 December, an attempt was made, under the direction of Captain Popham, to destroy Fort Rouge (6), a pile-built battery at the mouth of Calais harbour, by means of the fire-vessel *Susannah* and a couple of catamarans. The *Susannah* exploded, but did little harm; one of the catamarans drifted clear of the fort, the other failed to blow up ; and on neither side was there any loss.

Next year another futuristic weapon was brought into service when long distance bombardment with the new Congreve rockets was tried in December of 1805. Unfortunately, 'the rockets were fired without effect, some of them burst in our own boats and none of them went in the intended direction,' as Keith wrote. However over the next few months that useful man Captain Owen helped Congreve improve his weapon in range, hitting power, (comparative) accuracy and reliability, as well as to develop practical means to bring it into action. As a result Owen's major rocket attack on Boulogne (8 October 1806) was well planned and went off well with 400 rockets fired and fires started. The enemy did not seem to be aware of what had hit him, the confusion being aided by the bomb *Desperate* adding her own contribution with incendiary 'carcasses'. A subsequent rocket bombardment of Calais was not so successful.

6

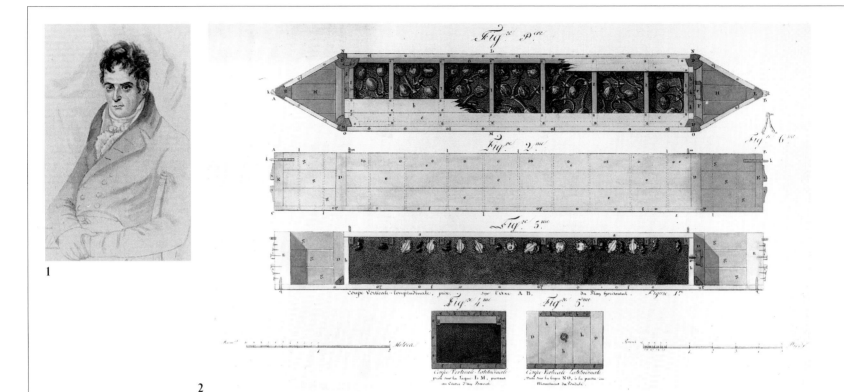

1

2

Fulton's Infernals

ROBERT FULTON (1) is best known to history as a steamboat pioneer, but after a short career as a painter and then a canal engineer his earliest real achievements were in the field of underwater technology. By his own account, he was driven to experiment with submarines and mines by an idealistic desire to free the high seas of the tyranny of navies, but since this sentiment was most strongly expressed after he returned to his native United States, it sounds like an *apologia* for the time spent working on behalf of France and Britain.

Fulton had been trying off and on since 1798 to inter-

est the French government in his prototype submarine, the *Nautilus*, as well as what modern observers would term mines, although Fulton called them 'torpedoes' after the electric ray, a species of stinging fish. His interest in steam also manifested itself early, in a proposal to employ steamships to speed Napoleon's planned invasion of Britain on its way. On the face of it, the British could be expected to give no encouragement to devices likely to challenge their conventional superiority at sea, but the French proved dilatory and costive with cash, so eventually Fulton accepted a discreet invitation to place his expertise at the disposal of the British government.

On his arrival in Britain in May 1804, Fulton (for security reasons known as Mr Francis) had to submit his proposals to a high-powered committee, comprising scientists like Sir Joseph Banks, Henry Cavendish and the engineer John Rennie; but it also included technically minded military men like William Congreve, an artillery expert who had developed the incendiary rocket, and Captain Home Popham, whose newly invented telegraphic code would be used to send Nelson's most famous signal at Trafalgar. At this point in time the country's attention was firmly fixed on the threat of the Boulogne Flotilla, and the Navy in particular was becoming ever more frustrated by its inability to interrupt the preparations for invasion. The committee reflected this priority, and although they thought the submarine technically feasible, they regarded the 'torpe-

3

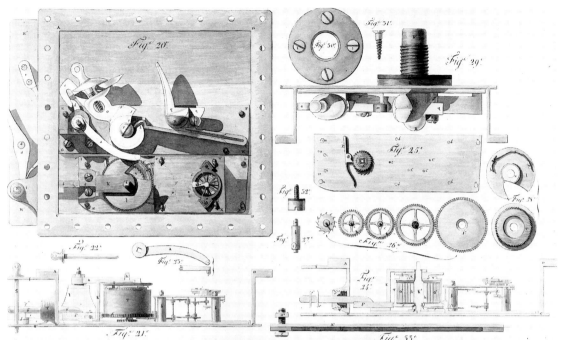

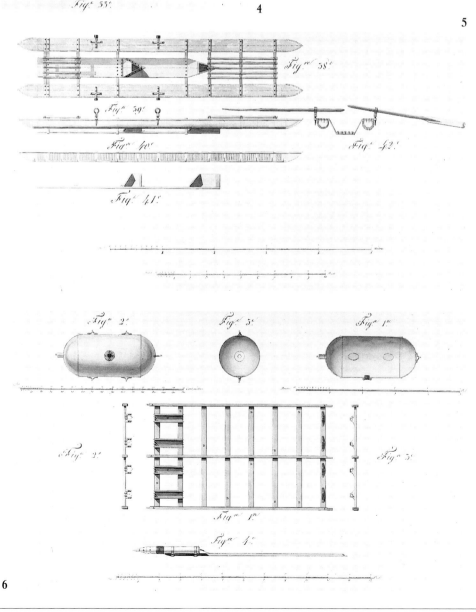

does' as more likely to be effective militarily. A contract was soon drawn up between Fulton and the government, and preparations put in hand immediately for what became known as the Catamaran Raids on Boulogne and Calais.

The technology was new, secret and of protean terminology so it is not surprising that the exact nature of a 'plunger', 'catamaran' or 'torpedo' have confused historians as much as they confused the public at the time. However, the National Maritime Museum possesses a portfolio of original technical drawings produced by a French engineer showing the devices used in both the 1804 and 1805 raids, and clearly taken from examples which did not explode, catch fire or otherwise work as intended.

For the October 1804 attack, Fulton himself said he had prepared '5 large coffers, 5 small, and 10 hogsheads', and two of these types are easily identified in the French portfolio. (2) is almost certainly a large coffer, and fits the description of the single carcass about 21ft long confusingly called a catamaran in William James's account of the attack. The hogshead is also depicted, in (3), and this seems to have been a recent invention. On 17 August 1804 Home Popham reported to Lord Keith:

> We have tried an experiment with a tin lantern . . . having a tube fixed in the lower part, and that tube fitted with slow fire composition and put in a cask charged with gunpowder and combustible balls; the cask has ballast boxes below it to keep it steady, and each boat may carry two to throw overboard when it may be judged expedient to do so. They are about the size of a forty-gallon cask . . .

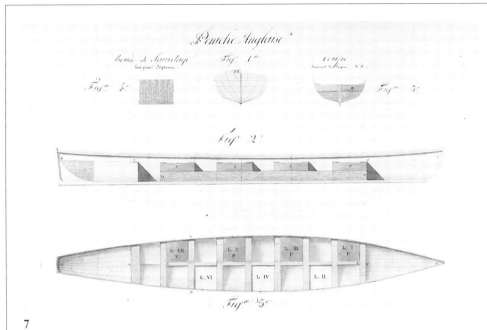

7

1. 'Robert Fulton Esqr', brown engraving by W S Lency after an original by Chappel and Miss Emmett, no date. The manuscript notes call him 'Inventor of the Steam boat. Was a man of rare mechanical ingenuity; inventor of the Catamaran system of blowing up vessels – his infernal machine . . .'
NMM ref PAD3249

The illustrations of the weapons are from a portfolio in the National Maritime Museum catalogued as GUN/19. An undated letter pasted inside the cover from a M Garriguer addresses the drawings to 'Monsieur Guillemard, ingénieur de la Marine, Rochefort'.

2. 'Machines Incendiares, Dirigées par les Anglais contre la Flotille Impériale, dans la nuit de dix au onze Vendémiare An 13', Plate 1.

3. 'Machines Incendiares, Dirigées par les Anglais contre la Flotille Impériale, dans la nuit de dix au onze Vendémiare An 13', Plate 2.

4. 'Machines Incendiares, Dirigées par les Anglais contre la Flotille Impériale, dans la nuit de dix au onze Vendémiare An 13', Plate 4.

5. 'Machines Incendiares, Dirigées par les Anglais contre la Flotille Impériale, dans la nuit de dix au onze Vendémiare An 13', Plate 5.

6. 'Machines Incendiares, Dirigées par les Anglais contre la Flotille Impériale, dans les nuits du huit au neuf Vendémiare et du 28 au 29 Brumaire An Quatorze', Plate 6.

7. 'Machines Incendiares, Dirigées par les Anglais contre la Flotille Impériale, dans les nuits du huit au neuf Vendémiare et du 28 au 29 Brumaire An Quatorze', Plate 7.
NMM negs D9059B-D9059G

The ballast boxes and the 'combustible balls' (enlarged in the right-hand figures) are clear in (3). The same letter expresses concern about tardy progress by the clock makers, since all the devices were fired by a timer comprising a clockwork mechanism setting off a flintlock, all sealed in a water-tight case. The portfolio reproduces these in loving detail at full size (4).

It is not clear how much input Home Popham had in these developments, but an earlier letter implies that he was a significant if not major partner in the design of the 'delivery system'. It was a rowing craft intended for minimal visibility—one experiment in a night of strong moonlight proved it was barely discernible at 25 fathoms and totally invisible at 35, even from halfway up the rigging—'and although the thing did not row so fast as I expected, yet it had more buoyancy and the men went in it with much confidence . . . and I am pretty confident it will now row three knots as soon as it is completed.' Popham called them 'plungers' and said they were rowed with two pairs of sculls, so must be the craft delineated in (5).

Since Fulton called his submarines 'plunging boats', or *plongeurs* in French, this has led some historians to believe that Popham was working on a diving boat, but the craft was simply an early example of 'stealth' technology; the crew even dressed in black and were masked. Of course, the craft had a catamaran hull and this feature took over as its identifying feature. Keith, for example, told Fulton: 'Of the catamaran I must beg leave to inform you that I have no good opinion. It has no power whatever on a substance of any considerable weight in a tide's way, or curl on the water's surface, and the persons on it are endangered.' This also explains the famous gibe in the satirical ballad published in *Cobbett's Political Register*:

Catamarans are ready
(Jack turns his quid and grins)
Where snugly you may paddle
In water to your chins

According to Captain Edward Owen, who was much involved with them, the mode of operation was to row across the bow of the target and drop two connected 'machines', one either side of the anchor cable to float down with the tide and make contact with the sides of the ship. Obviously the huge 21ft carcasses could not be meant, if it is assumed that the slatted platforms fore and aft of the sculling position were intended to carry the 'payload'; the big carcasses must have been towed into position, and Fig 6 of (2) shows a towing bracket. However, Owen appears to be describing the later attacks which benefited from some development in the weapons.

By this time more streamlined copper carcasses were being mentioned, far more sophisticated than the lead-lined wooded boxes shown in (2). In fact, two drawings in the French portfolio relate only to weapons used against them in October and November 1805, and one of these (6) shows what is probably a small copper carcass. It is certainly closer to Owen's notion of a lead-covered copper cylinder, but is nowhere near 18ft long, so must represent the smaller model. In a letter of 6 January 1805 to Fulton, Keith himself seems to have suggested tethering them in pairs, 'or attached to a buoy by cork floats and with hooks like fish jiggers fastened to it . . .' (see Fig 11 in '3'). Thereafter the carcasses were employed in pairs, and this has added a further level of confusion since the term 'catamaran' became transferred to them.

The portfolio also includes two other devices used in these attacks. One is a gig, one of those described in the 1806 inventory of the effects left over from the operations as 'fitted with cork as lifeboats' (7), used to rescue the crews of the plungers and explosion vessels. The other is the Congreve rocket and its quadruple launching frame (6), another weapon of the future given its first naval outing during these attacks on the invasion flotilla.

Popham referred to Fulton's inventions as the 'New Curiosities' but to most in the Navy they went by the traditional term for explosive and fiery devices, 'infernals'. Fulton finally demonstrated the potential of underwater weapons by blowing up the anchored brig *Dorothea* in Walmer Roads in October 1805 with two of his torpedoes, but in the changed atmosphere after Trafalgar the British lost interest, and having failed to extort large sums of money from the government to preserve the secrets of these weapons, Fulton sailed for America at the end of 1806

1

Anti-Flotilla operations: the North Sea

THE DUTCH contribution to the assembly of the National Flotilla (1), at Flushing and Ostend, was watched by a squadron under the flamboyant Commodore Sidney Smith. On 15 May 1804 the inshore part consisted of the brig sloops *Cruiser* and *Rattler*, under Commander Hancock. Twenty-three gun-vessels were seen to haul out of Ostend harbour (2), and anchor. As darkness came on, Hancock got under way with his two sloops, and re-anchored within long range of the pier batteries to prevent the escape of the enemy. In the morning a Dutch flotilla, under Rear-Admiral Verhuell, was sighted consisting of the *prames Ville d'Anvers* (flagship) and *Ville d'Aix*, nineteen schooners, and thirty-eight schuyts, mounting more than one hundred long guns between them, with 4000 troops. *Cruiser* and *Rattler*, using the tide, closed. An hour later, the wind becoming favourable to the sloops, Verhuell turned back.

Smith's 50-gun *Antelope*, with the frigates *Penelope* and *Aimable*, was coming up but the sloops pressed on, and took a schuyt. In the meantime the wind had slightly shifted; and Verhuell turned back towards Ostend. A little later, a shift of wind placed both sloops upon the lee beam of the flotilla. The *Ville d'Anvers* and several

schooners and schuyts opened a heavy fire, as did the Blankenberghe batteries. Despite this the British pair drove ashore the *Ville d'Anvers* and four of the schooners. Shortly afterwards the *Aimable* followed by *Antelope* and *Penelope* also began to drive other schooners and schuyts ashore. Finally Smith signalled to cease firing, his ships being nearly aground (3). The remnants of Verhuell's flotilla, covered by the gun-vessels, got into Ostend. Next morning four gunbrigs were sent in to endeavour to destroy or capture the grounded *Ville d'Anvers*; but she was so well covered by guns and mortars on the beach sand dunes, that they were beaten off. On the 19th, assisted by the sloops *Galgo*, and *Inspector*, they made another ineffectual effort. Ultimately the *Ville d'Anvers* and five out of eight grounded schooners and schuyts were re-floated.

On 23 October 1804 two *prames* and eighteen armed schuyts left Ostend for the westward, and were chased by the brig sloop *Cruiser*, the gunbrigs *Blazer*, *Conflict*, *Tigress* and *Escort*, and the hired armed cutters *Admiral Mitchell* and *Griffin*. The headmost *prame* was brought to action, and soon silenced; but as the tide was falling, darkness was increasing, the vessels were in very shoal

2

3

water, and the sands and currents were unfamiliar, the *Cruiser* hauled off and anchored. The *Conflict*, however, had grounded, and, when they found that they could not get her off, her crew abandoned her, and pulled for the *Cruiser*. An attempt to bring her off was afterwards made by the *Admiral Mitchell* and *Griffin*; but by that time the *Conflict*, high and dry, was held by the enemy, who were supported by field pieces and howitzers on shore, so the British had to retire .

The spring of 1805 saw the part of the Franco-Batavian

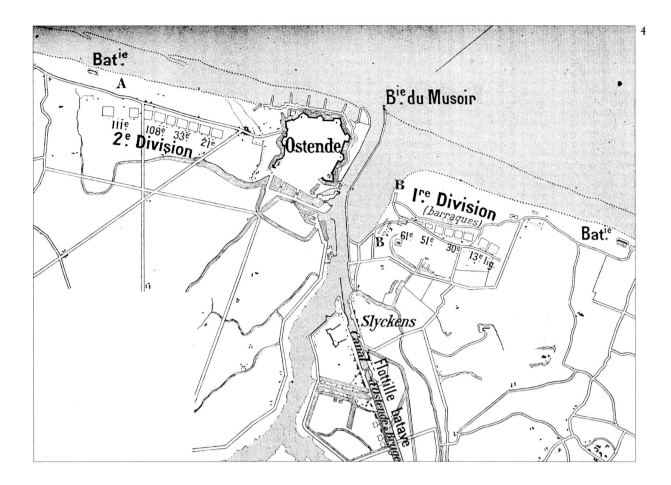

flotilla which had been driven into Ostend (4) by Smith moved as far to the westward as Dunkirk, whence it crept piecemeal along the coast to Ambleteuse. On a dark night with a fresh wind blowing, thirty-three gun-vessels and nineteen transports had safely passed Gravelines and Calais; but, just before dawn on 24 April, they were thrown into some confusion by a shift of wind, and change of tide. Most made for an anchorage near Cape Gris-Nez, although eight schuyts were too far to follow. At daybreak the enemy was discovered by the *Leda*, two sloops *Harpy*, and *Railleur*, a bomb, and eight gunbrigs. The squadron chased, and the *Gallant*, and the *Watchful* closed the schuyts, which were aided by gun-brigs and shore batteries. The *Gallant*, struck between wind and water, had to haul off; but the *Watchful* took one schuyt, and the *Railleur*, with the *Locust*, and the *Starling*, presently coming up, took six more. The following morning *Archer* captured another schuyt which had drifted off. The rest reached Ambleteuse, assisted by launches sent from Boulogne.

Nearly all the remaining part of the Ostend division was assembled by the end of May at Dunkirk under Verhuell, blocked by unfavourable winds until 17 July, when most of it got under way. Certain small craft remained behind, with instructions to follow if it should be seen that Verhuell was intercepted by the British.

Verhuell had with him four *prame*s and thirty-two schooner rigged gun-vessels and he formed his flotilla into two overlapping lines. The British squadron off Gravelines, the *Ariadne*, 20, three or four sloops and bombs, and some five gunbrigs, attacked, driving ashore or disabling eleven of the gun-vessels, and damaging one *prame*, in spite of the very heavy fire kept up both by the flotilla and by the batteries. About midnight, the rest of the division anchored off Calais. The noise of the firing brought more British ships from the Downs including a 50, and the British attacked again. But the Dutch were too well protected by the forts and, after a two hours' cannonade, the British were drawn away westward. For Rear-Admiral Lacrosse, at Boulogne, had ordered several divisions of gun-vessels to get under way as if to attack Owen's squadron, which then drove them under the batteries near Wimereux.

Verhuell started again on 18 July, taking with him Marshal Davout. The batteries kept off the British until near Wissant where sloops and gunbrigs succeeding in driving six of the gun-vessels ashore. The frigates, drawing too much water to get within effective range of the smaller vessels, managed only to drive ashore two gun-vessels. The British vessels had to withdraw to repair damages; and, while they were away, the whole of the Franco-Batavian flotilla reached Boulogne.

1. 'Vue du Chantier de l'Amiraute de Zelande a Flessingue en 1779', etching by J Arends after his own original, 1780. After 1803 these facilities were turned over to the production of Napoleon's Flotilla craft.
NMM ref PAH2245

2. 'View of the Town & Harbour of Ostend', Plate CXLIV from the *Naval Chronicle* XI (1804), published by Joyce Gold.
NMM neg D9042

3. 'To Commodore Sir William Sidney Smith . . . This View of the Squadron under his Command engaging the Enemy's Flotilla consisting of fifty-nine sail, Brigs Schuyts Schooners & Praams near Ostend on the 16th May 1804 is . . . inscribed by . . . Robert Dodd', aquatint published by Robert Dodd, no date.
NMM ref PAH8010

4. Plan of the defences of Ostend as in 1804, from an original map in the French Archives de Guerre, published in E Desbrière, *Projets et Tentatives de Débarquement aux Iles Britanniques*, Vol 3 (Paris 1902)

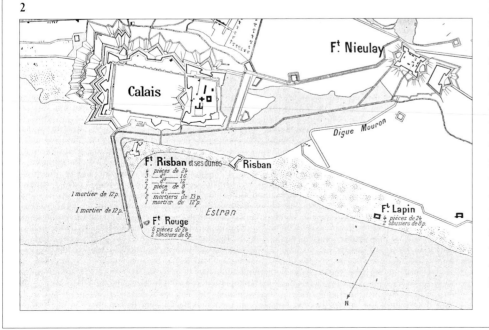

1

French naval bases: Boulogne and the invasion ports

ETWEEN 1803 and 1805 the chief focus of the war was on the French coastal city and fishing port of Boulogne and its environs (1). When the Franco-Spanish fleet retreated to Cadiz following Calder's action, the *Grand Armée* began to march away from its camp on the heights towards Ulm and Austerlitz (on 26 August 1805, though Napoleon himself stayed until 3 September), giving up their dreams of invasion for the reality of victory against Austria and Russia. It then reverted to just another harbour for the British squadrons to watch, but for two years those vessels had been standing by for the launch of an invasion attempt centred on that port. It had also fulfilled the same function in the period running up to the Peace of Amiens, after

Austria had left the war and when Britain stood alone. As shown in an earlier volume of this series, Nelson's attacks on the port at this time had proved both costly and fruitless (see *Nelson against Napoleon*, pages 138-140).

As a haven Boulogne had grown out of the gap made by the estuary of the small river Liane in the cliffs of the French coast. The Romans had used it as their continental headquarters for the *Classis Britannicus* (British fleet—the chief maritime defence against the Saxon raiders who would take over what would become England), with a lighthouse which matched the one at Dover on the other side of the straits. By the middle ages the city had become a double settlement. The port itself was down by the Liane, whilst on the hill behind it was the high town, with its thirteenth-century ramparts. Its importance had declined since the Hundred Years War and the conflicts of the sixteenth century when it was an important frontier fortress, marking its English opposite number at Calais (until that town fell to the Duke of Guise), and defending against attack from Flanders further east. By the later eighteenth century, however, it had acquired the significance as a packet port for trade with England that it still retains, whilst both here and at neighbouring Calais English debtors and others wishing to live cheaply had settled in some numbers—though they were temporarily dispersed by the war, as Napoleon had, against previous practice, seized and interned all male Britons of military age immediately war broke out. He had also made Boulogne an administrative centre for a special commissioner with responsibility for the northeast frontier region of France.

Round the corner of Cape Gris-Nez lay the other, and

2

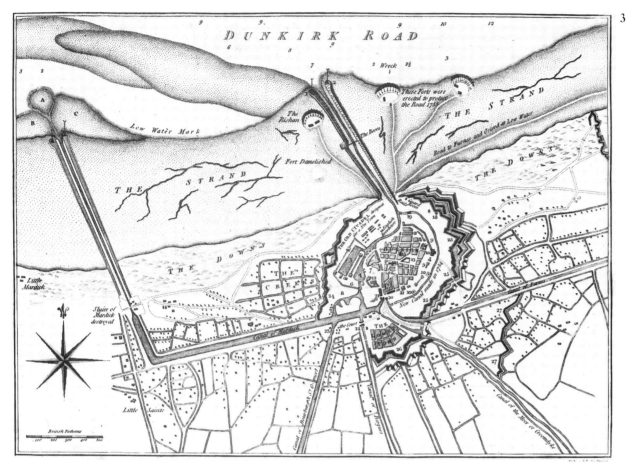

1. A seaward view of Boulogne as it was in July 1804; note the camp on the heights surrounding the port. Plate CXCIII from the *Naval Chronicle* XIV (1805), published by Joyce Gold. *NMM neg D9051*

2. Calais and its defences in 1804-5 from an original map in the French Archives de Guerre, published in E Desbrière, *Projets et Tentatives de Débarquement aux Iles Britanniques*, Vol 3 (Paris 1902).

3. 'Plan of the town, fortifications & Environs of Dunkirk', engraving by Neele, published by I Wallis, 25 August 1793. *NMM ref PAI5334*

4. Étaples and the mouth of the river Canche in 1804-5 from original maps in the French Archives de Guerre, published in E Desbrière, *Projets et Tentatives de Débarquement aux Iles Britanniques*, Vol 3 (Paris 1902).

5. Wimereux in 1804-5 from an original map in the French Archives de Guerre, published in E Desbrière, *Projets et Tentatives de Débarquement aux Iles Britanniques*, Vol 3 (Paris 1902).

6. Ambleteuse in 1804-5 from original maps in the French Archives de Guerre, published in E Desbrière, *Projets et Tentatives de Débarquement aux Iles Britanniques*, Vol 3 (Paris 1902).

7. 'View of Dunkirk', Plate CLXXII from the *Naval Chronicle* XIII (1805), published by Joyce Gold. *NMM neg PAI8504*

8. 'Vue de Dieppe Prise du fond du Port', coloured aquatint engraved by Ambroise Louis Garneray, published by Basset, no date. *NMM ref PAH9973*

more important, packet port of Calais (2), once an English possession and still, then and now, the chief entry port for English visitors to France. The two are at the narrowest point of the sea passage between England and France, which explains their role in the cross-channel passenger transit trade, minimising the exposure to sea-sickness, just as an invasion launched from those points and their vicinity would lessen the exposure of

the French invasion force to defending ships and boats. However, Calais was less obvious as an invasion port than Boulogne. This may have owed something to the sandbanks which in common with its more easterly neighbours, Dunkirk (3) and Ostend, made access and egress trickier; and to the more obvious potential of Boulogne's river estuary for the rapid construction of the large basin needed for the harbouring of the hun-

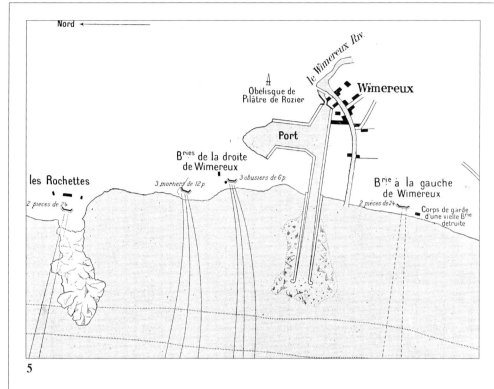

5

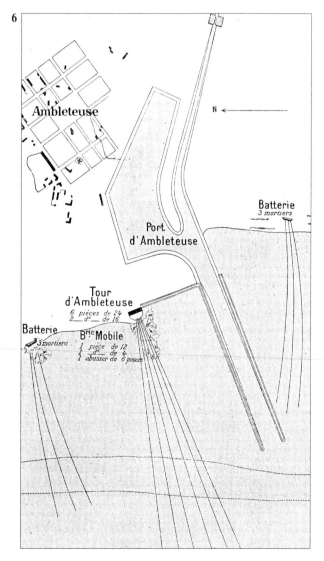

dreds of landing craft. Probably the fact that the high ground behind and either side of Boulogne gave elevated sites and therefore both better range and greater command to the shore batteries needed to keep the British cruisers at a distance also contributed to the choice. It also helped that this was a rich agricultural region with reasonable road communications with the rest of France, and not too far from Paris. Feeding the huge assemblage of soldiers and of draught and cavalry horses would not present the enormous problem that would be set by gathering an invasion force in the comparatively infertile and remote area of Brest.

All the harbours along this part of the French coast were small, cramped and not very adequate, and there were no anchorages safe enough from the weather or defensible against marauding British warships. Napoleon set to work with characteristic and demonic energy to modify the river-mouth harbours of Étaples (4), Wimereux (5), Ambleteuse, and, above all, Boulogne to accommodate the large flotilla needed to carry an army sufficient to overwhelm the British defences. Boulogne was given a semi-circular basin and had an enlarged, straightened and deepened access channel between long dikes. Much the same was done, on a smaller scale, at Ambleteuse (6), whilst similar labours had produced reasonably capacious harbours at the other two designated bases. All the ports were given extra forts and gun batteries.

Napoleon also worked on Ostend, Dunkirk (7) and Calais, where the reserve divisions of the Flotilla were based. Similar works were initiated and completed further afield to improve the ports, such as Dieppe and Le Havre, which were staging points and harbours of refuge for the steady flow of the invasion craft from their building ports further along the coast. The invasion never took place, but the preparations for it have benefited that part of the coast of France ever since. Also large numbers of forts and batteries were built to protect the ports themselves, and the coastal route by which the newly completed invasion craft slipped in from east and west. However, the sandbanks and difficult tides of that coast continued to obstruct access and cause as much danger and difficulty to the crews of the unwieldy invasion craft as the British gunboats and cruisers which were constantly trying to interrupt the coastal flow; and as the bombardments, secret weapons and cutting-out attacks the British produced in an attempt to destroy the craft in harbour.

The sheer size of the invasion force accommodated in the four main invasion ports and the three back-up ones can be found in the section on the National Flotilla in this book. The 160,000-strong *Grande Armée* which it was to carry was based in a vast tented township on the

7

heights to the north of Boulogne (at Moulin-Herbert). With its attendant civilians, official and unofficial, this must have been one of the greatest concentrations of population in the Europe of the day, and all organised with the military precision and tireless energy characteristic of Napoleon. There were other formations based not far away at Saint Omer and elsewhere, within a day or two's marching from the invasion ports. It was, however, at Boulogne that, on 16 August 1804, Napoleon made the first presentation of his new decoration, the *Légion d'Honneur*. It was also from here that the soldiers marched down for the practice embarkations which would never have any practical result, except for the unfortunates who perished in the full dress rehearsal carried out in bad weather. After the *Grande Armée* marched away, the camp continued in use for concentrating troops, accommodating them and training them. It was here that the new divisions that fought the Austrians in 1809 were formed, and here that much of the French part of the army that invaded Russia in 1812 was assembled. The site is now commemorated by a memorial pillar on the heights from which the troops could sometimes see the coastline of an England they would never manage to invade and, closer to, the ever-present sails of the blockading flotilla whose presence forbade that project.

8

Part III

THE FRENCH GRAND STRATEGY

BY THE end of the summer of 1804, Napoleon had come to realise the limitations of France's traditional concentration on military warfare by land, and her inability to match British seapower throughout the previous decade of hostilities. Now, while the British commmanded the sea, the French navy was confined to port. If the Royal Navy suffered the trials, wear and tear, and losses by wrecking that arose from close blockade, the French navy deteriorated faster by remaining without exercise at sea. Blockaded in every port, the French navy could not even begin to drill its seamen—who were anyway in short supply—or to establish that confidence in its officers which would permit them to engage and defeat the British fleet in battle. Above all, unless the French navy was able to protect the National Flotilla, Napoleon could not realise his ambition of invading Britain. In the first five months of 1804 not a single French naval vessel put to sea from Brest, and even in August a sally lasted only a few hours.

To clear the British from their blockade stations, the Royal Navy had either to be drawn aside or driven off, probably both. Realising this, by degrees Napoleon began to develop a grand strategy which he would attempt to follow throughout the months that led up to the Battle of Trafalgar on 21 October 1805. His first consideration was for the appointment of officers who would be capable of following his orders. In June 1804 he dismissed Vice-Admiral Laurent Truguet from his command at Brest and replaced him with Vice-Admiral Honoré Ganteaume. In mid August 1804 the death of Admiral Latouche-Tréville, in command at Toulon, gave him the opportunity to replace him with the forty-one year old Vice-Admiral Pierre-Charles-Jean-Baptiste-Silvestre Villeneuve. At Rochefort he appointed Rear-Admiral Edouard-Thomas de Burgues Missiessy. All three of his new commanders were to play their part in Napoleon's strategy.

Their opponents, as they were late in 1804,

were Vice-Admiral Lord Nelson off Toulon, commanding, at least nominally, thirteen ships of the line and twelve frigates, besides smaller vessels. Off Brest, Admiral Sir William Cornwallis had thirty-three ships of the line, though only a squadron of perhaps six stood guard off the harbour at Brest itself; another six at least, including his flagship, kept station nearby off Ushant; while other squadrons hovered off Cherbourg, Lorient, Rochefort and Ferrol. The latter port, though Spanish, contained five French vessels which were kept, quite deliberately, under 'observation'. Finally, in the Downs, Lord Keith commanded twenty-one ships of the line and twenty-nine frigates, dispersed in squadrons off the Texel, Heligoland and Helvoet, off the Flemish coast and along the Flotilla ports as far south as Le Havre.

As Napoleon may have been informed by French intelligence, rarely did these British fleet commanders have at their disposal their full complements of ships: generally around half were replenishing, refitting, convoying or on passage to or from their particular stations. Nevertheless, the British presence was constant, and in sufficient force to present a challange to any French ships that might venture forth. Napoleon had to devise a means by which both the French fleet could be consolidated and the omnipresent British squadrons might be swept aside. On 2 July 1804 he came up with the basis of the strategy which he would pursue for the next fifteen months. He proposed that the Mediterranean squadron sail from Toulon to Rochefort and Cherbourg, engaging if necessary the British squadrons its way, permitting the Brest fleet to emerge, to command the Channel and allow the flotilla to sail.

By the end of September, Napoleon had developed this idea further, incorporating instructions for both the exercise of the French fleet and the relief of French colonies. On 29 September 1804 he ordered Villeneuve to sail from Toulon with at least ten ships of the line,

if possible avoiding Nelson's Mediterranean fleet, to collect one French vessel in Cadiz, and to sail for the northern shore of South America where they would land 5600 troops in Surinam. There Villeneuve would be joined by Missiessy from Rochefort with another six of the line, who would previously have deposited troops on Martinique and assisted towards the repossession of St Lucia and St Domingue. Meanwhile a third smaller French expedition would sail from Toulon, take St Helena, land troops at Senegal, retake neighbouring Gorée and attack British settlements down the coast of Africa.

Napoleon supposed that, reeling from the impact of these sudden assaults, the British government would hardly expect its own shores to come under attack. The invasion attempt would thus benefit from an element of surprise. Together Villeneuve and Missiessy would return from the Caribbean, pick up the five French ships blocked in Ferrol and the remainder in Rochefort, and arrive off Boulogne ready to escort the National Flotilla across the Channel. The British would hardly expect the flotilla to sail, for Ganteaume would already have sailed from Brest with his twenty-one of the line to land 18,000 men in Lough Swilly Bay on the north of Ireland where they would be instructed to march straight for Dublin. They would be reinforced by 25,000 Dutch and French troops sent out from the Texel. Ganteaume would then return to the Channel to join with Villeneuve and Missiessy, reinforcing the combined French fleet to more than forty vessels.

Though planned like a campaign on land, where Napoleon's victories had been achieved by speed, surprise and overwhelming force, he nevertheless realised the sea brought unforeseeable obstacles and accidents which might prevent any one of his objectives being achieved. Yet he saw himself reaching either England or Ireland: 'one of these two operations must succeed . . . in either event we will have won the war.' He had not anticipated actually what would happen. Ganteaume's orders were intercepted by the British and all related instructions had to be cancelled.

Once conceived, however, the strategy stuck. In October Napoleon revived part of the plan. On the 26th of that month Missiessy was directed to retake St Domingue and St Lucia, and reinforce Martinique and Guadaloupe. The instructions were modified on 23 December, and he sailed with six of the line and two frigates on 10 January. Six days later Villeneuve was also directed to sail for the Caribbean and to seize Cayenne, Surinam, Berbice and Demerara. He sailed on 18 January but was forced to put back into Toulon, and his part in a combined operation was cancelled. Missiessy began operations in the West Indies, but in March 1805 received instructions to return to Rochefort. Though having done everything he could to comply with his instructions, he returned to expressions of disappointment from Napoleon, partly because the latter had, in further instructions, ordered Missiessy to remain in the West Indies, for by then event were raising the campaign to a new level.

In October off Cadiz British ships took three Spanish frigates, one carrying silver, and sank another, also carrying treasure; on 12 December 1804 Spain declared war on Britain, and effectively placed at Napoleon's disposal nine ships of the line in Ferrol, six in Cartagena, and sixteen in Cadiz. The Spanish Commander-in-Chief, Admiral Don Frederico Gravina, energetically set to work to make the ships ready. Then at the end of February, French fears of Austrian hostilities having been allayed by pacific reassurances from the Emperor at Vienna, plans for a land campaign on the Rhine and in Italy were cancelled. For a while Napoleon was freed to concentrate on his invasion plan.

On 2 March new instructions issued to Ganteaume visualised the Brest fleet of twenty-one of the line releasing the Spanish nine and surviving French four ships in Ferrol and sailing with them for Martinique where they would rendezvous with Missiessy, whom Napoleon hoped had remained in the West Indies, and with Villeneuve with his eleven of the line and as many Spanish vessels as were ready to sail. From Martinique, Villeneuve would return to the Channel with over forty of the line. At Brest, the embarkation of troops began on 23 March and the fleet shifted to Bertheaume Bay preparatory to sailing on 27 March. That day, however, twenty-eight British sail of the line appeared off the Ile de Béniguet. Instructed not to engage the British fleet, Ganteaume put back into Brest.

That very day, 30 March 1805, Villeneuve sailed from Toulon with eleven of the line and six frigates, with 3070 soldiers on board. He was to rendezvous with the other squadron at Martinique then return to Euope via St Domingue, the Canaries and Cadiz, where he would receive further directions for invading the Channel. Off Toulon two British frigates noted his departure, but both immediately departed to inform Nelson, who at that time was off the Sardinian coast. Heading southwest between the Balearic Islands and mainland Spain, Villeneuve made Cathagena on 7 April but, delaying only eight hours, sailed again without the eight Spanish vessels in harbour. Passing Gibraltar on the 9th, British frigates from Sir John Orde's squadron off Cadiz went off in haste to warn him. That night, Villeneuve anchored off Cadiz, Orde keeping his distance, but again, impatient to be off, Villeneuve gave the Spanish squadron of six of the line under Admiral Gravina and a single French 74 time only to weigh before heading out into the Atlantic. Straggling after him, only one Spanish vessel overtook him on 11 April; the others eventually caught up with him at Martinique on 16 May.

Meanwhile what had happened to Nelson? Having instituted a loose blockade of Toulon, open enough to permit a French force to sail, but keeping the port under observation, Nelson with the core of his squadron had taken up a winter station in the Maddalena Islands off the north coast of Sardinia. Some might have argued that his blockade was too loose. On the occasion of Villeneuve's breakout from Toulon on 18 January he had suffered a desperate search for him. Then Villeneuve had been seen sailing southeast, but Nelson's frigates had lost sight of the French squadron and he had been forced to search for it as far east as Alexandria, only to discover that it had put back into Toulon when he reached Malta on 19 February. Virtually the same search was to be re-enacted after Villeneuve's departure on 30 March, though this time Nelson sent his few frigates in seach and waited himself with the main force of his squadron close to the island of Ustica, north of Palermo, Sicily. It was 18 April before Nelson heard that Villeneuve had passed through the Straits of Gibraltar ten days before heading west.

Nelson thus set out in chase, though keeping his options, for when he passed through the Straits, completely open. Still he was wracked by doubts as to the precise destination of the French, as were the other British squadron commanders off Ferrol and Brest. They had contingency plans. When Villeneuve had reached Cadiz, leaving observation frigates, Orde with his five of the line had fallen back to reinforce the Channel fleet off Brest. Sir Robert Calder off Ferrol was also prepared to fall back on Ushant. Nevertheless, by the time Nelson reached Gibraltar the lack of news of Villeneuve in European waters seemed to suggest he had crossed the Atlantic; off Lagos, Rear-Admiral Campbell, then in Portuguese service, positively assured Nelson that Villeneuve had sailed for the West Indies. Nelson made up his mind. Leaving Rear-Admiral Bickerton in command in the Mediterranean, on 11 May with his ten of the line he sailed in chase.

Nelson's report of his decision to sail himself to the West Indies reached the Admiralty in London on 5 June. Lord Barham at the Admiralty responded at once, formally approving his decision. In London, by a process of elimination, Villeneuve's destination had been surmised, but Barham had had no clear preference who should go in pursuit, though clearly to reinforce the squadron in the West Indies one of the admirals at his disposal had to follow. If Nelson had not gone, Barham had expected Nelson either to stay in the Mediterranean or to retire on Ushant in reinforcement of the Channel Fleet and on 9 May had issued orders to Nelson to that effect. Had Nelson taken either of these two other options, Barham had intended to despatch Collingwood to the West Indies, and had given directions to him to prepare for that destination on 10 May and a week later, as he prepared to sail for Lisbon, sent to him the following logistical instructions.

If you have positive knowledge that the Combined Fleet has sailed for the West

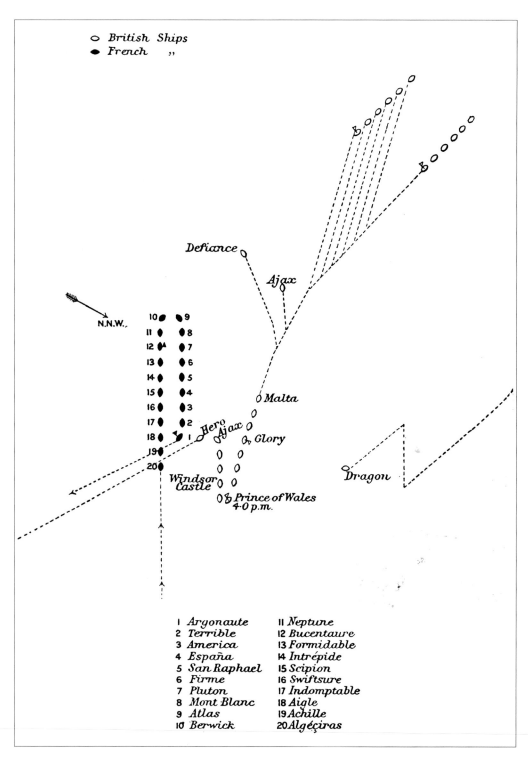

British Ships
French   "

Defiance

Ajax

N.N.W.

10 ● ● 9
11 ● ● 8
12 ● ● 7
13 ● ● 6
14 ● ● 5
15 ● ● 4
16 ● ● 3
17 ● ● 2   Malta
          Hero Ajax
18 ●   1   Glory
19 ●
20 ●   Windsor
       Castle   Dragon
           Prince of Wales
              4·0 p.m.

  1 Argonaute   11 Neptune
  2 Terrible   12 Bucentaure
  3 America   13 Formidable
  4 España   14 Intrépide
  5 San Raphael   15 Scipion
  6 Firme   16 Swiftsure
  7 Pluton   17 Indomptable
  8 Mont Blanc   18 Aigle
  9 Atlas   19 Achille
 10 Berwick   20 Algéçiras

*A diagrammatic representation of Calder's Action, 22 July
1805. From Julian Corbett,* The Campaign of Trafalgar
(London 1910).

Indies and *that Admiral Nelson has followed them,*
you will detach thither such a number of
your ships of the line that Lord Nelson may
have a total of twelve of them, provided
that the enemy force is not more than eighteen. But if this should be the case, you are
to give Lord Nelson in addition as many
ships as the Allies have in excess of eighteen
. . . If Lord Nelson has not followed the
enemy to the West Indies, you are to pursue
them to the Barbadoes with twelve of the
line, if the enemy has not more than eighteen; and, should they have more than
eighteen, you will take with you in addition
to the first mentioned twelve as many more
as they have in excess of eighteen.

By this time, however, Nelson was on his
way to the West Indies, and Villeneuve was
approaching Martinique and St Lucia, which
were sighted on 14 May. By 16 May, furthermore, the remainder of the Spanish squadron
from Cadiz and the French 74 had joined
Villeneuve; also on 30 May two ships of the line
with 861 soldiers from Rochefort. He now had
twenty ships of the line under his command.
Yet the French admiral here felt obliged to kill
time. His instructions of 2 March directed him
to wait for Ganteaume from Brest until 22
June. He thus detached three frigates to cruise
to windward to gain intelligence, harrass
British trade and gain supplies; also to retake
from the British the Diamond Rock, an islet off
the southwest point of Martinique, which
commanded entry to its harbour and ham-
pered the trade of the island.

On 30 May, however, Villeneuve received
new instructions, dated 14 April, directing him
to return to Europe and join with the fifteen
French and Spanish ships in Ferrol, then join
with Ganteaume's twenty-one at Brest and
enter the Channel with over fifty ships of the
line. He was also conscious of running down
his provisions. Nevertheless, aware of the need
for troops in Europe, he took on board soldiers
from Martinique and Guadeloupe to make his
land forces up to 8600 men, and sailed on 5 June
passing Antigua to leeward. To the north on 8
June he took a valuable British convoy. Possibly
from them, he heard that Nelson was searching for him and promptly headed for Europe.

On the very day that Villeneuve set sail,
Nelson also sailed from Barbados. There he had
taken under his command two ships of the line
left there by Cochrane, making his own force
up to twelve. He himself suspected Villeneuve
would have attacked one or more rich British
sugar islands like Antigua or Jamaica, to the
northwest. Yet he received from Lieutenant-
General Sir William Myers, Commander-in-
Chief of the British forces at Barbados and in
the Leeward Islands, a note from General
Brereton at St Lucia of a report from Gros Islet,
between St Lucia and Martinique, that the
enemy fleet had passed there sailing south
towards, Brereton supposed, Barbados or
Trinidad. Myers supported Brereton as a
source. Nelson thus steered south.

However, three days later he was writing
furiously that Brereton's information must

have been 'very incorrect'. Off Grenada on 9 June he received another report, this time from General Prevost at Dominica that three days before the Franco-Spanish fleet had been sighted there passing north. At Antigua on 12 June this was confirmed, and Nelson rightly concluded 'that some cause, *orders*, or *inability* to perform any services in these seas, has made them resolve to proceed direct to Europe'. Four days later, he report to the Admiralty that he too was returning to Europe and that, he supposed, he was no further behind Villeneuve than 80 leagues, or 240 miles. In fact, the Nelson and Villeneuve were on diverging courses, the former heading for the Azores and the Straits of Gibraltar, the latter for the more northerly latitude of Ferrol.

Nelson reached the southern tip of Spain on 18 July, where he found Collingwood blockading Cadiz. Nelson was completely exhausted. He had just sailed about 3500 miles, having not been out of the *Victory* since 16 June 1803. Willingly, as he himself wrote, did he embrace the Admiralty permission to return to England to recoup his health. Sailing north, he left his squadron with Cornwallis off Ushant, and landed in England on 19 August 1805 to begin what was to be his last long leave.

Meanwhile, at that very time, Villeneuve continued to fulfill Napoleon's instructions and bring together the squadrons of the Franco-Spanish navies. Returning from the West Indies on his more northerly route, on 22 July, 39 leagues east-southeast of Ferrol, Villeneuve encountered the squadron of fifteen of the line under Vice-Admiral Sir Robert Calder. The latter's objective was to prevent Villeneuve uniting with the vessels in Ferrol, but in baffling winds and poor visibility—a thick haze intensified in patches to impenetrable fog—it was late in the day, 3.20pm, before Calder signalled for his squadron to tack and engage the enemy, and another two hours before the enagement began. The six Spanish vessels forming the head of Villeneuve's line took the brunt of the attack and two surrendered. But at 8.25pm Calder discontinued the action, which was never resumed, though for two days the two forces kept one another under observation. By 25 July they were sufficiently far apart for Villeneuve to steer away for Vigo Bay. There he left two battered ships

before slipping into Ferrol on 31 July. When Calder returned to his station off that port on 9 August, he was alarmed to find twenty-nine French and Spanish vessels inside, opposed to which he had but nine. Recognising the odds against him were too great, Calder retired on Ushant for reinforcement.

But Villeneuve was not to remain where he was. In Ferrol he learned that Rear-Admiral Allemand was at sea with the Rochefort squadron. Putting out a frigate to attempt to find Allemand, on 9 August Villeneuve himself sailed with the same intention. He took with him all twenty-nine ships of the line. Had he found Allemand probably he would have headed for Brest and the Channel. But he did not do so, and instead turned south for Cadiz where, pushing Collingwood's small squadron aside, he took refuge on 20 August. In Cadiz, six Spanish ships of the line were ready for sea, giving Villeneuve thirty-five of the line to contest the Channel. So far, in spite of a variety of obstacles, Napoleon's strategy had succeeded.

The reason why Villeneuve did not make contact with Allemand was that the frigate he sent on this mission was captured. 'Capture of Le Didon Augt 10th 1805. By Phoenix off Corunna', coloured aquatint engraved by Thomas Sutherland after an original by Thomas Whitcombe, no date.   NMM ref PAD5694

1

1. 'Admiral Sir William Cornwallis 1744-1819', engraving by Charles Turner Warren after an original by Thomas Uwins, published by J Stratford, 22 June 1805. *NMM ref PAD3291*

2. 'Chart of the Road and port of Brest', Plate XLVIII from the *Naval Chronicle IV* (1800), published by Joyce Gold. *NMM neg D9053*

The blockade of Brest

AS SOON as war was declared Admiral Sir William Cornwallis (1) sailed on 16 May 1803 to reimpose the blockade of Brest, the linchpin of British naval strategy. Having succeeded St Vincent in command of the Channel Fleet in 1801, this was a return to familiar waters (2), and he was again entrusted with establishing a close blockade, initially with only a handful of ships cruising off Ushant, but in increasing force as the Navy found the men and stores to put its ships into service. As ships came available, the two- and three-deckers with Cornwallis were augmented by an Inshore Squadron of three line of battle ships and two frigates patrolling in the entrance to Brest (3); however, Cornwallis' concerns also included the French ships at the Biscay ports or returning thence from the West Indies, Dutch ships at Ferrol and the British frigates cruising in the Atlantic to protect the homeward bound trade (and, not incidentally, to press desperately needed seamen for the fleet).

Mainly due to the lack of frigates, five French ships of the line returning from San Domingo were able to elude Rear-Admiral Sir George Campbell's squadron and reach Corunna in mid July, later passing on to Ferrol. These ports thus had to be watched, and a squadron was detached for this duty under initially Sir Robert Calder, relieved in September 1803 by Sir Edward Pellew, who showed high diplomatic skills in treating with Spain's uneasy neutrality.

The continuous blockade of Brest and the Biscay ports was the most arduous of tasks, hard on men and ships, but the vital necessity of which could allow no breakdown. Life was hardest in the smallest vessels, the few

2

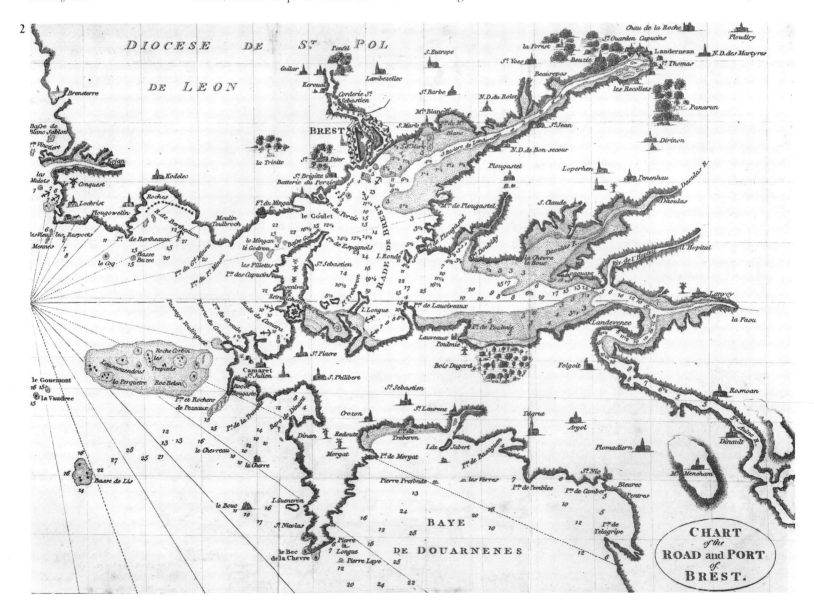

3

cutters, schooners and brigs which could be spared—Cornwallis was always conscious of the 'great want of small vessels' and Rear-Admiral Collingwood, in command of the Inshore Squadron, wrote as early as July 1803 of the 'great use a cutter or two would be'—and it was to them that the most hazardous duties regularly fell. The number and readiness for sea of the French ships had to be regularly (and closely) reconnoitred, the convoys of coastal traffic supplying Brest to be disrupted, as well as clandestine operations, and cutting-out raids—but the most gruelling aspect was, quite simply, the keeping at sea in all but the most extreme conditions (4). By September the schooner *Pickle*, for one, was a 'discontented and very wet' vessel. Life in the frigates and

ships of the line was little easier. Collingwood wrote in December: 'I came in from sea to refresh my ship's company, and, poor creatures, they have been almost worked to death ever since.' The ships were also worn out with the strains of constant blockade—'we have been sailing for the last six months with only a sheet of copper between us and eternity,' Collingwood lamented of the state of his flagship HMS *Venerable*.

In all classes of vessel, the provision of fresh supplies was a constant concern: any ship sent into port for any reason (usually weather damage) was first to dispose of her stores throughout the squadron. Eventually specialised victualling craft became available (5), and every ship joining the fleet carried its quota of fresh beef and

3. 'La Parquette Rock, near Brest, at half tide', Plate CCCCLXVIII from the *Naval Chronicle* XXXVI (1816), engraved by Baily and published by Joyce Gold. *NMM neg D9040*

4. 'Fighting vessels at sea in a storm', watercolour by Charles Oldfield Bowles, no date. Although the location is not specified, this watercolour from a naval officer's sketchbook could well represent the tribulations of the Inshore Squadron off Brest. *NMM ref PAF8397*

5. 'Beef Boat at the Nore', black pen and ink by Lt Edward Bamfylde Eagles, c1810. The bullock symbol on the sail is noteworthy. Being at the Nore this cutter was probaly used to victual the North Sea squadron, Channel victuallers probably being larger and more seaworthy vessels. *NMM ref PAF2685*

6. The Channel Fleet coming in to Torbay. Plate CLXXVIII from the *Naval Chronicle* XIII (1805), engraved by Baily and published by Joyce Gold. *NMM neg D9045*

7. 'France Maritime. Vaisseau école de Brest', etching by Thevenon after an original by Gilbert, published by Baillieu 1838. *NMM ref PAD7327*

8. 'H.M.S. Hibernia', watercolour by Lt Humphrey J Julian, no date. It is a postwar view, the ship having been modified in detail. *NMM neg A972*

4

5

6

masthead, earning Cornwallis the nickname 'Billy Blue' (to add to 'Mr Whip', 'the Coachee' and 'Billy-go-tight'). Over a dozen ships were back off Ushant by 12 January, guarding the seventeen French ships readying for sea in Brest. On 25 March the *Magnificent*, 74, struck an uncharted reef near the Black Rocks and was lost, the crew saved by the boats of the Inshore Squadron.

Napoleon personally devised a form of training programme for his ships and men, many of them mere soldiers, to exercise them in gunnery and the rudiments of seamanship—even just raising anchor and simple evolutions under sail within the harbour would be useful (7). The ineffective French commander at Brest, Vice-Admiral Truguet, who voiced his objections to Napoleon taking the style of Emperor, was sacked and replaced by Vice-Admiral Honoré Ganteaume in mid June. Ganteaume took over a fleet that by now had grown to twenty-three ships of the line.

Napoleon's intention at this time was that the fleet should embark General Augereau's 30,000-40,000 troops and break out of Brest in November, eluding the blockading force, and land them at Lough Swilly. He was then to make his way to Boulogne, collecting Dutch ships and troop transports off the Texel: having then successfully joined with Villeneuve's twenty sail of the line, the force would be complete and in position for the safe passage of the invasion of England. In the event there was only one tentative excursion by five ships and a couple of frigates in July of 1804. When the fog that masked their exit suddenly cleared to show the Inshore Squadron under Rear-Admiral Sir Thomas Graves

vegetables for distribution, but the fine calculation of how long a vessel could remain on station before stores ran dangerously low, whether victuals, water or naval stores, was always a high priority.

With the onset of winter, a succession of westerly gales eventually drove all the fleet to their anchorages in Cawsand Bay and Torbay (6), Cornwallis' flagship *Ville de Paris* and the other three-deckers *San Josef* and *Dreadnought* being the last to seek shelter at the end of December. All the while his ship was at anchor, replenishing and repairing with furious haste, the Blue Peter flew at the

7

forming line of battle, they tamely returned to harbour.

In June 1804 Captain Puget (for whom Puget Sound was named) of the *Foudroyant*, 'having turned my thoughts to the possibility of annoying the French fleet' put forward a detailed plan for a fireship attack, which Cornwallis promoted favourably to Lord Melville, First Lord of the Admiralty. However, the Sea Lords refused to believe the enemy could be so 'supine beyond example' as to allow any chance of success, and scotched the proposal in September, when preparations were well advanced.

After enduring another winter off Ushant, with the additional factor of Spain's entry into the war to be borne, in February Cornwallis detached five ships under Vice-Admiral Sir Robert Calder to watch Ferrol, leaving himself for a time with only eleven ships in front of Brest, where Ganteaume had twenty-one. The 'unwearied perseverance' of the blockade finally forced Cornwallis ashore for his health and he struck his flag in the *Ville de Paris* on 20 March 1805, succeeded on 3 April by Admiral Lord Gardner in the new 110-gun ship *Hibernia* (8). A week later the fleet, now back to twenty-one sail of the line, was driven off station, but regained their position by the 15th, when they formed line of battle to meet the French who appeared to be getting under way. Ganteaume retired to port, declining the glory offered by Napoleon ('Vous tenez dans vos mains les destinees du monde') and any chance of a junction with Villeneuve.

Cornwallis reassumed command of the Channel Fleet

in July in the *Ville de Paris*, when he found the batteries around Bertheaume and Camaret greatly augmented. On 20 August Ganteaume with twenty-one sail of the line anchored outside the Goulet; next morning Cornwallis formed line of battle and moved forward, but after a token broadside or two the French fleet retired under covering fire of their shore batteries and returned to harbour. Cornwallis was hit (but not injured) by a spent shell fragment; more importantly to him, he was denied his fleet action.

8

1

'Dangers of the sea': shipwreck

STATISTICALLY SPEAKING, by far the most likely cause of a Royal Navy ship-loss during the years 1793-1815 was by wreck – the destruction of the ship by striking the shore or an isolated rock, from navigational error, sheer stress of weather or, very occasionally, incompetence. Taking only major ships of 28 guns and up, Professor Michael Lewis calculated that of 101 accidental losses in the course of these wars, 84 were by wreck, 7 by foundering, and 10 through fire or explosion. This loss to what the Naval Prayer called 'the dangers of the sea' contrasted starkly with a mere 10 attributable to 'the violence of the enemy', although this is a net figure, excluding British ships captured and later retaken.

For the enemy the figures are dramatically reversed: only 24 major ships lost to accidents (6 per cent), but 377 to British action, whereas over 90 per cent of the Royal Navy's major losses were accidental. At first glance this suggests the Royal Navy's fighting skills exceeded its seamanship, but this hypothesis survives not a moment's analysis. Not only did the British fleet spend vastly more time at sea than its opponents, but it was also employed in a manner which exposed it to far greater risk of shipwreck. This can be demonstrated by a closer look at

2

some of the losses incurred during the period covered by this book, approximately thirty months between the renewal of war and the end of 1805, when nine major warships were wrecked: the 74s *Magnificent* and *Venerable*, the 50-gun *Romney*, and the frigates *Resistance*, *Seine*, *Circe*, *Shannon*, *Hussar*, *Apollo*, *Severn*, *Sheerness* and *Doris*. This is close to average for the 1793-1815 period as a whole.

Looked at geographically, it is noticeable that the single area of greatest danger was the west coast of France, and if the Netherlands is added then a quarter of all British warship wrecks occurred on these littorals. This must be associated with the policy of blockade, which in the case of France meant operating on a predominantly lee shore, and in the North Sea and Channel in tricky and shallow waters, with powerful currents and large tidal ranges. This implied a level of navigational accuracy which before the era of Satnav systems was virtually impossible, and a period of fog or heavy weather could throw out the calculations of even the most experienced navigator—although, having said that, the court-martial enquiries that followed the loss of every ship often found the pilots guilty of ignorance or negligence.

A case in point is the loss of the *Romney* on 19 November 1804. The ship was joining the Dutch blockade squadron in stormy conditions with drifting fog when she ran on the Haak Sand and broke her back (1), the wreck being surrendered to the Dutch. The two pilots who were conning the ship were held responsible, fined and banned from piloting HM ships in future; the senior was also imprisoned for a year.

Originally the blockade of Brest had been a rather loose affair in which the main fleet was only on station in favourable conditions. However, the demands of this kind of service were considerably enhanced by the introduction of year-round constant blockade, which had been applied in the Channel Fleet by St Vincent from 1800 and was continued in the new war under Cornwallis. Frigates and small craft bore the brunt of the close-in service, but there was also an elite Inshore Squadron of two-deckers designed to prevent the cruisers being driven off station by small detachments of the enemy fleet. Considering the time the Royal Navy spent on this uncomfortable and dangerous station off Brest, one would expect the waters to be exceptionally well charted, but this was apparently not the case, for the largest loss of the period was occasioned by running on an isolated rock that was not accurately positioned on any of the ship's charts, including the standard *Neptune François*. The 74-gun *Magnificent* was just off the notorious Black Rocks when she struck the Boufoloc rock on 25 March 1804, eventually capsizing, but not before virtually all the crew had been rescued by a superbly efficient rescue operation by the boats of the fleet (2).

3

For refitting and resupply, the fleet still used Torbay, but its crowded waters required sure seamanship if minor accidents were not to become disasters, as happened to the *Venerable*, 74, in November 1804. While the fleet was getting under way in deteriorating weather, the ship lost a man overboard from the anchor party, and then lost a boat crew trying to recover him. Failing to weather Berry Head, as night came on the ship was forced to thread her way through a bay full of ships on different tacks trying to get to sea, and having lost her bearings eventually *Venerable* blundered ashore (3). Signal guns brought help from the fleet, and thanks to the rescue efforts of small craft like the cutter *Frisk* (4), only eight men were lost.

4

5

6

It might be argued that this last was an accident that might as easily have occurred in peacetime, but most shipwrecks were more closely linked to the special pressures of wartime. An extreme example was the case of the frigate *Doris*, which had been badly damaged by striking a rock in January 1805, but before repairs could be properly completed, her captain was informed by the schooner *Felix* of the escape of Missiessy's squadron from Rochefort. Judging that the strategic importance of the news outweighed the danger to his ship, he set sail only to find the leaks opened up again, and eventually the crew was transferred to the *Felix* and the *Doris* was set on fire and abandoned (5).

In parallel with the struggle between the main fleets, another war was being fought in the narrower waters of the Channel against the would-be Invasion Flotilla. Taking the fight right up to the enemy's tideline was clearly a high-risk strategy, and many small craft suffered the penalty of slight pilotage errors. This was primarily a conflict of gunboats and gunbrigs – ten of which were lost during the period under review in circumstances in which grounding played a part. Some would attribute the losses like those of the *Conflict*, *Bouncer* and *Woodlark* to enemy action, but none would have been lost without first having gone ashore. A larger example was the frigate *Shannon*, detailed to blockade Le Havre, which ran aground near Cape Barfleur in bad weather on 10 December (6). Stranded, she was forced to surrender, but although a British sloop was sent to burn the wreck a week later, it is very unlikely that the ship would ever have sailed again.

The losses of big ships seized the attention, then as now, but small craft suffered more, partly because they existed in greater numbers but also because being small they were more vulnerable and being cheap they were put at greater hazard. For the record, between May 1803 and the end of 1805, while major shipwrecks amounted to nine, the following numbers of the lesser rates were lost from the same cause: one post ship, eight sloops, ten gunboats or gunbrigs, one fireship, one bomb vessel, three cutters, three schooners, a storeship, and even one prison hulk.

It was, in Kipling's phrase, the Price of Admiralty.

Nelson takes over in the Mediterranean

1

AT THE renewal of war in 1803, the French Toulon fleet numbered seven sail of the line ready for sea, two almost ready and a further five either under construction or on order. The British blockading squadron under Sir Richard Bickerton (1) numbered nine sail of the line, so there was a danger that the balance of naval power in the region would soon be lost by the British. It was decided that the command of the Mediterranean Fleet should fall to a flag officer whose distinction and experience would intimidate the enemy, and it was duly offered to Nelson, who accepted it enthusiastically on 16 May 1803. As his flagship he is supposed to have asked specially for the *Victory*, 104 guns, which had been rescued from ignominious harbour service and given a complete refit (2). With Samuel Sutton as his flag captain, Nelson sailed in the old ship on 18 May in company with the frigate *Amphion*, 32 (Captain Thomas Masterman Hardy) bound for the Mediterranean.

His orders were to report to the Brest blockading squadron under Admiral Cornwallis, and if required the *Victory* was to be transferred to the squadron, with Nelson proceeding to Malta in the *Amphion*. The *Victory* with *Amphion* arrived off Ushant on 22 May, but a gale had blown the Channel Fleet off station. After searching for two days Nelson decided to take advantage of the good northerly wind and shifted his flag to the *Amphion* and proceeded onwards, leaving Sutton and the *Victory* to find Cornwallis. The frigate made good progress and arrived at Valletta (3) on 15 June after calling at Gibraltar on the 3rd to inform the Governor of the declaration of war, the first official news the Rock had received since the renewal of hostilities.

During his passage, Nelson must have reflected on Mediterranean strategy. His orders were to prevent the French from breaking out of Toulon and joining the fleet at Brest or if the opportunity offered, to bring them to a decisive action. However, another objective for the British forces in the Mediterranean was to check Napoleon's eastwards ambitions in the Ottoman Empire, the Kingdom of the Two Sicilies and the island of Malta. This last was the only British base in the Mediterranean east of Gibraltar, and although it was of great strategic importance as a military garrison and an outwork on the route to India, it was of little immediate value for maritime operations, lying too far to the south of Toulon.

Therefore, Sicily and Sardinia were crucial to the maintenance of the British blockade, but it was essential not to compromise their continued neutrality in the eyes of the French. The British did not have the forces to keep the

French army out of Naples in 1803, but they would be able to hold Sicily by reinforcing Messina from the garrison at Malta. However, if Britain moved too quickly to secure Sicily, it might actually provoke the French in to taking Naples. Although Naples was dear to his heart, Nelson knew that its territories could not be reinforced at present, but wrote to the chief minister, 'A ship of war, and generally one of the line, on some pretence or other shall always be in the Bay of Naples to prevent the worst of all incidents, the loss of the Royal family.'

2

3

4

The *Amphion* arrived off Naples on 25 June (4) where Nelson expected to find Bickerton, but the admiral had taken the fleet to blockade Toulon on hearing the news of the war. It was there that Nelson finally fell in with them on 8 July. The *Victory* arrived some weeks later, after proving her renowned sailing qualities by overtaking and recapturing the ex-British frigate *Embuscade*, taken by the French in 1798. Nelson transferred his flag to the three-decker and also took Hardy as his flag captain, Captain Sutton assuming command of the *Amphion* in exchange. Hardy (5) had served under Nelson at St Vincent in 1794 as a lieutenant and then as Nelson's flag captain aboard the *Vanguard* after the Nile in 1798, and in the *St George* during the Baltic operations in 1801 against the Danes.

Nelson had at his disposal ten sail of the line and three frigates although he kept a main force of six of the line with him off Toulon, detaching the remainder on various duties. His most immediate problem with the fleet was their material state. Although belied by their smart external appearance, their hulls were in need of dockyard attention, and their running rigging and sails needed replacing. Furthermore, their stores had been run down, and each ship of the line was approximately 100 men short of a full war complement. Representations to the Admiralty were pointless, St Vincent replying simply, 'We can send you neither ships or men', for every vessel in the Navy seemed to be employed.

Nelson was determined not to take the fleet into port and set about replenishing and refitting the ships on sta-

5

tion. Arrangements were made for transports to bring out water, provisions and supplies directly to the ships, and when the weather prevented this, he would anchor the fleet in a roadstead rather than divide the force. For the next year Nelson managed to preserve the blockade whilst keeping the fleet stored for a long chase should the circumstances arise. With justifiable pride, he was able to write to St Vincent, 'I have the pleasure to acquaint you that the squadron under my command is all collected except the *Gibraltar*, and in perfect state of readiness to act as a the exigency of the moment may determine.'

---

1. 'Sir Richard Bickerton Bart, K.G., Rear Admiral of the White', stipple engraving by William Ridley after an original by T Maynard, published by Joyce Gold, 31 October 1804.
NMM ref PAH5905

2. 'Victory, Portsmouth', etching by Henry Moses after his own original, no date.
NMM neg B4970

3. 'His Majesty's Ship Phoenix beating into Marsamashet Harbour (Malta)', grey wash by J Bushman, 1819. *Amphion* was a similar looking ship in most essentials.
NMM neg 7989

4. 'The Victory in Naples Bay, 25 June 1804', watercolour by Nicholas Pocock (1740-1821), 1810. This seems to be a rare mistake by the otherwise meticulous artist: *Victory* was off Toulon at this time, and the painting is probably meant to represent Nelson's visit to Naples in June 1803, but he arrived in the *Amphion* and not the *Victory.*
NMM neg 9956

5. 'Captain Hardy. Sir Thomas Masterman Hardy 1769-1839', photogravure after an original by Lemuel Francis Abbott, engraved and published by W H Ward & Co, no date.
NMM neg 5103

Ships of the Royal Navy: gunboats and gunbrigs

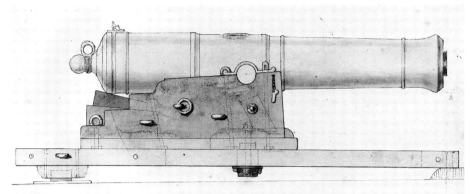

1

AS A dominant blue-water force, the Royal Navy did not traditionally expend much effort on such an inherently defensive type as the gunboat, but there were times and situations in which they were the only answer. The defence of Gibraltar was one, since the Spanish made use or oared vessels which in the frequent calms of the region could be deadly to both merchantmen and small warships trying to enter or leave the bay. Early gunboats were very boat-like, and may well have been derived from the flat-bottomed landing boats so widely employed in eighteenth-century amphibious operations – the addition of a gun to these craft to support the landings would be natural, and in very sheltered waters their value would have become speedily apparent.

Boats of this type, with a single gun, usually forward and on a slide (1), were built during the American Revolutionary War, and some were deployed to defend British estuaries, creeks and minor harbours. They averaged about 40 tons, but from 1794 a new type of far larger gunboat, of around 150 tons, began to be constructed. The hull form was very flat and square-sectioned, shoal draught, and probably inspired by the small coastal traders of the time, with which the Surveyors would have been familiar, both as naval hired vessels and in slightly smaller forms as Dockyard service craft. They carried two long 24pdrs firing forward and twelve 18pdr carronades as broadside and stern-chase armament, and the design stressed the requirement to be rowed by eighteen oars, which meant a very shallow draught and poor sailing qualities (2).

Initially rated as 'gunboats', then 'gun vessels', they were soon rerigged as brigs and a radical attempt was made to improve their sailing qualities by fitting Schank's novel 'sliding keels', an early form of the daggerboard familiar in modern sailing dinghies. Originally simply numbered, their enhanced status was confirmed when they were quickly named; the new rating 'gunbrig' was coined at the same time, and each was placed under the command of a lieutenant. St Vincent believed they destroyed promising lieutenants by driving them to drink, the stress of commanding such unseaworthy vessels with minimal support from junior officers being too much for many of the younger and less experienced. However, when first introduced, gunbrigs were largely defensive and rarely saw duty outside estuaries and the occasional coastal convoy; although with care they could accompany colonial expeditions, once they arrived they were only actively employed inshore. However, as the war expanded more aggressive employment forced them to take on roles for which they were not really suited.

The design progress from the original *Conquest* class, through the *Acute*/*Courser* classes of 1797 to the *Bloodhound*/*Archer* classes of 1800-1 is clear and consistent: the designs get marginally larger, the hull forms become deeper, sharper and more seaworthy, and the bow armament less dominant in the overall conception (3). This process culminates in the 180-ton *Confounder*s of 1804, which are not very different from a small brig sloop – in fact, as the gunbrigs grew so there was an exactly opposite movement to reduce the smaller brig sloops, from around 300 tons to the 235 tons of the 1807 *Cherokee* class. Both developments were driven by the need for the maximum numbers of cruisers, and in the case of gunbrigs

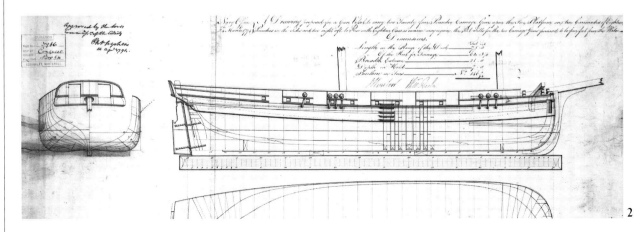

2

3

4

5

what were originally decidedly inshore craft became committed to increasingly offensive duties (the same needs that drove the Second World War 'Flower' class coastal corvettes into the Battle of the Atlantic).

The employment of gunbrigs can be seen as a three-stage expansion: initially they were hardly to be found outside British coastal waters; then towards the end of the French Revolutionary War they were deployed off the French and Dutch coasts as part of the anti-invasion operations; and finally in the Napoleonic War they were sent to almost all parts of the world. A crude measure of this expansion can be found in the losses suffered by the various classes – only two before 1801, but thereafter the quantity went up rapidly, and the large number wrecked or driven onto the French Channel coast underlined the fact that they were in the front line of anti-invasion patrols. Because the invasion flotilla comprised very shallow draught vessels that rarely strayed from their harbours, the gunbrigs sent to take, burn or destroy them were obliged to run serious risks. Ordered close inshore in areas demanding the greatest experience of treacherous tidal and weather conditions, it is neither surprising that so many gunbrigs were lost, nor that so many of their youthful commanders were driven to drink.

As the invasion threat receded and British domination of the waters around Europe increased, enemy trade was largely driven from the high seas. Only coastal shipping, creeping from port to port under the protection of shore batteries wherever possible, had any chance of survival. Similarly, the blockade so bottled up the Napoleonic main fleets, that only minor warships could reasonably expect to get to sea. So to complete the Royal Navy's stranglehold on Continental seafaring, the gunbrigs were sent inshore to disrupt coastal convoys and prevent the escape of small commerce raiders. At first it was mostly confined to the Atlantic and North Sea coasts, but after 1807 the economic blockade vastly widened the European areas of gunbrig activity, and such was their value inshore that many were transferred to other parts of the world as well.

When in 1801 it was decided that Parker's fleet for the attack on Copenhagen needed gunbrigs to counter Danish gunboats, their 24pdrs and attendant equipments were carried across the North Sea in ships of the line; seven years later gunbrigs were operating independently off Denmark, Norway and in the Baltic – not to mention crossing the Atlantic, and reaching the East Indies. Whatever their origin, by this date gunbrigs were thought capable of going anywhere, although this is more of a tribute to the seamanship and *esprit de corps* of the Royal Navy than to any quality in their design – gunbrigs were never true blue-water cruisers and always tended to operate inshore, although they were clearly

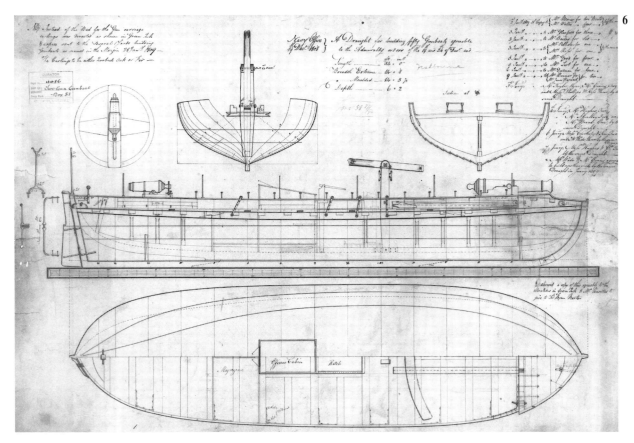

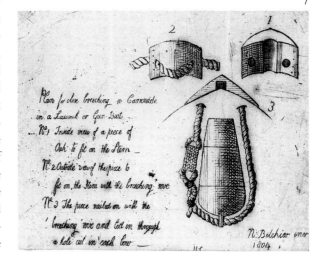

capable of making safe passages to their designated stations. In an attempt to make them easier to handle with small crews, some were rerigged as barques (4), and this was a common peacetime rig postwar (5).

As so often happens in warship development, when one type outgrows its original function, so another comes along to replace it. The evolution of the gunbrig into a cruiser–albeit more suited to coastal waters–left a gap to be filled by a more modest gunboat, and large numbers of the traditional launch-like oared craft were built. Best known of the specific designs is 'Commissioner Hamilton's gunboat', designed by Captain Thomas Hamilton, a Commissioner of the Transport Board, and a man with many ideas on naval architecture. His gunboat had one long gun forward on a slide that seems to have allowed limited traverse, and a carronade aft on a turntable (6). They were clinker built, with a sharp section that suggests they probably sailed well; the single mast was fitted in a tabernacle, so could be lowered aft when the craft was rowed. The first six were shipped to Gibraltar in 1805 and proved so successful that, with some modifications, eighty-five more were ordered in 1808. They were widely used on the coasts of Spain, in support of the Peninsular campaigns, but some saw action in the North Sea as well. These gunboats were commanded by Midshipmen or Master's Mates, and judging by the recorded losses were employed, like gunbrigs, in some unlikely locations–two were lost in the estuary of the Elbe on the other side of the North Sea, although most of the remaining losses were around Gibraltar. Unlike the early gunbrigs, they were never named, although their crews seem to have given them unofficial soubriquets.

It should also be remembered that virtually all warships were, in effect, equipped with a 'gunboat', in the form of the ship's launch, which by this time regularly carried a carronade (7). As deep-water actions became rarer, ever increasing employment was found for ships' boats, in cutting-out expeditions, army co-operation, and even occasionally 'cruising' as an independent tender.

1. A pen and wash drawing of a pivot gun on a slide from one of the sketchbooks of Nicholas Pocock (1740-1821). A typical gunboat mounting, although the slide did not pivot in all types. *NMM ref PAI1298*

2. Design draught for the *Conquest* class of 1794, the first of the gunboats of the French Revolutionary War period. It is not certain how they were originally rigged, but some were noted as being converted to brigs; some were also fitted with sliding keels later. *NMM ref DR3786*

3. 'Etchings of ships. Gun brig close hauled', etching published by R Lamb, 1 August 1820. *NMM ref PAD7703*

4. Portrait of the *Confounder* class gunbrig *Resolute* rigged as a barque 1812, from the journal of Lt W Pringle of *Conqueror*, 74, kept from about 1805. *NMM neg D9055A*

5. 'Mastiff gun-brig anchored in calm waters', anonymous grey wash, no date. One of the last of the *Confounder* class, *Mastiff* may be shown here as fitted for a survey ship in 1836. *NMM neg X1996*

6. Design draught for the group of Hamilton gunboats ordered in December 1808. Note the carronade on a turntable aft, and the mast in a tabernacle. *NMM neg DR4086-58*

7. 'Plan for close breeching a Carronade in a launch or gun boat', etching after an original by Admiral Nathaniel Belchier, 1804. *NMM ref PAI2674-5*

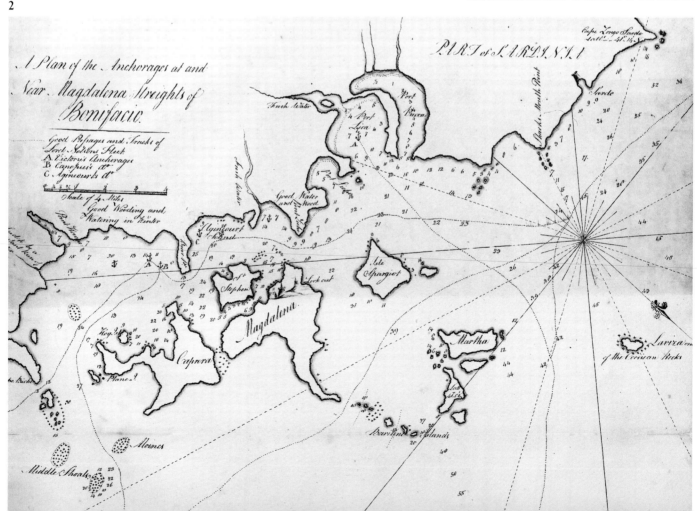

Watching Toulon

ALTHOUGH NOT as obviously formidable to blockade as Brest, Toulon had its own difficulties. Chief amongst these was the surrounding high ground (1) that gave the blockaded a good view of the blockaders. Since Nelson was more interested in luring the French out, where he knew he could destroy them, than in simply bottling them up, the lay of the land made it difficult to ambush any squadron that did sortie. There was also no safe anchorage locally in which to base the main fleet.

In October the fleet made for what was to become its new anchorage, named Agincourt Sound after the ship that had first surveyed it in 1802, in the Maddalena Islands off Sardinia (2). They returned to station off Toulon toward the end of November, but as Nelson later said when receiving the thanks of the Corporation of London for 'blockading Toulon', he had in fact given the French every opportunity to put to sea.

On 9 April 1804 the *Amazon* came under fire from shore batteries while off Cape Cepet (3). Three frigates, followed by four other ships, made a sortie from Toulon to intercept, but returned to port when the *Donegal*, 74 and the *Active*, 38 arrived to support *Amazon*. Further reinforcements arrived for Nelson throughout May 1804; in Toulon (4) the French had seven ships of the line, including Vice-Admiral Latouche-Treville's new-built flagship *Bucentaure*, ready for sea, with several more fitting out in the inner harbour.

On 24 May, as the *Canopus*, *Donegal* and *Amazon*, detached from the fleet to look into Toulon, tacked inshore with the body of the fleet out of sight, a number of gunboats made a dart at the frigate; *Canopus* fired on them, at which four French line of battle ships and two frigates made sail from Toulon 'determined' in the words of one of *Canopus*' officer 'to make a grand push out after us'. After a brief exchange of gunfire, the British withdrew in face of the superior force; the French 'fearful of being drawn too far, and decoyed into the jaws of the Viscount', stood back into harbour.

Three weeks later, on 14 June, as Lord Nelson in the *Victory* led the inshore division (*Canopus*, *Belleisle*, *Donegal* and *Excellent*), while Bickerton cruised some sixty miles offshore with the remainder, the frigates *Amazon* and *Phoebe* went in chase of two French frigates which came to anchor off Porquerelles under the protection of a battery. As the two English frigates prepared to engage them, supported by the *Excellent*, the whole French fleet in the outer road of Toulon was seen to get under way, whereon the three ships were recalled. Seeing Latouche-Treville apparently making a determined sortie with eight powerful ships of the line and several frigates, Nelson formed line of battle with his division, but the French squadron, having saved their comrades, declined the invitation to battle – Nelson initially thought little more of it. However, Latouche-Treville made much of it. To Nelson, writing on the 18th, Latouche-Treville had 'cut a caper off Sepet, and went in again'; Latouche's report to Paris, that he had 'pursued Nelson till night; he ran to the South-East', earned him a promotion within the Legion d'Honneur and the position of Inspector of the Coasts of the Mediterranean. Nelson wrote to his friend Davidson 'I have kept Monsieur la Touche's letter; and if I take him . . . I shall make him eat it.'

Perhaps more importantly, Napoleon's letter to Latouche-Treville of 2 July informing him of his rewards also contained the first draft of a plan of operations. The Toulon fleet was to embark 1600 soldiers, stripping the cruisers and pressing seamen from Marseilles if necessary to make up the crews of the ships of the line. Eluding Nelson's blockade, they were to pass through the Straits, collect the six sail of the line at Rochefort and make for Boulogne, either directly or northabout the British Isles, where, given a projected departure date of July 28th, he would arrive in September. This was the first inkling of the operations that led the fleets to Cape Trafalgar, but Latouche-Treville had no part in the coming events. He died on board his flagship the *Bucentaure* on 18 August, still in the harbour at Toulon.

3

1. 'Geometrical Survey of the Environs of Toulon (18 Dec 1793)', etching by Thomas Foot, published by William Faden, 1 May 1794. *NMM ref PAH7846*

2. Anonymous manuscript and watercolour chart of the Maddalena anchorages: Agincourt Sound is above 'Magdalena', between the little island of St Stephen and the Sardinian mainland. It is one of a folio of watercolour charts of anchorages drawn up in one of the ships of the Mediterranean Fleet about this time; NMM ref NVP/12. *NMM neg D9057*

3. 'Cape Brun to Sepet, Toulon. Drawn on the Spot by Captn Knight R.N.', coloured aquatint engraved by Francis Jukes after an original by Captain Knight, published by W Faden, 31 March 1794. *NMM ref PAH2317*

Spanish gold

SINCE THE Treaty of San Ildefonso (1796), Spain had been bound to furnish France, on demand, fifteen ships of the line and a body of troops. After war between France and Great Britain was resumed in 1803, Napoleon informed Spain that he would prefer to receive an equivalent aid in money (thus leaving Spain nominally neutral). When Spain protested that the conditions were onerous, Napoleon gave her a straightforward choice: pay the subsidy; or declare war herself on Great Britain; or have war declared against her by France. On 19 October 1803, Spain reluctantly decided that the least of these evils was to pay the subsidy. She was promptly informed by London that Great Britain reserved the right to regard such payment as a *casus belli* should she decide to do so at any time. Further formal warnings followed, that—unless the preparations increasingly taking place in Spanish naval ports were

suspended—war would ensue. Activity in the ports continued, under French orders; and the cabinet in Madrid was warned that, unless satisfactory explanations were forthcoming, the British ambassador would depart.

Against that background (certainly, one of diplomatic tension, but where there had been no recalling of ambassadors, still less any formal declaration of war), the British government decided on a pre-emptive strike. Towards the end of the summer of 1804 it received intelligence from Rear-Admiral Cochrane (commanding the squadron off Ferrol) that an armament was fitting out in Ferrol, that a considerable Spanish force had already collected there and that French troops were on their way. The information later proved to be false, but it tipped the balance. London despatched a squadron to loiter off Cadiz to intercept and detain, 'by force or otherwise', the squadron of four Spanish frigates known to be homeward bound for Cadiz from Montevideo, loaded with the specie from the New World which would pay the subsidy.

On 3 October 1804, two frigates from Cornwallis' fleet, the *Indefatigable*, 44 and the *Lively*, 38 joined two 18pdr frigates from Nelson's fleet, the *Amphion*, 32 and the *Medusa*, 32 at a rendezvous off Cape Santa Maria. Wishing to make the squadron so strong that resistance would clearly be pointless, Nelson had also despatched one ship of the line (the *Donegal*, 74), but she failed to arrive at the rendezvous in time. At 6am on 5 October 1804, the four frigates were cruising some 9 leagues southwest of Cape Santa Maria when they sighted four large sail. This could only be the awaited treasure fleet. The British squadron wore and made sail to close the unsuspecting Spaniards.

Two hours later, they came up with the Spanish squadron, which formed line of battle ahead: *Fama*, 34; *Medea*, 40; *Mercedes*, 34; and *Clara*, 34 (1). The Spanish squadron was weaker than the British (but not, as Nelson had intended that it should be, hopelessly out-

2

matched). It was also totally unprepared. *Medusa* placed herself on *Fama*'s weather bow, and *Indefatigable* and *Amphion* paired off with, respectively, *Medea*, and *Mercedes*. *Lively*, the fastest sailer in the British squadron, placed herself strategically abeam and to leeward of the *Clara*. As the senior British officer, Captain Moore of the *Indefatigable*, hailed *Medea* to shorten sail and, receiving no reply, put a shot across the forefoot. *Medea* took the hint and shortened sail; and Captain Moore sent across to tell Rear-Admiral Bustamente that he had orders to detain the Spanish squadron and to urge him to surrender without bloodshed. Honour compelled Bustamente to refuse, and the boat returned to the *Indefatigable* with that answer. At 9.30 the *Indefatigable* bore down on *Medea*; *Mercedes* fired into *Amphion*; *Medea* opened on *Indefatigable* and a close action immediately followed. Nine minutes later, with a tremendous explosion, *Mercedes* blew up alongside *Amphion* (2). In another twenty minutes *Medea* and *Clara*, too, had struck. According to one account, the *Fama* had earlier struck to the *Medusa* but, when *Medusa* ceased fire, rehoisted her ensign and tried to escape. At all events, by 10am only the *Fama* was left, drawing away from the *Medusa*. *Lively* was despatched to join in the chase and, being an excellent sailer, slowly but surely overhauled the fleeing *Fama*. By 12.45 *Lively* was able to open fire on *Fama* with her bowchasers and half an hour later *Fama* struck.

In the meantime boats from *Indefatigable* and *Amphion* had been attempting to rescue the unfortunate survivors of the *Mercedes*. One officer and 45 men were saved; the remainder, including several women and children, perished. Apart from these losses, Spanish casualties were 27 killed and 80 wounded. British losses were very slight (2 killed and 7 wounded). The three captured prizes were worth about £1,000,000. Perhaps as much as a third again went to the bottom with the *Mercedes*. On 12 October 1804 Spain, outraged, declared war on Great Britain. The pre-emptive strike was certainly expedient. It was almost equally certainly illegal. Had the roles been reversed one can certainly imagine the indignation at foreign foul play.

An immediate result of the declaration of war was a naval convention between France and Spain in which the latter undertook to fit out a substantial portion of her fleet to co-operate with Napoleon's plans. Cornwallis was forced to detach a squadron from Brest to keep an eye on Ferrol and Corruna, ultimately to be commanded by Sir Robert Calder. Further south, a 'Spanish' command had been separated from the Mediterranean Fleet in October 1804, and given to Sir John Orde (3) – much to Nelson's disgust, who thought Orde would grab all the prize money – and on the outbreak of war it was promptly sent to renew the blockade of Cadiz (4).

3

4

Missiessy's raid

ON 11 January 1804, taking advantage of the temporary absence of Sir Thomas Graves' blockading squadron, Rear-Admiral Burgues Missiessy with five ships of the line—a First Rate and four new 74s (1)—three frigates and two brigs, with 3500 soldiers embarked, slipped out of Rochefort 'the weather ominous and snowing' by his report. The squadron was sighted by the frigate *Doris* and the schooner *Felix*, who shadowed them, while *Doris* went in search of Graves. Already damaged in the gale that kept Graves from his station, the *Doris* sank two days later; the crew was saved by the *Felix*. The report of Missiessy's escape finally reached Graves on the 16th: the storm made immediate pursuit impossible.

Because of the storm the British expected them to return to a French port; their absence from Rochefort, Lorient or Brest caused disquiet when these ports could again be investigated a full three weeks later, after the series of gales finally blew out. Opinions and information

1

2

3

differed about whether the expedition was headed for the Mediterranean or the West Indies, and Sir Alexander Cochrane's squadron of six ships was detached from the blockade of Ferrol to reinforce Nelson if the enemy ships had entered the Mediterranean, or to cross to Jamaica, gathering Commodore Samuel Hood's Leeward Islands squadron on the way. After calling for intelligence at Lisbon and a rendezvous with the squadron blockading Cadiz, neither of which yielded a lead, the pursuit set off for the West Indies some weeks behind Missiessy, finally reaching Barbados on 5 April.

In fact the severe weather of which Missiessy complained and which covered his all-but unseen departure had caused great damage aloft in the ships of the necessarily inexperienced French squadron, and his force crossed the Atlantic under jury rig. They reached Martinique (2) on 20 February, with one prize, the transport *Prince of Asturias*, taken from a convoy chased in the St Lucia Channel. On the 22nd a landing was made on Dominica. Surprise was complete; the island's governor General Prevost, taken in by the false British colours the ships initially showed, actually sent one of his staff on board the flagship in welcome. The local militia were allowed to surrender, but Prevost resourcefully improvised a resistance with his regular garrison which could not be quickly overcome, not least due to a failure of inter-service co-operation between Missiessy and his military force commander, General LaGrange. Having

to be content with levying a contribution of 100,000 francs, and some trophies and prisoners, the French expedition sailed on the 27th for Guadeloupe with the score of small vessels taken in the roadstead.

For some reason no attempt was made on St Lucia, but the pattern employed on Dominica was followed on St Kitts on 5 March, then Nevis (3), and Montserrat (4) on the 9th: a landing by troops, imposition of a financial levy (a total of 280,000 francs), and destruction of coasting vessels. On 14 March at Martinique, instead of the expected rendezvous, despatches from France told Rear-Admiral Missiessy that Villeneuve had not broken out, and the squadron, by now very much reduced in manpower, must return to France. After supplementing and supplying the besieged garrison of St Domingue Missiessy's squadron put to sea again, and anchored in Aix Roads on 20 May, undetected by any blockading squadron or cruiser.

Despite the considerable damage he had done in the islands, the British position in the Leeward Islands was still powerful, and Missiessy had not pleased Napoleon. He felt that Dominca should have been taken and held, Barbados should have been attacked and more done for the forces at St Domingue. That was not all: 'I choked with indignation when I read he had not taken the Diamond Rock,' he wrote. Broken in health and in disgrace, Rear-Admiral Missiessy was replaced, and not employed for some years.

1. French three-decker and two-decker, painting by Antoine Roux, 1809. Although a newer ship, the *Commerce de Paris*, the three-decker shown here, might represent Missiessy's flagship, *Majestueux* of 120 guns.
Peabody Essex Museum, Salem MA, neg 2498

2. 'Fort George Martinique', watercolour by Edward Pelham Brenton, about 1802.
NMM ref PAF8427

3. 'The Islands Redonda and Nevis in the West Indies', coloured aquatint engraved by Hall after an original by G T, published by Joyce Gold, 30 April 1808.
NMM neg A4178

4. 'Montserrat, N.E. 3 miles', coloured lithograph engraved by Thomas Goldsworth Dutton after an original by W S Andrews, printed by Day & Sons, no date.
NMM neg A783

4

1

A naval officer's view

GOING TO sea at an early age, the average naval officer of the Nelsonic era was very lucky if he had been able to acquire much formal education. His profession, on the other hand, rapidly taught him to observe – wind and weather, the stars, coastal features, methods of identifying ships – and he was encouraged to commit his observations to paper in journals and logs using both word and illustration. Some moved on from simple sketches to become reasonably accomplished artists, usually in a medium like line and wash or watercolour that did not require professional accoutrements and did not take up much space in a crowded wardroom. The National Maritime Museum at Greenwich possesses a number of sketchbooks that belonged to officers of the period, and they offer the modern viewer two great advantages over the work of the professional artist; firstly, the officer always understood the technicalities of what he was depicting, and secondly, free from the tyranny of patronage, he could please himself what he portrayed, so often celebrated the everyday aspects of a navy at work that would otherwise go unrepresented.

One such is Daniel Tandy, whose sketchbook is dated 1798 on the cover. No high-flyer, Tandy became a Lieutenant in 1790 and served without promotion until 1806, when he came ashore suffering from yellow fever picked up in the West Indies; he did not go to sea again

2

and retired with the rank of Commander in 1825. There **3** is no annotation to his sketchbook, so identifying subjects is a matter of speculation. Only a few can be linked, even tentatively, with known events of his career, but (1) is a possibility. He was First Lieutenant, and the officer in charge of the *Gibraltar*, 80 guns, when she and the 74s *Culloden* and *Courageux* were driven from their anchorage in December 1796; *Courageux* was wrecked, but Tandy's seamanship saved his ship, and he may have felt this traumatic event worthy of recording.

Otherwise, most of the sketches seem devoted to more mundane aspects of sea service, and herein lies their value. Tandy served for much of the 1790s in the Channel Fleet and judging by the topography these are the waters depicted (he was also in the Mediterranean, but all the small craft in this selection belong in the Channel), so the sketchbook represents an officer's view of Britain's most important naval force going about its wartime business. A squadron is seen getting under way in (2), possibly in Torbay, the fleet's usual refuge; the

4

5

the same event at a slightly different moment, but it emphasises the high quality of shiphandling required by such close-quarter manoeuvring, especially in these boisterous conditions.

St Vincent believed that the seamanship of the Channel Fleet bore no comparison to his crack Mediterranean squadrons, but even relatively sloppy station-keeping made an impressive sight (4) as two divisions in close line-ahead rolled down to the usual blockading grounds off Brest. Off duty, ships of the line spent time in Torbay, but maintenance requirements might take them to Portsmouth or Plymouth. The flat-sheered hoy in (5) has the look of a dockyard craft, and the 74 with her topgallants sent down may be lying off Plymouth, perhaps in Cawsand Bay; the three-decker beyond looks like a Second Rate, and it might be noted that Tandy served in the *Barfleur*, 98.

After the big ships of the battlefleet, Tandy's favourite subject seems to have been boats. It is easy to forget that in the days before auxiliary power, boats were an essential ajunct to the sailing ship, but they certainly play a major part in Tandy's work. Almost every drawing, like (2), (3) or (5) contains at least one portrait of a boat, and usually achieving that lively sense of motion displayed by small craft in a seaway. Some are warships' boats, but fishing vessels and workboats were equally dear to him, one of the best examples being (6), where the foreground boats dominate the composition.

flagship, centre right, has fired a gun to emphasise her signal, and the two-decker on her portside already had men aloft letting go the topsails and main course; the three ships already under sail are tacking back and forth, waiting to take station. If it were not that the ships have sent down their topgallant yards, (3) might well depict

6

Note that the following descriptions are as catalogued by the NMM, and are not from the sketchbook itself.

1. 'Two fighting vessels in collision off a headland in choppy seas', water-colour by D Tandy, *c*1798-1805. *NMM ref* PAF0472

2. 'British men of war, one firing a salute, with other vessels and ships' boats off a coast', watercolour by D Tandy, *c*1798-1805. *NMM ref* PAF0453

3. 'British man of war and a smack off a mountainous coast', watercolour by D Tandy, *c*1798-1805. *NMM ref* PAF0423

4. 'Fleet of naval vessels at sea', water-colour by D Tandy, *c*1798-1805. *NMM ref* PAF0486

5. 'Men of war at anchor by a hilly wooded shore, with small craft', watercolour by D Tandy, *c*1798-1805. *NMM ref* PAF0452

6. 'British naval vessels and small craft off a headland', watercolour by D Tandy, *c*1798-1805. *NMM ref* PAF0479

1

Villeneuve's first sortie

AT THE beginning of 1805 Nelson was troubled by two strategic problems. The final success of British diplomatic attempts at a coalition with Russia had resulted in the planning of combined operations in the Mediterranean. Russia had secured a foothold in the area by occupying the Ionian Islands in the previous war, and had established a headquarters in Corfu (1). Britain was to send 5000 troops under General Sir James Craig to the Mediterranean to act in concert with Russian forces from the islands, the principal aim being to secure the Neapolitan kingdom, or at least its island territory of Sicily. In due course the Mediterranean Fleet was ordered to protect and support the expedition as required, which included the organisation of transports for the passage of Russian troops. There were a few Russian warships (2) outside the Bosporus, but they were not sufficient for the planned expedition.

A more pressing difficulty was the unexpected eruption of Villeneuve's squadron. Napoleon had instructed his admirals to break out of Toulon and Rochefort and to rendezvous in the West Indies. As seen in the previous section, Missiessy's division sailed from Rochefort on 11 January 1805, but it was not until the 17th that Villeneuve thought conditions right for his escape – a gale from the north-northwest. Villeneuve's strategy for evading the blockading squadron was to take the course that allowed him to make the best speed to lose any pursuers, then to settle on his intended course. It was an evasion tactic that was to work well and give so much anxiety to Nelson.

Villeneuve came out of Toulon with eleven sail of the line, seven frigates and two brigs, carrying a total of 3500 troops under the command of General Lauriston. Nelson had taken the British fleet to Agincourt Sound for victualling on the day Missiessy sailed, but the frigates *Active* and *Seahorse* were left to keep watch over Toulon. On the morning of 18 January, the two frigates were chased off by one of Villeneuve's divisions, but they managed to stand out to sea, and later at 6.30pm sighted the French ships heading south. *Active* and *Seahorse* shad-

2

3

owed until 2am the next morning, when they broke off and under a press of sail set course for Agincourt Sound. They arrived some thirteen and half hours later and signalled the *Victory* that the French were out. At 4.30pm the British fleet weighed and put to sea. Nelson had with him eleven sail of the line plus the two frigates.

As ever, Nelson was concerned for the east, but did not commit the fleet until he had further information, taking it down the east coast of Sardinia while *Seahorse* probed to the south. By now the wind was blowing a full gale and the fleet was mainly under storm staysails. Off Cagliari on 21 January *Seahorse* encountered the French frigate *Cornélie*, 40, but poor visibility prevented her from ascertaining whether any other ships were at the Pula anchorage or in Cagliari. Further forays by *Seahorse* and *Active* found nothing. Nelson was indeed perplexed. He wrote to General Acton, the Neapolitan minister, on 25 January, 'I have neither ate, drank or slept with any comfort since last Sunday.' The Admiral was not the only person in discomfort, for the British fleet had been cleared for action since they had quit the anchorage at Agincourt Sound, the men sleeping at their guns.

On 26 January the frigate *Phoebe* joined with information that a week earlier she had come upon the *Indomptable*, a French 80-gun ship lying crippled and dismasted at Ajaccio on the west coast of Corsica. This led Nelson to believe that either the French had been storm damaged and returned to Toulon, or had eluded him around Sicily and were heading east for Egypt. Nelson sailed eastward and rounded Stromboli during the early hours of 29 January (3), sailed through the straits of Messina (4) and pressed on to Alexandria. He simultaneously despatched all three of his cruisers in search of information, with orders to rendezvous off Toulon and resume

4

the watch on the French if they were found to be there.

On communicating with Alexandria on 7 February, Villeneuve was nowhere to be seen, and with much haste Nelson started west again. Arriving off Malta on 19 February, he received his first definite intelligence of the French: Villeneuve had been driven back by the gales to Toulon after his ships had been crippled by storm damage. Nelson, with a weight off his mind, took the fleet back to Sardinia and was anchored in Pula Road (5) by the 28th, before taking his ships to Palma Bay to complete their victualling. By 9 March he was again off Toulon, no damage having been done by Villeneuve's short sortie.

5

1. 'View of Corfu, ancient Corcyra', coloured aquatint engraved by W I Bennett after an original by W Walker, published by the artist, 1 December 1804.
NMM ref PAI0147

2. 'Portraits of two Russian Men of War', engraved by Baily after an original by Nicholas Pocock, published by Joyce Gold, 1 October 1799.
NMM neg D9039

3. 'The Victory off Stromboli', watercolour by Nicholas Pocock (1740-1821), no date but part of a series done about 1810.
NMM neg A373

4. 'The Streights (or fare) of Messina, with His Majesty's Ship Foudroyant', aquatint engraved by Hall after an original by Nicholas Pocock (1740-1821), published by Joyce Gold, 30 April 1807.
NMM neg B1579

5. 'Ruins of Theatre at Nora. Coast at Pula, Bay of Cagliari, Sardinia 1857', watercolour by Admiral Sir Edward Gennys Fanshawe, June 1857.
NMM ref PAI4687

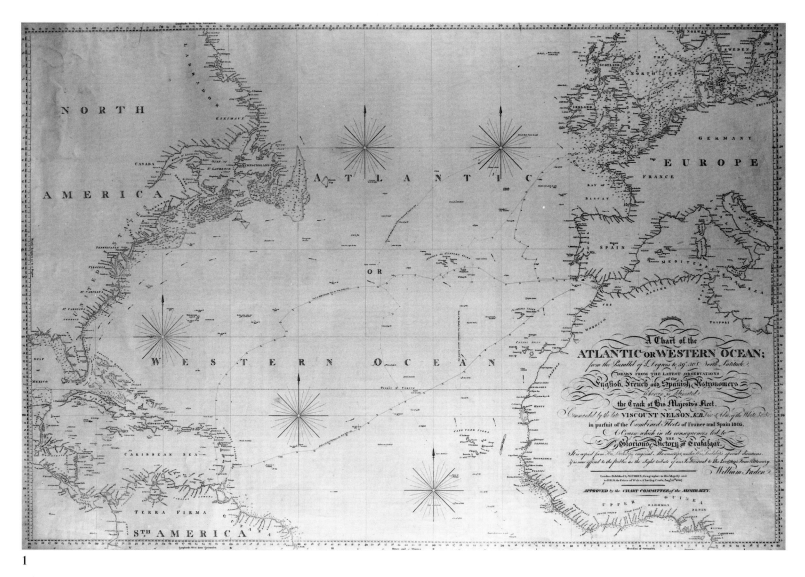

1

Villeneuve escapes

AD WEATHER had ruined Villeneuve's first attempt, in January, to play his part in Napoleon's elaborate strategy for concentrating his squadrons in the Channel for long enough to get his invasion force across. As Allied commander-in-chief, Villeneuve's orders were to collect the Spanish squadron at Cadiz, and then to make for Martinique, the French stronghold in the West Indies, where he was to wait forty days for the arrival of Admiral Ganteaume's Brest squadron. On the morning of 30 March there was a fresh breeze from the northeast, and Villeneuve put to sea with eleven sail of the line, with 3000 troops embarked, and sailed on a course of south-southwest. Villeneuve believed Nelson to be off Barcelona, where he had previously been sighted, and therefore his plan was to pass well to the east of the Spanish coast.

At the time of the breakout, the British fleet was just finished victualling in Palma Bay, with the frigates *Active*

and *Phoebe* left to watch over Toulon; on sighting the French fleet thirty miles off Cape Sicié, *Phoebe* bore up for Palma. *Active* continued to trail the French but lost them as darkness fell upon the fleet. News of the escape presented Nelson with the same dilemma he had faced in January, and he reacted with the same concern for Sardinia, Sicily and the east, stationing his fleet between Sardinia and the north African coast. He then despatched all his cruisers in search of intelligence, but it was not until 18 April that he learned that the French had passed Gibraltar.

In fact, by 9 April the French were through the straits and standing into the bay of Cadiz, Orde's inferior squadron retiring before them. Villeneuve waited only long enough to order the Spanish to sea and with the exception of one ship the rest of the Spanish did not catch up before he arrived in the West Indies. Apart from knowing Villeneuve had left the Mediterranean, Nelson

had little to go on, since the French had a number of possible destinations. Nelson's pursuit was delayed by the need to cover the important convoy carrying Craig's expeditionary force to Malta and then later by foul winds preventing him from passing through the straits. In the meantime, by a process of elimination he came to the conclusion that Villeneuve must be headed for the West Indies, and on 11 May he finally sailed from Lagos Bay on the epic chase across the Atlantic (1).

He was a month behind Villeneuve, who arrived at Martinique (2) on 14 May and the laggardly Spanish two days later. On his way into Port Royal he had been engaged by 'HMS' Diamond Rock, the British possession which was causing so much aggravation to the authorities at Martinique (see pages 36-39). The reduction of this 'insult' was one way of usefully filling the forty-day wait for Ganteaume, and to do the job he detailed a powerful force comprising the *Pluton*, 74, *Berwick*, 74, *Sirène*, 36, *Argus*, 16, an armed schooner and eleven gunboats with 350 troops under the command of Commodore Julien Marie Cosmao-Kerjulien, an able, energetic officer who was to become a hero for the sortie he led after Trafalgar.

The attacking squadron met bad weather and was unable to fetch the rock until 31 May which gave the British time to prepare. Unfortunately, while trying to work up to the Diamond the French squadron was spotted from St Lucia apparently heading south, and it was this report which misdirected Nelson to Trinidad when he arrived at Barbados a week later.

The French attacking force was overwhelming (3), and Commander Maurice, the British officer in charge, abandoned the lower parts of the rock, and concentrated his defence from the upper reaches. At 8am the French opened fired; Diamond Rock returned fire from two 18pdrs (Diamond Battery) and the carronade of Hood's battery. The British positions might have been impregnable, but an accident had caused all the drinking water to leak from the garrison's cistern, so the defence was carried out in blazing heat with virtually no potable rations. The French bombardment lasted until 4.30pm on 2 June when the British, with their ammunition almost expended and collapsing from thirst, hoist-

ed a flag of truce and advantageous terms of surrender were concluded. The action had cost the British 'sloop' two killed and one wounded out of a complement of 107. The French had lost 50 killed or wounded, plus three gunboats sunk or disabled. Maurice was not only later acquitted at his court martial for the loss of his command but was highly commended for his defence.

Whilst the attack on Diamond Rock was progressing, Villeneuve had received new orders brought by the frigate *Didon*, 40 to seize St Vincent, Antigua, Grenada and if possible Barbados. After waiting in the Antilles he was then to take the fleet to Ferrol. Consequently, the Allied fleet weighed on 4 June and proceeded north, and was lucky enough to fall in with a homeward-bound British convoy on the 8th, capturing fifteen merchantmen with cargoes valued at £200,000. However, from the prizes Villeneuve also learned that Nelson had arrived in the West Indies, and was at that moment searching for him. This news instantly changed his mind, and he decided to return to Europe immediately, orders notwithstanding.

1. 'A Chart of the Atlantic . . . wherein is delineated the Track of his Majesty's Fleet Commanded by the late Viscount Nelson . . . in pursuit of the Combined Fleets of France and Spain 1805 . . . It is copied from His Lordship's original Manuscript, under His Lordship's special directions . . . ', engraved and published by William Faden, 12 August 1807. *NMM neg A1258*

2. 'St. Pierre. Martinique. T. 1er Page 113 Album Maritime', etching by Fortier after an original by L Garneray, published by Baillieu, 1838. *NMM ref PAD7313*

3. 'Prise du Rocher le Diamant, 25 Juin 1805, Galerie Historique de Versailles', steel engraving by Chavanne after an original by M Meyer, published by Diagraphe et Pantographe Gavard, no date. *NMM neg 5191*

1

Nelson in the West Indies

ELSON FINALLY arrived at Barbados on 4 July, and anchored the fleet in Carlisle Bay (1). When off Madeira he had already sent the *Amazon* ahead to warn the local commander, Admiral Cochrane, of his forthcoming arrival and his need for reinforcements. Cochrane, who had been pursuing Missiessy, had information that suggested Jamaica was threatened, so left only the 74s *Northumberland* and *Spartiate*. As pointed out in the previous section, a sighting of the force sent against Diamond Rock was misinterpreted, and an attack on Tobago and Trinidad was assumed. At Carlisle Bay, General Myers and 2000 troops were embarked by the fleet, and on the following morning Nelson sailed for Tobago en route to Trinidad.

Nelson had drafted a new order of battle to include the latest additions – *Northumberland* and *Spartiate* – so he was presumably prepared to engaged the combined Allied fleet if the circumstances were in his favour. However, his main intention against such a fleet, superior only in numbers, seemed to be to keep contact until such reinforcements joined him to enable complete annihilation. He is reported to have said to his captains, 'We won't part without a battle. I think they will be glad to leave me alone, if I will let them alone, which I will do until we approach the shores of Europe or they give me an advantage too tempting to be resisted.'

On 7 June the brig *Curieux*, which had been stationed ahead of the fleet, brought news that the Allied fleet was indeed believed to be at Trinidad. The British fleet cleared for action and formed in order of battle on the approach to the Gulf of Paria, Trinidad (2). Nelson had been lead to believe that the enemy had landed and commenced amphibious operations. The confusion had arisen from British forces on the island believing the approaching fleet to be that of the French. The army fell back from the shore to their concentrated positions, setting fire to blockhouses on the way. The ensuing flames and smoke which followed this action the British assumed to be the result of an Allied landing and expected to find the Combined Fleet at anchor in the harbour.

Once it was clear that Trinidad was still safe under the British flag, the fleet immediately reversed course. On the following morning Nelson was off Grenada, and it was here that he received news from a cruiser out of Dominica that the Allied fleet had been off Guadeloupe three days before and was moving north. Villeneuve in fact had sailed for the Azores on 10 June, unnerved at hearing that Nelson was indeed in the West Indies. Believing Nelson had arrived with fourteen of the line and been reinforced by the whole of Cochrane's squadron, Villeneuve wanted to avoid an action at all costs. He no longer had freedom of action against British possessions in the region, nor could he wait any longer for

2

3

Ganteaume. He therefore committed his recently captured prizes to the protection of a frigate, disembarked his troops into crowded cruisers to return to their respective garrisons, and sailed for Europe. One of Villeneuve's junior officers was to note, 'We have been masters of the sea for three weeks with an army of 7000 and have not been able to attack a single island.' This decision could only adversely effect the morale of his fleet.

On the day Villeneuve had sailed for home waters, Nelson was off Montserrat. He had received weak intelligence that the Combined Fleet had been sighted off Guadaloupe, with the intention of attacking Antigua. Nelson proceeded north and arrived off Antigua to find no sign of the enemy. On the 12th he came in to St John's harbour (3) where he disembarked General Myers and his troops. Nelson received word that day that French

troops had been disembarked at Guadeloupe. He now believed, although with no certainty, that Villeneuve had sailed for Europe. However, just as Nelson had made his decision to quit the Caribbean in pursuit, the schooner *Netley* arrived confirming Nelson's belief.

The brig *Curieux* was dispatched (4) to inform the Admiralty of Villeneuve's return and Nelson's intention to follow; she sighted the Combined Fleet on the 19th and hurried on with her information, arriving in enough time to allow the Admiralty to make final adjustments to the waiting squadrons. Leaving Cochrane's flagship, the *Northumberland*, at Antigua, the British fleet sailed on 13 June with eleven of the line to give chase. Nelson was now only a matter of days behind Villeneuve, but they were heading for different landfalls, Nelson for Cadiz and Villeneuve for his unexpected rendezvous with Calder's squadron off Finisterre.

1. 'Watering place for the ships lying in Carlisle Bay, Barbados', watercolour dated 15 January 1794 from a sketchbook of the Rev Cooper Willyams.
NMM neg D9056

2. 'Entrance to the Gulf of Paria, or Dragon's Mouth, Trinidad (West Side)', coloured lithograph engraved by Thomas Goldsworthy Dutton after an original by W S Andrews, published by Day & Son, no date.
NMM ref PAD0947

3. 'St Johns Harbour, Antigua', engraving by J Medland after an original by N Pocock, published by Joyce Gold, 30 June 1804.
NMM neg D9043

4. 'View of St John's Harbour, Antigua. The Fleet at anchor and the Curieux brig making sail with despatches for England', watercolour by Nicholas Pocock, 1810.
NMM ref PAF5884

4

Ships of the Royal Navy: the 50-gun ship

1. 'British 50-gun ship, ca. 1775', etching by Robert Pollard after an original by T Mitchell, published by William Mitchell 18 November 1808. The ten lower deck gunports but two-level stern gallery suggest the *Experiment* of 1774.
NMM ref PA12614

2. An unidentified 50-gun moored off Malta about 1770. The ship wears a commodore's broad pendant at the main truck. The neat harbour stow of the topsails and line of marines on the gangways implies the kind of ceremonial 'showing the flag' which was so often the peacetime lot of the 50-gun ship.
NMM ref PAD8514

3. The lines and profile draught for the *Salisbury* of 1814, the last traditional 50-gun design.
NMM neg DR1435

4. The profile draught of the purchased East Indiaman *Glatton*, showing the high arched gunports on the upper deck that allowed her carronades the elevation to fire carcasses at Copenhagen.
NMM neg DR8073

AT THE beginning of the eighteenth century the 50-gun ship was the smallest unit of the battle line, but as the century progressed the 50 seemed increasingly inappropriate for fleet engagements. From the 1760s France ceased to regard small two-deckers as part of the battlefleet, although such ships continued to hold a more important position among the second-rank powers like the Netherlands and the Baltic states.

The Royal Navy, concerned as always with fleet size, found it expedient to carry on building smaller ships, albeit after about 1750 in decreasing numbers (1). By 1793 some naval officers would have considered the 50-gun ship an obsolescent type, and indeed many of the earlier examples were converted to auxiliary roles, like troopship or storeship, where their relatively spacious gundecks would prove valuable. Nevertheless, for most of the Great French Wars a reasonably consistent number were always in Sea Service commission, although the total numbers dwindled steadily: 7 in 1793, 9 in 1801, 7 in 1810 but only 2 by 1814. Furthermore, three were under construction at the outbreak of war, and a new design was ordered as late as 1810.

The fact is that the 50 had a distinct, if relatively minor, role for which there was a small but constant demand. Structurally, the 50 was usually the smallest rate fitted with two levels of stern cabins, so were regarded as providing the bare minimum accommodation for a flag officer. The 50 was also reasonably economical of manpower, so found considerable favour in peacetime as flagships on distant or unimportant stations. In 1792 the flagships of the Mediterranean (2), North America, Newfoundland, Leeward Islands and Jamaica stations were all 50s, and another was the senior officer's ship on the Coast of Africa; and during the conflict, out-of-the-way stations continued to be commanded from 50s.

Even when not carrying a flag officer, there was a tendency to consign 50s to lesser stations, like the Cape and East Indies. Here they provided the local ship of force, but more often than not much of their workload was humdrum convoy protection duties, a defensive role for which their powerful 24pdr lower battery and lack of performance under sail would appear to suit them. However, they were not ideal cruisers: the lower deck battery was too near the water to be regarded as usable in all weathers, which put them at a real disadvantage when faced with a tenacious frigate. The *Jupiter* on the Cape station in 1799 was unable to use her lower deck guns against the 12pdr frigate *Preneuse*, which escaped with minor damage, while the *Centurion* was outfought by the 18pdr frigate *Cybele* off Mauritius in 1794. On the other hand, *Centurion* cleverly used her shallower draught to stay inshore and out of the fatal reach of the French 74-gun *Marengo* in 1804.

The one home theatre in which the 50 saw much

action was the North Sea. The Dutch navy was composed of ships which were smaller and less powerful on average than those of Britain, France or Spain, and the shadowing British North Sea squadron was a cinderella fleet of older and smaller ships. *Leopard*, *Isis* and *Adamant* served with Admiral Duncan, and the last two fought at Camperdown, a battle in which the Dutch included four 50-gun ships in their line. *Isis* was later to fight at Copenhagen as well. One factor which made 50s particularly well suited to the North Sea was their relatively shallow draught—about 17ft mean compared with about 22ft for a Common Class 74. This was particularly important among the shoals and swatchways of the Dutch coast, allowing blockading small craft to have a ship of force much closer in for potential support. Not surprisingly, the 50-gun *Isis* was chosen by Vice-Admiral Mitchell as his flagship for the 1799 landings in Holland, despite the presence of far more powerful ships in his squadron.

This suitability as a shallow-draught flagship was developed during the Great French Wars into the only entirely new role for the 50 of the period—as a kind of

control craft for coastal forces on anti-invasion duties. Although the threat of a French descent was not new, the Napoleonic plan was novel in its scale and in its detail. Bonaparte's record meant that serious defensive measures were required against the putative invasion, but the assembly of a mosquito fleet of would-be landing craft in the Channel ports also suggested that vigorous counter attacks might bear fruit. The 50-gun ship was involved with these anti-invasion measures in both the defensive and counter-offensive roles: indeed, such was the demand for ships that some, like the *Trusty* which had been relegated to trooping duties, were returned to full establishment as guardships, leading small flotillas in the narrow waters of the Thames Estuary, the Downs, and the East Coast. Others found more aggressive employment, perhaps none more so than *Antelope*, acting as the flagship of Sir Sydney Smith off the Low Countries in 1804. After the battlefleet itself, these squadrons were the second line of anti-invasion defence, and as flagships of these units the 50-gun ships probably made their most significant contribution to the wars of 1793-1815. Such limited requirements meant that a few

2

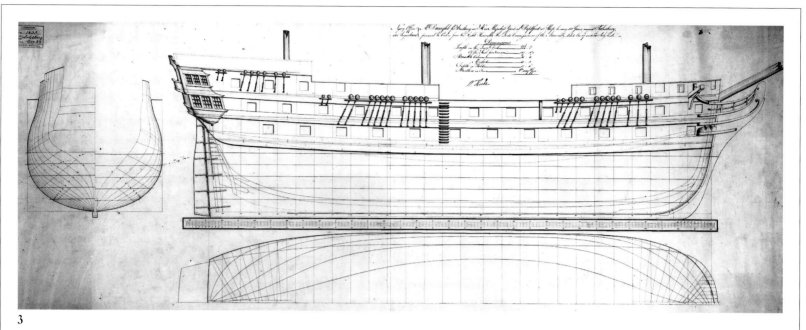

3

ships were under construction even as the long wars against Napoleon were coming to an end (3).

During the wars a few Dutch 50s were captured, but none saw any cruising service. There was, however, one other source of Fourth Rate two-deckers and that was the Honourable East India Company. In 1795 nine large East Indiamen were purchased in various stages of completion in a desperate attempt to increase the size of the fleet in response to a sudden widening of the conflict. They were armed with twenty-eight 18pdrs and twenty-six or twenty-eight 32pdr carronades, rating as 54- or 56-gun ships accordingly. Structurally they were un-naval in their two flush decks with virtually no superstructure – only a tiny topgallant forecastle platform and a quarterdeck that was no more than a roof for the great cabin. They were clearly stopgap measures and as soon as the crisis seemed less pressing four were converted to storeships or transports. The remainder were consigned to minor stations and were mostly utilised for colonial expeditions: *Madras* took part in the 1796 attack on

Martinique and *Malabar* was lost after successfully leading a squadron against Dutch possessions in the Leeward Islands; *Abergavenny* was a virtually stationary flagship at Port Royal, Jamaica between 1797 and 1798.

One exception in both armament and activity was the *Glatton*, which was fitted out to the specification of her carronade-crazy captain, Henry Trollope. His spectacular rout of a French squadron of four frigates, two corvettes, a brig and a cutter was illustrated in *Fleet Battle and Blockade* in this series so needs no further comment. Under the less flamboyant command of 'Bounty' Bligh, the ship was heavily engaged at Copenhagen, accomplishing the rare feat of setting fire to the Danish *Dannebrog* with carcasses (incendiary shells) fired from the upper deck carronades (4). However, the latter battle showed up the unhandiness of the ex-East Indiamen under sail and Nelson was to complain that *Glatton* and *Ardent* (another John Company purchase) 'sail so heavily that no rapid move could be made with them in the Line or the Order of Sailing'.

4

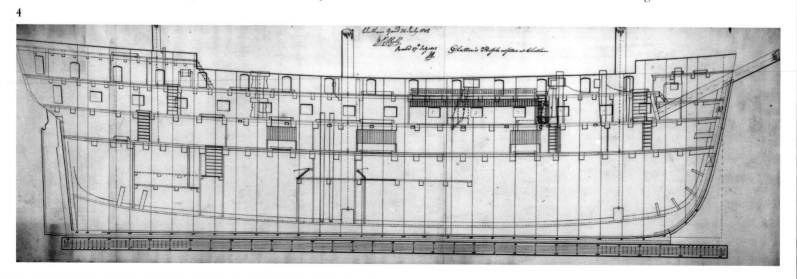

Calder's Action

A BATTLE which marks the final foiling of the enemy's grand strategic design, one in which a numerically inferior fleet captures two of the enemy whilst receiving less damage than it hands out, yet a battle considered so much of a disgrace that the commander has to ask for a court martial to clear his name—Calder's action off Cape Finisterre is one of the odder incidents in British naval history.

Warning from Nelson that the Allied fleet was probably on its way back to Europe reached the Admiralty just before midnight on 8 July 1805. Lord Barham, the irascible First Lord, had gone to bed and no one wanted to disturb him. When he did see the dispatches next morning he was furious at the waste of time, and still in his nightshirt, wrote an order to Cornwallis to detach Rear-Admiral Stirling, with five sail of the line to join Vice-Admiral Calder (1) who was to station himself westward of Cape Finisterre, while Cornwallis himself, with the Channel Fleet, was to cruise between Cape Finisterre and Ushant to catch the returning Villeneuve. This classic order, the necessary (and unsurprising) reaction of a skilled seaman and strategist, sealed the doom of Napoleon's landlubberly scheme. The order reached Cornwallis on the 11th, and was immediately acted upon. Calder had earlier been detached to assume the blockade of Ferrol, and had found on it six ships of the line.

Calder cruised from 90 to 120 miles westward of Cape Finisterre on the lookout for the Allies, who, he believed, had only seventeen of the line. When at about 11am on 22 July the enemy emerged from the fog, the enemy had twenty sail of the line, besides seven frigates, two brigs, and the recaptured galleon *Matilda.* At noon Calder signalled to prepare for battle. An hour later he ordered line of battle, and signalled for close order. His own forces were: four 98s, including his flagship *Prince of Wales*; the 80-gun *Malta*; nine 74s; one 64; two frigates, a lugger and cutter. The larger Allied fleet was made up as follows: the Spanish 90-gun *Argonauta* (Gravina's flagship), one Spanish and four French 80s, including *Bucentaure* (Villeneuve's flagship), two Spanish and ten French 74s, and two Spanish 64s, plus seven frigates and a couple of corvettes. Therefore, the only British advantage was in three-deckers (four to one).

The British were on the starboard tack, the Allies, on the port, in a close and well-formed line, with a frigate ahead of them, the *Sirène*, with the recaptured galleon *Matilda* in tow, astern. Calder's fleet, which could barely see the enemy through the mist, was nearly abeam about seven miles off, but the frigate *Sirius* had reported on the enemy to Calder. Villeneuve and Calder seem to have signalled their respective fleets to tack in succession at about the same time in the late afternoon; but, in the foggy conditions neither fleet saw what the other had done. The British tacked to prevent their opponents escaping them on the opposite tack; but the allies wore

1

2

3

round to protect their rear, alerted by guns fired by the *Sirène.* She was alarmed by the British frigate *Sirius* moving in to attack. Suddenly through the haze *Sirius* saw the alarming sight of the enemy's van ship, the *Argonauta,* approaching. The *Sirius* turned away but was not fired on until about 5.15pm when the *Hero,* the leading British ship of the line came into view, head to wind coming round onto the other tack. Instantly the Spanish ships opened fire, the *España* on the *Sirius,* which suffered a few casualties, but then escaped.

The captain of the *Hero* had tacked without signal because he saw what, owing to the mist, his commander could not see, that the enemy had come round on the

starboard tack. At 5.20pm, she opened fire, and the *Ajax* astern turned away to hail Calder to tell him of the change of position of the two vans; and, when she had done that, she took a place in the line astern of the *Glory.* The ships astern of *Ajax* turned with *Hero.* By 5.50pm, when a signal to tack in succession was hoisted, the *Triumph, Barfleur, Agamemnon, Windsor Castle,* and *Defiance* had already done so without orders (2). The flagship followed, and soon the engagement became general (3). By 6pm, all the ships, except the *Dragon,* which was still working up from leeward, had come round on the starboard tack; and most of them had found opponents; but, as smoke was added to mist and the obscurity deepened, a confused melee resulted. *Windsor Castle, Malta,* and *Ajax* were the worst hit.

On the other side, the *San Rafael, Firme* and *España,* which had dropped to leeward, were very badly damaged by overwhelming British fire. The gallant and pugnacious French captain Cosmao-Kerjulien in *Pluton* gallantly bore out of line for a time, in a hopeless effort to save the *Firme,* and a more successful attempt to relieve the *España.* Just after 8pm, the *Firme,* then almost mastless, struck, as did, a little later, the *San Rafael* (4). Both vessels, soon after surrendering, lost all their masts. At 8.25pm, his fleet scattered, the fog and smoke as thick as ever, and night drawing on, Calder signalled to discontinue the action. Several ships did not see the signal, and desultory firing went on some time. In the meantime the *Dragon* had taken in tow the *Windsor Castle,* which had lost her fore topmast. The two prizes had suffered 476 killed and wounded and the Allies' other vessels, 171; a total 647, as against only 198 on the British

4

5

side. It is an indication of the thickness of the weather that it was not until next morning that Villeneuve knew that he had lost two ships.

By the morning of 23 July, the centres of the two fleets were about seventeen miles apart, with neither moving appreciably, the weather being still hazy with little wind. Calder concentrated his command, and then placed the rest of his fleet between his crippled ships (*Windsor Castle*, *Firme*, and *San Rafael*, the first towed by the *Dragon*, the second by the *Sirius*, and the third by the *Egyptienne*) and the enemy (5, 6). Temporarily deceived by the beginning of these moves into thinking Calder was fleeing, Villeneuve, sent some of his frigates to inform his captains that he intended to bring on a decisive action, but the wind was too feeble to renew battle before nightfall. Also Villeneuve had probably remembered that he had been ordered, if he decided to join the Brest fleet, he should try to do it without fighting. Subsequent wind shifts brought the Allies nearly astern of the British, who might, perhaps, have made their enemy fight again on the morning of the 24th. Yet Calder made no attempt of

the kind and by early evening the fleets were out of sight of one another. Villeneuve went to Vigo, and eventually proceeded to Ferrol.

Calder had won a victory with an inferior force, though the French declared that he had fled the Allied fleet; the Admiralty suppressed part of his official letter in which he gave reasons for not following up his advantage; and there was a press clamour against his lack of aggression. Calder therefore demanded a court martial, at which he was severely reprimanded for not having done his utmost to renew the engagement, but acquitted of cowardice. It was an unfortunate end to a confrontation which had been reasonably successful tactically. Strategically Calder's Action was a thundering success; it was this confrontation and not Trafalgar which put the stopper on Napoleon's over-ingenious invasion plans. The credit for this, however, rests not with Calder, but the elderly nightshirted figure of Charles Middleton, Lord Barham, writing the orders which swung the far-flung squadrons of the Royal Navy into action to block Villeneuve.

1. 'Sir Robert Calder, First Captain to Admiral Earl of St Vincent &c &c', stipple engraving by Edward Orme after an original by Lemuel Francis Abbott, no date.
NMM ref PAD4575

2. 'Sir Robt Calder's Action, July 22nd 1805. Defiance, Windsor Castle, Prince of Wales, Repulse, Raisonable; Ferrol 23 July 1805', coloured aquatint engraved by Thomas Sutherland after an original by Thomas Whitcombe (born c1752), 1 March 1817.
NMM neg B3587

3. 'Admiral Sir Robert Calder's action off Cape Finisterre, 23 July 1805', oil painting by William Anderson (1757-1837), no date.
NMM ref BHC0540

4. 'Sir Robert Calder's Action with the Combined Fleet of French & Spaniards on the 22nd July 1805, as seen from the Frisk Cutter at an interval of the Fog clearing away', aquatint and etching by Robert Dodd after his own original, published by the artist November 1805.
NMM ref PAI6129

5. 'Situation of the hostile Squadrons on the Morning of the 23rd July 1805', coloured aquatint engraved by Thomas Sutherland after an original by Thomas Whitcombe (born c1752), no date.
NMM neg B3588

6. 'Admiral Sir Robert Calder's action off Cape Finisterre, 23 July 1805', oil painting by William Anderson (1757-1837), no date.
NMM ref BHC0539

6

Part IV # TRAFALGAR

FROM OFF Ushant in August 1805, the logistics Cornwallis had under calculation were uncertain and challenging. Although the French and Spanish fleets were attempting to avoid close action, they were clearly no longer content to remain confined to port and their sallies and mergers demanded the most careful redisposition of the British blockading squadrons, for even the most naive strategist in the British fleet had to link the manoeuvres of the combined fleets to the massed invasion craft lining the coasts around Boulogne. The return of Villeneuve from the West Indies demanded the greatest redisposition. On 17 August Cornwallis despatched Calder back to Ferrol with twenty of the line, including eight of Nelson's earlier Mediterranean fleet. When Cornwallis received news of Villeneuve having emerged from Ferrol, Calder was urged in chase and was to move south with his force to reinforce Collingwood off Cadiz where the Franco-Spanish Combined Fleet then amounted to thirty-five ships of the line.

However, the British forces under his own immediate command were thereby reduced and the enemy squadrons in the French ports were equally troubling. On 17 July Captain Zacharie Allemand had broken out of Rochefort with five ships of the line and had since taken in the Channel a British 16-gun brig and the 54-gun *Calcutta*. Villeneuve had hoped to link up with Allemand on emerging from Ferrol, but, unbeknown to Cornwallis, without success. When this attempted juncture failed, after cruising the Bay of Biscay, Allemand would eventually return into Rochefort safely.

Meanwhile Cornwallis himself was left off Brest with only seventeen of the line to blockade Ganteaume with twenty-one. Though not so far successful in sailing, the manoeuvres of the Brest fleet continued to look threatening from time to time. On 22 August Ganteaume again moved to the outer roads with his full

force, and only retreated within the headlands when Cornwallis bore down with his full seventeen. The latter was fortunate at that time in having his squadron up to strength, for at other times a significant proportion of his squadron was usually away replenishing or refitting.

At the end of August Cornwallis took leave, his command off Ushant falling to Sir Richard Strachan. At the same time, Nelson sailed to relieve Collingwood off Cadiz. He reboarded the *Victory* on 14 September and she sailed the following day, with five more of the line to follow as they became ready. Nelson joined the British fleet off Cadiz on 28 September. There, by now, were twenty-nine British ships of the line, but six were due for revictualling and watering at Gibraltar. On finding 'thirty-six Sail of the Line looking me in the face', Nelson acknowledged his force was 'not so large as might be wished' but intended, as he claimed, to do his best: 'I am not come forth to find difficulties, but to remove them'.

Prior to Nelson's arrival, Collingwood had kept his blockading squadron only about 15 miles off Cadiz. Nelson moved his main force to cruise some 50 miles to the westward, leaving observation frigates close off the town, and four or five of the line between them and his main fleet. Under such a loose blockade, there was the always the possibility that the Cartagena or Rochfort squadron might attempt to force their way in; but against that Nelson considered the Combined Fleet would be continuously tempted out against what appeared an inferior force; at the same time, there was less risk, in the event of a westerly gale, that the British fleet would be forced off station into the Straits and the Mediterranean.

On 10 October the Combined Fleet moved to the entrance to Cadiz harbour to sail at the first opportunity. Villeneuve had received intructions dated 17 September from Napoleon to take his fleet into the Mediterranean to deposit the troops he carried at Naples and to gain further reinforcement from ships built at Toulon

and Genoa. Napoleon had not undertaken to instruct the Spanish to sail, but the Spanish government, thinking Gravina could unite with the Cartagena squadron, ordered him to sail with Villeneuve.

Ironically, in the way long-term plans are altered on account of short-term emergencies, the instructions signed by Napoleon and sent to Villeneuve on 17 September were motivated now not by thoughts of the invasion of England or Ireland but from that gathering Third Coalition of European states allied to Britain which Pitt had gradually constructed since May 1804. Russia, Sweden and Britain had drawn together by April 1805; Prussia had allied with Russia in May; and Austria with Russia in June. In August 1805 Austria signed a treaty with Britain and agreed to invade Bavaria, France's ally, on 11 September. From 23 August Napoleon was poised to strike his camps around Boulogne and to march on Vienna. Austria had to be distracted and an invasion of the Two Sicilies—being courted to join the coalition by Britain—would draw her land forces into Italy. Whether, under these war conditions, an invasion of England could go ahead was doubtful. If Villeneuve managed to break out of the Mediterranean again and reach the Channel, and if an invasion army was still at Boulogne, perhaps it could. But Napoleon was more inclined to think the combination of arrangements necessary for an invasion was no longer tenable, at least in the immediate future. He was thus considering splitting Villeneuve's force into raiding squadrons once he had collected the ships in the Mediterranean ports.

None of this was known to Nelson, and little to Villeneuve. Nelson was solely preoccupied with Villeneuve's movements. With five ships sent to water early in October, and with two new arrivals from England and Gibraltar, on 10 October Nelson's fleet amounted to twenty-six ships of the line. Conscious of his persisting inferiority in numbers, that day he completed and issued the memorandum that foreshadowed the plan of attack later actually carried out. After declaring his intention that the order of battle should be the order of sailing and that the British fleet should form in two columns, he went on:

> If the enemy's fleet should be seen to windward in line of battle, and that the two lines . . . could fetch them, they will probably be so extended that their van could not succour their rear. I should therefore probably make the second in command's signal to lead through about the twelfth ship from the rear, or wherever he could fetch, if not able to get so far forward. My line would cut through about their centre . . . The whole impression of the British fleet must be to overpower [from] two or three ships ahead of their commander-in-chief—supposed to be in the centre—to the rear of their fleet. I will suppose 20 sail of the enemy's line to be untouched. It must be some time before they could perform a manoeuvre to bring their force compact to attack any part of the British fleet engaged, or to succour their own ships; which, indeed, would be impossible without mixing with the ships engaged . . .

In actual battle, Nelson believed that British ships should be one-fourth superior to the enemy cut-off, but beyond that knew success was ultimately the effect of initiative and courage on the part of the commanders of ships. 'Something must be left to chance. Nothing is sure in a sea-fight . . . Captains are to look to their particular line as their rallying point; but, in the case signals cannot be seen or clearly understood, no captain can do very wrong if he places his ship alongside that of an enemy.' Collingwood was to lead the second line and on 10 October he shifted his flag from the slow-sailing *Dreadnought* into the newly refitted and faster *Royal Sovereign*.

For his part, Villeneuve was also preparing for battle and anticipated the instructions issued by Nelson. He informed his captains:

> The enemy will not confine himself to forming on a line of battle parallel with our own and with engaging us in an artillery duel . . . he will endeavour to envelope our rear, to break through our line and to direct his ships in groups upon such as ours as he shall have cut off, so as to surround them and defeat them.

However, he proposed no method of countering the British tactic he anticipated, simply explaining that, should it be adopted, 'in this case, a captain in command must consult his own daring and love of honour far more than the signals of the Admiral who, being perhaps engaged himself and shrouded in smoke, may no longer have the power of making any'. Strangely, Villeneuve did not develop any plan

One event from Nelson's short final leave which appealed to printmakers was his only meeting with Wellesley, then known as the victor of campaigns in India but not yet the great Duke of Wellington. 'The Army and Navy. This Print representing the only interview between those great commanders Wellington and Nelson . . .', mezzotint engraved by Samuel William Reynolds after an original by John Prescott Knight, published by Lewis & Johnson, no date. NMM neg A3403

or tactic of attack for his own ships other than in line. Possibly, intent on achieving Napoleon's instructions and conscious of the defensive strength of the line, he was more concerned for his fleet to reach the Mediterranean than for it to destroy the British fleet.

A significant loss to Nelson on 14 October was the three-decker *Prince of Wales*, Calder's flagship. With the arrival of the *Victory*, Calder learned from newspapers and from the letters of friends of the growing body of opinion against him for failing to achieve more against the Combined Fleet on 23 July and he requested a court martial on his conduct. Out of sympathy for Calder, who felt his integrity under attack, Nelson allowed him to sail for England in his own ship rather than a frigate. The decision was taken amid the arrival and departure of other ships until 19 October when, as preparations to sail were detected in the Combined Fleet in Cadiz, the British fleet off Cadiz was held at twenty-seven of the line.

Gales prevented Villeneuve sailing between 10 and 17 October. That day the wind moderated and shifted to the east. On 18 October Villeneuve heard rumours that his intended replacement, Vice-Admiral François Etienne Rosily, had reached Madrid. Napoleon had not been pleased that Villeneuve had sailed south from Ferrol to Cadiz, rather than attempting to reach Brest and Boulogne, and, considering his admiral had betrayed France, on 18 September ordered Rosily to do better. A month later at Cadiz, in the hope of redeeming his reputation by performing Napoleon's instructions before he could be replaced, on 18 October Villeneuve ordered the fleet to sail next day.

On 19 October there was little wind and only twelve of the Combined Fleet got out of harbour; they were joined on the 20th by another twenty-one, consisting altogether of eighteen French and fifteen Spanish ships of the line. Villeneuve sailed southwest to clear Cape Trafalgar, then turned south southwest. Their exodus was communicated to Nelson by the new telegraphic signals developed by Sir Home Popham, but he with the bulk of his fleet was still 50 miles from Cadiz. He ordered a general chase southeast, but as the fleet approached the Straits, he put it back on a northwesterly course, and early on the 21st on to a northeast-

erly, then easterly, course which placed the British fleet to windward of the Combined Fleet and prevented it from returning into Cadiz.

As the two fleets sighted one another in the first light of 21 October they were 11 miles apart. Fearing a night attack, Villeneuve had already ordered his fleet into a rough order of battle, a manoeuvre executed in the dark, resulting in squadrons becoming mixed up in several adjacent lines. These he reorganised into '*ordre naturel*' when day broke, requiring many ships to back and fill into their pre-arranged order of battle. The confusion somewhat worried Nelson, who wondered what they were doing, concern that was enhanced between 7.15 and 8.30am as Villeneuve ordered his fleet to wear together and form in reverse order. Had the wind strengthened, its new direction might have brought the Combined Fleet back to Cadiz. As ships attempted to reform on the new tack, the rear composed of Gravina's division was congested, forcing some vessels to bunch and sail to leeward of others. So the Combined Fleet took on an overlapping crescent formation.

Before dawn Nelson too had brought his fleet roughly into two columns, lee and weather lines, that formed more regularly in Collingwood's and Nelson's wakes in the light of day. The two fleets were gradually converging and, in the light winds, after the Spanish wore Nelson and Collingwood had only to alter direction slightly to maintain the course which would bring about their collision with the Combined Fleet. It was nevertheless 11.40am, nearly six hours after first light, before the two fleets were close enough for Nelson to signal to Collingwood his intention to pass through the head of the enemy line to prevent them getting into Cadiz. It was followed by his attempt to 'amuse' his fleet with the signal which, though initially beginning 'Nelson confides . . . ', was altered on the suggestion of *Victory*'s signal lieutenant, to 'England expects that every man will do his duty'.

It was about noon when the first shot was fired, on the *Royal Sovereign*, at the head of the lee line. She began the engagement first, cutting through the enemy line about fifteen ships from its rear, immediately astern of the Spanish *Santa Ana*, flagship of Vice-Admiral

Alava. Owing to the slow pace of sailing, it was 15 minutes before she was supported by the *Belleisle*. As other ships in Collingwood's rear came up, they engaged the ships astern of the *Santa Ana*. Seeking to gain advantageous positions and to support other British vessels, progressively a melee developed. The bunching of ships in the rear of the Combined line gave it in places a double or even triple strength which permitted the Spanish to absorb the onslaught. However, at close quarters, confidence and rate of fire could more than make up for sheer size and number of guns. Thus the *Dreadnought*, Collingwood's 98-gun former flagship, which could fire three broadsides every three and a half minutes, later successfully engaged Gravina's 112-gun *Principe de Asturias* as well as the 74 *San Juan de Nepomuceno*, combative courage that was repeated throughout the British fleet.

Nelson's column, lead by the *Victory*, came under fire 20 minutes after the lee line. As she approached the Combined Fleet, her course was altered to steer for the Spanish four-decked 130-gun *Santísima Trinidad*, flagship of Rear-Admiral Don Baltaser Cisneros, and the two ships ahead of her. While the *Victory* approached, the Combined Fleet held its fire: a minute or two of awful silence ensued and then, as if by signal, seven or eight of the closest enemy ships opened 'such a fire as had scarcely before been directed at a single ship'. As the engagement began, Villeneuve's flag broke out on the *Bucentaure*, following the *Santísima Trinidad*, and Nelson directed the *Victory* to bear away to starboard and engage her stern. The *Bucentaure* was closely supported by the *Redoutable* and *Neptune*, and the ships closed to point-blank range.

Astern of the *Victory* the British weather line had bunched as they pressed into action. As the centre of the Combine Fleet's line became a melee, so the rear of the British weather column was able to choose opponents who appeared likely to escape the initial onslaught. At the head of the Combined line, Rear-Admiral Dumanoir Le Pelley was slow to react to what was happening astern of him and Villeneuve only signalled for the van to wear together at 1.30pm. Four French and Spanish vessels did get back to the windward side of the melee, but it was past 3pm before they were able to fire on the British ships. Collingwood had seen the movement and at his signal a few from the rear of the weather line came to windward on the port tack in line of battle to fend Dumanoir off. At 4.30pm Dumanoir gave up the attempt to support Gravina and set a course for the Straits.

On the quarterdeck of the *Victory*, Nelson was shot by a musket ball fired from the mizzen top of the *Redoutable* at 1.25pm. He was carried below and died at 4.40pm. By then, the battle was virtually over. Villeneuve continued to stride the quarterdeck of the *Bucentaure* until the ship was dismasted and unable to fight her guns. With all her boats damaged, he was unable to get to another ship and, unwilling to subject the crew of his helpless flagship to further suffering, he ordered the colours of the *Bucentaure* to be lowered and surrendered to Captain Israel Pellew of the *Conqueror*.

When firing ceased, seventeen of the thirty-three ships of the line in the Combined Fleet had surrendered to British ships, and another had caught fire and blown up. Of the remainder, four escaped southeast with Dumanoir and eleven under Gravina ran to the northeast, some under tow by frigates, to anchor off Rota, the height of the wind preventing them getting into Cadiz. Of the prizes, eight were totally dismasted and nine partially. As night came, the wind rose from the west-southwest, accompanied by a heavy swell, which pressed the crippled ships towards Cape Trafalgar, only six or seven miles to leeward. Collingwood prepared to anchor, which four vessels did, but towards midnight the wind swung south-southwest and, with heads to the west, the remainder of the British fleet and prizes survived the night drifting seaward.

However, a gale got up the following day and many of the prizes had to be abandoned. Also on 23 October the senior French officer in Cadiz, Commodore de Cosmao-Kerjulien made a sortie with five ships of the line and rescued the *Neptuno* and *Santa Ana*. As a result of the gale and the rescue attempt, only four of the prizes were to survive to be taken into Gibraltar. Nevertheless, three of Cosmao-Kerjulien's vessels were also effectively lost in the storms, one being captured before she too was wrecked on 26 October. The *Victory* got into Gibraltar on 28 October, where she was partially refitted before sailing for England, anchoring at Spithead on 4 December.

The four ships which had escaped to the southeast with Dumanoir on 21 October never again saw a French port. Knowing Rear-Admiral Thomas Louis and several British ships of the line were at Gibraltar, having been detached from Nelson's fleet to water before Trafalgar, Dumanoir decided to head for a French Atlantic port. On 2 November off Cape Finisterre he was sighted by ships from the

A diagrammatic representation of the stages of Strachan's Action, 3-4 November 1805. From Julian Corbett, The Campaign of Trafalgar *(London 1910). It is based on sketches by Dumanoir himself in his official report.*

squadron under Sir John Strachan, cruising off Ferrol. They were chased and on 4 November attacked by Strachan who at that time also had with him four of the line and four frigates. After intermittent action and tactical manoeuvring, all four French ships surrendered. The four prizes were all got into Plymouth and eventually added to the British navy.

Villeneuve took the same route in the frigate *Euryalus*. Repatriated at Morlaix in the spring 1806, he was found in the Hôtel de la Patrie at Rennes on 22 April with six deep knife wounds in and around his heart. A note to his wife was allegedly discovered with his body and his death was officially said to have been suicide, a claim to which Napoleon subscribed. However, his wounds could hardly have been self-inflicted and the Imperial police failed to conduct a real investigation so that his death was regarded by many as murder, possibly on behalf of the Emperor to whom he had become an embarrassment. Napoleon had made him a scapegoat for the failure of his invasion strategy. Yet his conscientious, officer-like character and patent attempts to perform his instructions contrasted starkly with Napoleon's account of him as a traitor and coward.

Nelson was buried in St Paul's Cathedral on 9 January 1806. His body was conveyed by the *Victory* to the Nore where it was sealed in the coffin made from the mainmast of the French flagship *Orient*, which had blown up at the Battle of the Nile, and a second lead coffin. From the Nore on 24 December it was taken in the yacht of the Sheerness Dockyard commissioner to Greenwich Hospital where it lay in state and was visited by nearly 100,000 people. On 8 January, at the head of a procession of boats and barges streching two miles, it was conveyed up the river to Whitehall steps and remained that night in the Admiralty building. The procession to the Cathedral next day included the Prince of Wales and members of the crew of the *Victory*; the service was attended by thirty-two admirals and over a hundred captains. The ceremony lasted five hours, but perhaps a better reflection of the public attitude to Nelson was the silent reverence with which the thousands of spectators watched the procession. The only sound to be heard, apart from the grate of wheels and shoes on cobbles, resembled the quiet murmuring of the sea as men respectfully removed their hats.

The British Fleet on 21 October 1805

SHIPS	GUNS	COMMANDER	KILLED	WOUNDED
WEATHER COLUMN				
Victory	100	Vice-Adm Lord Nelson	57	102
		Capt Thomas Masterman Hardy		
Temeraire	98	Capt Eliab Harvey	47	76
Neptune	98	Capt Thomas Fremantle	10	34
Leviathan	74	Capt Henry William Bayntun	4	22
Britannia	100	Rear-Adm Earl of Northesk	10	42
		Capt Charles Bullen		
Conqueror	74	Capt Israel Pellew	3	9
Africa	64	Capt Henry Digby	18	44
Agamemnon	64	Capt Sir Edward Berry	2	8
Ajax	74	Lieut John Pilford	2	9
Orion	74	Capt Edward Codrington	1	23
Minotaur	74	Capt Charles Mansfield	3	22
Spartiate	74	Capt Sir Francis Laforey	3	20
LEE COLUMN				
Royal Sovereign	100	Vice-Adm Cuthbert Collingwood	47	94
		Capt Edward Rotheram		
Belleisle	74	Capt William Hargood	33	93
Mars	74	Capt George Duff	29	69
Tonnant	80	Capt Charles Tyler	26	50
Bellerophon	74	Capt John Cooke	27	123
Colossus	74	Capt James Nicoll Morris	40	160
Achilles	74	Capt Richard King	13	59
Dreadnought	98	Capt John Conn	7	26
Polyphemus	64	Capt Robert Redmill	2	4
Revenge	74	Capt Robert Moorsom	28	51
Swiftsure	74	Capt William Ruthefurd	9	8
Defiance	74	Capt Philip Durham	17	53
Thunderer	74	Lieut John Stockham	4	12
Defence	74	Capt George Hope	7	29
Prince	98	Capt Richard Grindall	0	0
FRIGATES AND OTHER VESSELS				
Euryalus	36	Capt Henry Blackwood		
Naiad	38	Capt Thomas Dundas		
Phoebe	36	Capt Thomas Bladen Capell		
Sirius	36	Capt William Prowse		
Pickle, schooner	10	Lieut John Lapenotiere		
Entreprenante, cutter	8	Lieut Robert Young		

The Franco-Spanish Fleet on 21 October 1805

SHIPS	GUNS	COMMANDER	KILLED	WOUNDED	FATE OF THE SHIP
REAR					
Neptuno (Sp)	80	Capt Don Cayetano Valdés	42	47	Taken by *Minotaur* (W); retaken by sortie, 23 October, wrecked, hulk fired 31 October
Scipion	74	Capt Charles Bérenger	0	0	Escaped; taken by Strachan, 4 November
Rayo (Sp)	100	Capt Don Enrique Macdonnell		18 casualties	Escaped; sortied 23 October; captured by *Donegal*; wrecked, hulk fired 31 October
Formidable	80	Rear-Adm Dumanoir Le Pelley Capt J M Letellier		65 casualties	Escaped; taken by Strachan, 4 November
Duguay Trouin	74	Capt Claude Touffet		Few	Escaped; taken by Strachan, 4 November
San Francisco de Asís (Sp)	74	Capt Don Luis de Flores		17 casualties	Escaped; sortied 23 October, but wrecked 23 October
Mont Blanc	74	Capt J La Villegris	0	0	Escaped; taken by Strachan, 4 November
CENTRE					
San Agustín (Sp)	74	Capt Don F X Cagigal	180	200	Taken by *Leviathan* (W); burnt 30 October
Héros	74	Capt J B R Poulain		Few	Escaped to Cadiz
Santísima Trinidad (Sp)	140	Rear-Adm Don H de Cisneros Commod Don F X de Uriarte		Many	Taken by *Prince* (L); foundered 24 October
Bucentaure	80	Vice-Adm P Villeneuve Capt J J Magendie		209 casualties	Taken by *Conqueror* (W); wrecked 23 October
Neptune	84	Commod E T Maistral		?None	Escaped; sortied 23 October
San Leandro (Sp)	64	Capt Don José Quevedo		30 casualties	Escaped to Cadiz
Redoutable	74	Capt J J E Lucas	474	70	Taken by *Temeraire* (W); foundered 22 October
VAN					
Intrépide	74	Capt L A C Infernet		306 casualties	Taken by *Orion* (W); burnt 24 October
San Justo (Sp)	74	Capt Don M Gastón	0	7	Escaped to Cadiz
Indomptable	80	Capt J J Hubert		Few	Escaped; sortied 23 October; wrecked 24 October
Santa Ana (Sp)	112	Vice-Adm Don I M de Alava Capt Don José Gardoquí	97	141	Taken by *Royal Sovereign* (L); retaken by sortie 23 October; escaped to Cadiz
Fougueux	74	Capt L A Beaudouin		400 casualties	Taken by *Temeraire* (W); wrecked 22 October
Monarca (Sp)	74	Capt Don T Argumosa	100	150	Taken by *Bellerophon* (L); wrecked 25 October
Pluton	74	Commod J M Cosmao-Kerjulien		300 casualties	Escaped to Cadiz; sortied 23 October
SQUADRON OF OBSERVATION					
Algésiras	74	Rear-Adm C Magon de Médine Capt G-A Brouard		216 casualties	Taken by *Tonnant* (L); retaken from prize crew; escaped to Cadiz
Bahama (Sp)	74	Commod Don D A Galiano		400 casualties	Taken by *Colossus* (L); prize bought into the Royal Navy; broken up 1814
Aigle	74	Capt P P Gourrége		270 casualties	Taken by *Defiance* (L); wrecked 5 October
Swiftsure	74	Capt Hôpitalier-Villemadrin		250 casualties	Taken by *Colossus* (L); prize bought into the Royal Navy; broken up 1816
Argonaute	74	Capt J Epron		160 casualties	Escaped to Cadiz
Montañes (Sp)	74	Capt Don J Alcedo		49 casualties	Escaped to Cadiz
Argonauta (Sp)	80	Capt Don A Pareja	100	200	Taken by *Belleisle* (L); scuttled 30 October
Berwick	74	Capt J G Filhol-Camas		250 casualties	Taken by *Achilles* (L); wrecked 27 October
San Juan Nepomuceno (Sp)	74	Capt Don Cosmé Churruca		300 casualties	Taken by *Dreadnought* (L); prize bought into the Royal Navy; sold 1818
San Ildefonso (Sp)	74	Commod Don José de Vargas	34	126	Taken by *Defence* (L); prize bought into the Royal Navy; broken up 1816
Achille	74	Capt G Denieport		Nearly all	Caught fire in action with the *Prince* (L) and blew up on 21 October
Príncipe de Asturias (Sp)	112	Adm Don Federico Gravina Capt Rafael de Hore	41	107	Escaped to Cadiz
FRIGATES AND OTHER VESSELS					
Rhin	40	Capt Chesneau			
Hortense	40	Capt La Marre La Meillerie			
Cornélie	40	Capt de Martinenq			
Thémis	40	Capt Jugan			
Hermione	40	Capt Mahe			
Furet	18	Lieut Dumay			
Argus	16	Lieut Taillard			

Note: Exact numbers of Allied casualties will never be known. The French published no official figures, and while the Spanish made estimates for surviving ships, some are round figures and others do not differentiate between killed and wounded. The large numbers lost in the wrecks in the ensuing storm complicate the issue. Fraser in *The Enemy at Trafalgar* calculated total French losses as 3373 killed in action or drowned and 1155 wounded; Spanish 1022 killed, 1386 wounded; as well as 3000-4000 prisoners.

The Fate column shows British ship to which the prizes surrendered, and whether their captors were from the Lee (L) or Weather (W) division.

1

2

SIGNALS USED BY LORD NELSON AT THE BATTLE OF TRAFALGAR, OCTOBER 21st 1805.

Single and Double Pendants.

	Neptune	Royal Sovereign	Queen	Victory	Superb	Defiance	Unité	Tonnant	Colossus	Melpomene	Main	
	Lively	Phoebe	Chiffonne	Prince	Renommée	Decade	Kent	Amazon	Aimable	Agamemnon	Fore	
	Belleisle	Aurora	Etna	Britannia	Ambuscade	Revenge	Seahorse	Mars	Spencer		Mizen	
	Thunderer	Africa		Téméraire	Prince of Wales		Defence	Achille			Starbd	
			Minotaur	Bellerophon	Dreadnought		Polyphemus		Orion		Larbd	
	Canopus			Tigre	Donegal	Swiftsure	Sirius		Leviathan		Starbd	
	Ajax	Zealous	Hydra	Euryalus	Amphion		Niger	Naiad		Endymion	Larbd	
	Conqueror	Juno		Beagle	Weazle	Nautilus	Merlin	Morgiana	Jalouse	Martin	Starbd	
	Spartiate		Thunder	Bittern	Termagant	Childers	Euryale	Pickle	Halcyon		Larbd	
		Nimble			Entreprenante						Cross Jack Yard Arm	

Where hoisted as Single Pendants.

Topmast Head. Main Top Masthead Gaff Arm.

To Sir Thomas Lovingston Bart. Captain of His Majesty's Ship Renommée.

Memo/ When the double Pendants are used they will be hoisted where best seen.

Nelson & Bronte.

Given on Board the *Victory* off Cadiz the 29th Septr 1805.

London: A H Baily & Co 83 Cornhill.

3

The blockade resumed

ELSON ARRIVED off Gibraltar on 20 July at the end of his long chase to the West Indies. Exhausted and in poor health after two years continuously at sea, he returned with *Victory* to England for rest and recuperation at his beloved Merton Place. However, his stay was to be short—he was out of the *Victory* for only twenty-five days. Unhappy with the outcome of the events of the last two years, he offered the Admiralty his renewed services if required, and most of the country from the Prime Minister down expected him to resume his command.

Captain Blackwood shared the assumption and stopped at Merton first when carrying the news to Admiralty that the Combined Fleet had been discovered in harbour at Cadiz. As a result, Nelson once more hoisted his flag in the *Victory* and on 15 September 1805 put to sea to take over command of the blockading fleet off Cadiz from Collingwood (1). Blackwood's frigate *Euryalus* was sent on ahead on 26 September to inform Collingwood that Nelson wished his arrival to be marked by no salutes or recognition signals: should the Combined Fleet be alerted to his presence, there was less chance of its putting to sea. When the *Victory* arrived off Cadiz on the 28th, Nelson assumed command of a fleet at that moment comprising twenty-three of the line and two frigates.

On receiving his first confirmation that Craig's army of 6000 had successfully landed at Malta, and that Anglo-Russian operations were due to begin in southern Italy, Nelson was sure that Villeneuve's orders would send him to sea bound for the Mediterranean. Accordingly, Nelson adopted similar tactics to those employed off Toulon, moving the main fleet out to 50 miles west of Cadiz and stationed *Euryalus* and *Hydra* close inshore. He then placed five ships of the line at equal distance between the watching frigates and the main fleet to ensure the rapid relay of signals. Between 7 and 13 September, Nelson was reinforced by a further six of the line which included his first battleship command and self-confessed favourite, *Agamemnon*, 64; and the newly refitted First Rate *Royal Sovereign*, to which Collingwood transferred his flag. His frigate force was also reinforced with the arrival of the *Naiad*, *Phoebe*, *Sirius*, *Juno* and *Niger* (2).

Within the harbour of Cadiz (3) there were thirty-five ships of the line, seventeen Spanish (two unfit for sea) which were under the command of Admiral Gravina (4) and eighteen French under the command of Admiral Villeneuve (5), the Commander-in-Chief. Further threats to Nelson's position was the possibility of the Spanish division at Cartagena slipping through the straits and into Cadiz. More seriously, if the French should break out of Brest and elude Cornwallis, there was the prospect of Nelson's blockading squadron being attacked from the west.

With no indication of when the enemy might move,

1. 'Cadiz with the Combined Fleets at anchor previous to the Battle of Trafalgar', watercolour from from the journal of Lt W Pringle of *Conqueror*, 74, kept from about 1805. *NMM neg D9055-B*

2. 'Signals used by Lord Nelson at the Battle of Trafalgar, October 21st 1805 . . . Distinguishing Pendants of the Mediterranean Fleet . . . Given on board the Victory off Cadiz, the 29th Sept 1805', coloured etching published by Baily & Co, no date. *NMM ref PA15425*

3. 'Cadix. Vue prise de la pointe de la Vache', coloured lithograph engraved by Cavilier after an original by Chapuy, printed by Bernard Lemercier & Co, published by A Bulla, Paris, no date. *NMM ref PAH2386*

4. A contemporary portrait of Vice-Admiral Federico Gravina, plate from E Fraser, *The Enemy at Trafalgar* (London 1908). *Chatham Collection*

4

5

6

Nelson had to keep up the regular rotation of ships to water and revictual. Accordingly, Rear-Admiral Louis (6), much against his will, was detached to Gibraltar on 2 October with the *Canopus*, *Queen*, *Spencer*, *Tigre* and *Zealous*— a powerful loss, since the squadron included a 98, an 80 and two big 74s. Nelson's strength should have been twenty-nine of the line, but in a typically generous gesture on 14 October he allowed Admiral Calder to sail for England for his impending court martial in his flagship, the 98-gun *Prince of Wales*; the *Donegal* was also sent to Gibraltar two days later. Thus he was left with twenty-seven, the number that fought at Trafalgar.

On 9 October that he drew up his secret memorandum for the order of battle, but Nelson's tactics for his attack on the Combined Fleet had been born back in late August at Merton. He had spoken with Sir Richard Keats about a plan involving three columns: weather division, a lee division and a reserve division to act as directed. As he told Lady Hamilton on 1 October, he had already explained the 'Nelson touch' to his captains and its electrifying effect (7), and Nelson's plan of attack of 9 October specified two lines of battle and an 'Advance Squadron'. The lee division was to be commanded by Collingwood and the weather division by himself. The aim of the lee column was to break the line and attack the enemy's rear, whilst the weather column would break and engage the centre division just ahead of the flagship. The flying squadron would join either column as directed.

Nelson knew his enemy and believed it would be some time before the unengaged van could organise a counterattack. By the time they had worked round, the British would have beaten the two other divisions and would be ready to receive them. Nelson's planned approach to the enemy line was also unorthodox in that his ships were to be under full sail instead of the usual fighting sail which were topsails alone. This was done to ensure that his divisions got amongst the enemy as quickly as possible, minimising the inevitable damage the end-on approach would bring on them. The idea of two columns plus the 'Advance Squadron' was based on Nelson having forty ships of the line. As it was becoming evident that he would have to fight with only twenty-seven ships, the idea of the 'Advance Squadron' would most likely be abandoned.

Meanwhile, within the harbour of Cadiz, Villeneuve was making his own plans. On 28 September he had received his orders to embark troops and make preparations for a passage to the Mediterranean to interrupt Anglo-Russian operations in southern Italy. After his failure in the West Indies and the action with Calder, Villeneuve had finally exhausted Napoleon's patience, and his replacement, Admiral Rosily, was already on his

way. Somehow, Villeneuve had word of his imminent supersession, and was therefore very keen to put to sea in the hope of redeeming himself in the eyes of the Emperor. This was indeed a desperate measure, for the French admiral knew that as soon as he put to sea, he would be brought to a battle that he was unlikely to win. Even though his fleet was superior in numbers, it lacked the experience of its opponents, and faced with an enemy who were superior in seamanship, who could manage a higher rate of fire and who possessed 'the habit of victory', the morale of the Combined Fleet was very low. Nor was the reputation of the victor of the Nile and Copenhagen an insignificant factor.

Villeneuve, although praying for victory, was indeed expecting defeat. The French admiral made an educated guess that Nelson would concentrate on his rear division, isolate it and do much damage before it could be supported. His intention was therefore to form line of battle with only twenty-two of his ships and with the remainder form a reserve squadron to observe and act accordingly. With the news that his relief was due at Cadiz within days and also believing that Nelson's fleet was weaker in number than it was because of the detachment of Louis, Villeneuve, without consulting his allies, decided to put to sea as soon as was possible. Therefore, with a perfect northeasterly breeze on the morning of 19 October 1805, Villeneuve made the general signal 'prepare to weigh'.

The Allied fleet was at last coming out (8).

5. A contemporary portrait of Vice-Admiral Pierre-Charles Silvestre de Villeneuve.
Musée de la Marine, Paris ref 85905

6. 'Rear Admiral Sir Thomas Louis Bart, K.M.T. & K.F. &c. &c. &c.', mezzotint engraved by Joseph Daniell after an original by Richard Livesay, published by James Daniell, 15 August 1807.
NMM ref PAG9348

7. 'England expects every man to do his duty. Lord Nelson explaining to the officers the plan of attack previous to the Battle of Trafalgar . . .', coloured etching by James Godby after an original by William Marshall Craig, published by Edward Orme, 9 January 1806.
NMM ref PAD4050

8. The Combined Fleet putting to sea from Cadiz, 19 October 1805, panel from a panorama by William Heath.
NMM neg D3481-1

1

2

Ship decoration

THROUGH MOST of the period of sail it was possible for an experienced seaman to tell the nationality of a ship even at a distance from a number of clues in the construction, rig and – above all

– in the decorative scheme. Although much reduced from the baroque confections of the seventeenth century, the figureheads and stern carvings of ships at Trafalgar could still serve to identify their owners, and although individual vessels differed in detail within every navy, these were merely variations of quite different and independent national styles.

The sterns of British ships (1) followed a traditional pattern which had not altered much since the middle of the century. It still included a distinctive decorated taffarel and carved quarter pieces until the 1790s, but thereafter the sculpture became simpler, in low relief, and even in some cases painted rather than carved. In elevation the British stern was roughly rectangular, and architectural in composition, with features like columns, pilasters and mouldings mimicking in a more plastic form the facade of a building. The French navy also had a typical stern (2), the characteristic feature being a horseshoe-shaped arch combining taffarel and quarter pieces, sometimes with a low-relief carving in the segment between the row of stern lights and the decorated arch. The ship's name was included within a small but ornamental cartouche on the lower counter, whereas British ships carried no names before 1778 and then favoured large lettering painted on the counter below the lowest tier of stern lights. French 80-gun ships were often used as flagships, like Villeneuve's *Bucentaure*, and this ship has a stern walk at quarterdeck level, which was always popular with flag officers. In British ships, by contrast, this feature was being phased out, and in *Victory*'s pre-Trafalgar refit the stern was closed in.

In general the decorative schemes reflected the artistic and spiritual attitudes of different nations. The predominantly Roman Catholic southern European navies tended to employ both the iconography and ebullient styles familiar from traditions of church decoration, while the more secular and Protestant north was more likely to employ schemes based on classical motifs or derived from medieval heraldry. In France, although the traditional ties with the Church were to reassert themselves, at the height of the Revolution a radically new set of ideals were to find expression in every aspect of cultural life, including ship decoration.

At its most extreme, it was manifest in painting the battlefleet blood-red all over, to reflect the red flag of revolutionary fervour. *Le Northumberland* (3) was captured at Glorious First of June in 1794 wearing this scheme, but within a few years the less extreme administrations that followed allowed the navy to revert to more traditional and restrained paintwork. Red remained popular with the Spanish navy, but it did not have the same political overtones. As had happened in Britain after the Commonwealth, a new regime renamed many ships to erase embarrassments or to celebrate the new realities. A spectacular example of this political imagery was the renaming of the *Dauphin Royal*, a large three-decker, which became the *Sans Culotte*, with a new figurehead and stern carving to suit (4, 5). The biggest ships were always vehicles of prestige and propaganda, and there could be no stronger expression of *égalité* and *fraternité* than to name one of the country's largest warships after the working class — those that did not wear the *culottes* or knee-breeches of the gentry. The massive brooding figurehead, wearing the red bonnet of *liberté* and clasping the *fasces* of republican Rome, epitomises the Jacobin belief in the power of the people, and hints at the sense of injustice that precipitated the massive social convulsions of the time. The ship was again renamed following a political realignment, this time to reflect France's new ambitions in the East, and as *L'Orient* the ship was famously lost by fire and explosion at the Battle of the Nile in 1798.

One stern survives from a French ship that actually fought at Trafalgar. The *Duguay Trouin* escaped with Dumanoir to be taken later in Strachan's Action, and as the *Implacable* she survived in the Royal Navy until 1949,

3

when it was thought the hulk was past saving, and the old ship was scuttled. However, before this the stern decoration and figurehead were removed and eventually presented to the National Maritime Museum, which will give the reconstructed stern a prominent place in the new Neptune Court to be opened in time for the Millenium celebrations. It is not the original French horseshoe stern (6), which had been replaced by a more British design during her first refit at Plymouth after capture; but this later copy of the original drawing shows good example of the typical pattern, with the restrained ornament in vogue when the ship was built in 1800.

The trend towards simplicity was not just a French phenomenon, and most naval authorities were driven as much by the need for economy as by changing artistic tastes. In Britain this could be summarised by the following approximate budget figures for carved work:

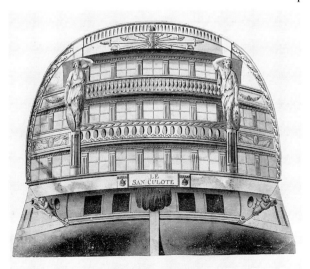

4

1. 'Arriere d'un Vaisseau de Ligne Anglais de 74. Plate 36 in *Collection de Toutes les Especes de Batimens . . . 5eme Livraison*', engraving by Baugean after his own original, published by Jean, 1826.
NMM ref PAD7412

2. 'Arriere d'un Vaisseau Francais de 80. Plate 57 in *Collection de Toutes les Especes de Batimens . . . 5eme Livraison*', engraving by Baugean after his own original, published by Jean, 1826.
NMM ref PAD7421

3. A watercolour portrait of *Le Northumberland* from the Duclos-Legris MS, NMM ref LOG/F/2.
NMM neg D9058-L

4. 'Le San Culote [*sic*] Revolutionary French ship ca. 1795', anonymous black and wash, grey pen and ink, no date.
NMM ref PAH0128

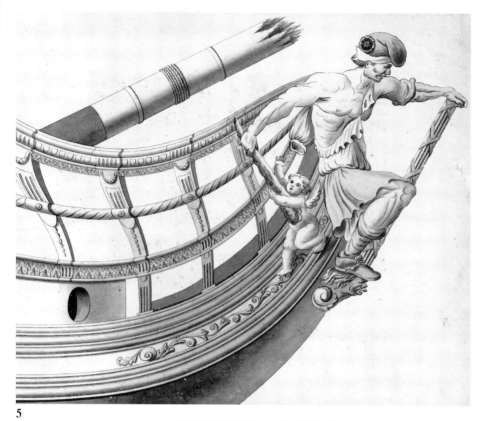

5

6

this time there is a noticeable reduction in the quality of what carving does survive, especially on lesser warships. The French navy, for example, even before the Revolution ordered a standard decorative scheme for each class from 1786. Figureheads were the single most complex and costly element, and so it is not surprising that attempts at simplification were made, and in the case of the new French rules frigates were to carry a non-figurative design—a badge bearing the national *fleurs de lys* emblem, as seen in a drawing of the *Réunion's* head sketched by a British officer after her capture in 1793 (7). Designed by Lubet, this pattern was not universally adopted as is obvious from many other French prizes which still had traditional figures when captured. However, when this ship was built, at Toulon during 1785-86, the ordinance was new and probably more vigorously enforced than later.

Other navies made similar attempts, the British going as far towards austerity in the 1790s as to specify billet-heads or scrollheads in place of figures. These entirely abstract carvings, looking like the head of a fiddle, violated the seaman's sense of the personality of his ship and the officer's pride in his command, so did not survive long—at least, not in ships much larger than gun-brigs—before more figurative emblems were restored. The Danish navy went through a similar cycle: when captured at Copenhagen in 1807 the 74-gun *Norge* (8) had a very simple crowned scroll designed by F C Willerup, master carver at the navy yard at Holmen, which was one of a number ordered by royal command to replace much grander figureheads designed by Willerup and

	Before 1700	After Nov 1700	From about 1717-37	After 1815
First Rate, 100 guns	£896	£500	£323-7s	£100
Fourth Rate, 50 guns	£103	£80	£40-2s	£24

Towards the end of the eighteenth century, ever larger numbers of ships were being built, stretching dockyard resources in both materials and manpower, and from

5. 'Le San Culote, figurehead Revolutionary French ship ca. 1795', grey pen and wash, no date. *NMM ref PAH0129*

6. 'Decoration de sculpture du Vaisseau le Duguay-Trouin', grey wash after an original by Delizy, July 1938. *NMM ref PAH5231*

7. 'Sketch of the bow of HMS Reunion', anonymous watercolour, no date. *NMM ref PAH4925*

8. 'The bow of the Norge a Danish ship of 74 guns, showing the new rounded bow for large ships', engraved by Nesbit after an original by N Pocock. *Naval Chronicle* XXI (1809). *NMM neg 5421*

9. 'Figurehead of the frigate Heldin, Dutch Warship', grey and yellow pen and ink and wash by Jan Rood c1795. *NMM ref PAG9650*

10. 'HMS Minotaur showing bow and figurehead', anonymous brown pen and ink, no date. *NMM neg B5500*

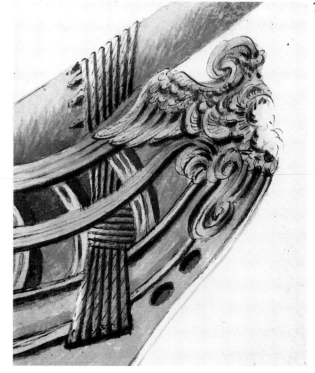

7

already gracing Danish capital ships. However, the fashion for austerity did not outlast the war that had inspired it, and the Danish navy also reverted to proper figureheads. Of more lasting significance, the Danish bow design was an influence in the introduction of the built-up 'round bow' in British ships, replacing the weak transverse beakhead bulkhead that provided so little protection during the end-on approach at Trafalgar.

An unlikely exception to the trend towards economy was the Dutch navy, which despite straitened circumstances seems to have continued devoting resources to decoration even at the height of the war. The frigate *Heldin*, for example, captured in 1799, was built at Amsterdam in 1796 with a full-length figure at the end of very ornate carved trailboards (9). This was not an exception, and surviving drawings of this period confirm the generally well decorated appearance of Dutch ships (for another example, see page 162 of *Navies and the American Revolution* in this series for the *Beschermer*).

In many navies warships' decorative work was an important matter, and often undertaken by artists of real talent (occasionally even by those with a reputation in the wider art world), so drawings and documentation tends to survive. However, in Britain carved work was usually undertaken by dockyard artisans, whose names are unknown to conventional art history, and archival sources tend to be thinner. A few models of figureheads survive — usually the complicated compositions favoured for First Rates — but drawings like that for *Minotaur*, a 74-gun ship launched in 1793, are rare indeed (10). First ordered in 1782, the ship was not laid down at Woolwich Dockyard until 1788. The decorative work was carried out by William Montague Burrough, the yard's principal carver, who is known to have worked on this ship between February and August 1792, in good time for her launch the following November, and may represent his initial sketch sent to the Navy Board for approval.

He was probably following a written brief, in this case outlining the story from Greek mythology of the Minotaur, a half-man, half-bull monster, the unnatural progeny of Pasiphae, wife of King Minos of Crete, and a white bull sent by the gods. The Minotaur was confined to the Labyrinth, the ultimate maze, and appeased with human sacrifice, until slain by Theseus. By the nineteenth century the figurehead tended to be a straightforward personification of the ship's name, but in earlier ages its relationship with the name was more elusive, such as an allegorical representation of abstract qualities associated with the name. In this case, Burrough chose not a portrait of the Minotaur itself, but a depiction of Theseus triumphally carrying the monster's severed head — a more heroic and human association for the ship than a creature of myth.

8

9

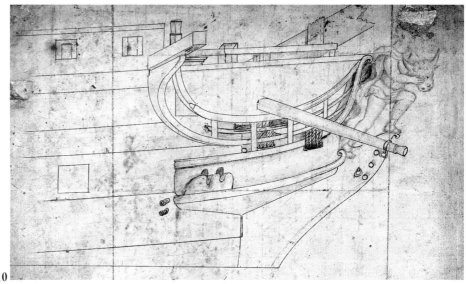

10

2

Trafalgar – the opening moves

1

ON THE morning of 19 October 1805 at 6am, *Sirius* made the signal 'Enemy have their topsail yards hoisted'. Then later came the more thrilling Number 370, 'The enemy is coming out of port or under sail.' As the light improved, the signal was relayed out to the fleet, via *Mars* of the Advanced Squadron, and by 9.30am the *Victory* had acknowledged. At that moment, the British fleet was 50 miles west of Cadiz. The signal for 'General Chase' was hoisted and immediately followed by 'Prepare for Battle'.

The Allied fleet was slow in coming out due to the light northeasterly breeze, but by 3pm the signal had been made that the French and Spanish fleet was at sea. However, in fact only twelve of Villeneuve's fleet had managed to get out of the bay; the rest remained at anchor and weighed during the early hours of the following day. The twelve stood out to sea on a port tack to

the north, shadowed on a parallel course by Captain Henry Blackwood (1) of the *Euryalus* and Captain Prowse of the *Sirius*. Nelson formed his 'Advance Squadron' and signalled the fleet to form order of sail. The British fleet held on a slow course for the mouth of the Gibraltar Straits, believing that was Villeneuve's intended destination, but by the following morning there was no sign of the enemy. The wind was coming up, visibility was poor and the weather was becoming foul with the fleet under close reefed topsails. Nelson was concerned not to be caught with a severe westerly wind so near Cadiz which could force his larger ships to sail through the straits.

With no enemy visible, Nelson signalled the fleet to wear and proceed northwest, taking the advantage of the stiff SSW wind to bring him back on to his original station. However, on doing this they were signalled by one of Blackwood's frigates that the enemy was to the north.

3

Nelson signalled again the order of sailing, and then hove the *Victory* to and summoned Collingwood on board for consultation. Collingwood was for an immediate attack, but Nelson was more cautious for reasons that are not entirely clear. The Admiral may have felt that they were too close to Cadiz to enable a decisive outcome or that it would mean engaging too late in the day.

Nelson was unsure of Villeneuve's intentions, having not found him at the straits. A telegraph signal to the *Victory* indicated that the Combined Fleet appeared to be intent on heading west. 'And that,' wrote Nelson in his diary, 'they shall not do, if in the power of Nelson and Bronte to prevent them.' Villeneuve was indeed heading west although he wanted to head for the Mediterranean, but the southwesterly winds had caused him to stand on. The French admiral began to form his fleet into battle order. As planned, he signalled his ships to form one column of twenty sail around his flagship, *Bucentaure*, and the remaining twelve to form the 'Observation column' under Admiral Gravina. However, the Allied fleet's manoeuvring was poor and for nearly three hours ships attempted to take up their positions. By 4pm the wind shifted round to the west and Villeneuve, keen to make progress south, signalled the fleet to wear and head south. This manoeuvre brought even more confusion to the fleet's attempted line, and his line was only accomplished by the fleet forming on the leeward-most ships.

As the Combined Fleet wore and headed south, Nelson shadowed their motions, but with no real prospect of bringing on an action that day, Nelson signalled Blackwood to keep contact with the enemy during the night. This the *Phoebe*, *Sirius* and *Euryalus* managed until they were chased off by Gravina's 'Observation squadron', which had orders to fend off the frigates but to return to the main fleet by nightfall. The *Aigle*, part of the detached squadron, signalled that at 7.30pm she had seen eighteen British ships in line of battle to the south. On receiving this news Villeneuve wore his fleet round to stand towards the northwest. Subsequently, at 8.40pm Nelson also wore his fleet round to the southwest, and wore again at 4am the next morning to head north by east. As dawn approached the next day, the two battlefleets were 11 miles apart and approximately 21 miles north by west from Cape Trafalgar (2).

To Villeneuve's dismay, he found that the British fleet was stronger than he had expected, and were to windward of him. This discovery led Villeneuve to disregard his plan of battle and he ordered his fleet to form one single line of battle and make for the southwest. On sighting the Combined Fleet, Nelson ordered his fleet to form two columns and make full sail (3). Nelson had arranged his forces so that both columns were spear-

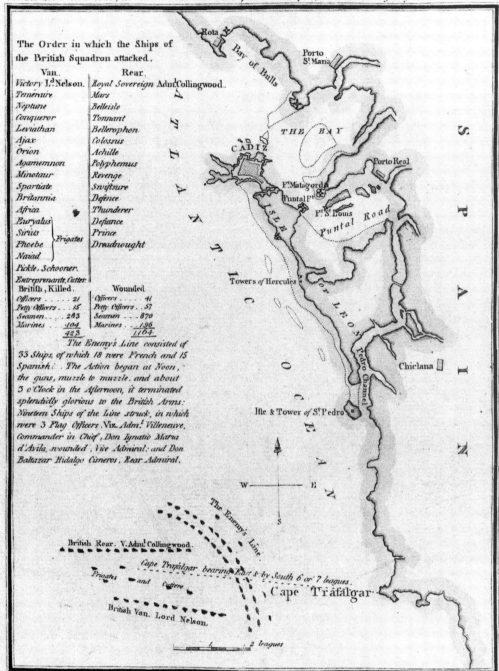

headed by powerful ships, although the poor sailing of the 100-gun *Britannia* and 98-gun *Prince* reduced his options. In the event *Victory* led the weather column, seconded by the three-deckers *Temeraire* and *Neptune*, while the *Royal Sovereign* (Collingwood's flagship) led the lee line.

Villeneuve, now realising that action was imminent, wore his line to keep Cadiz under his lee should he need to retreat. As previously, the manoeuvre was poorly exe-

5

cuted, and 'Even when the evolution had been completed, the allied line was very ill formed and crowded up, some ships being to leeward and some to windward, and some ahead and astern, of their proper stations, much of the column being two and even three ships deep, and part of its centre sagging away to leeward.' Villeneuve's fleet was now under topsails and topgallants, the Spanish *Neptuno* leading the van, steering north with Nelson's two lines bearing down from the east (4).

Whilst the two fleets were slowly converging, Nelson took time to tour the *Victory*'s decks with Hardy. The mood below decks was jubilant at the expectation of another great victory. Nelson came across a young Irishman who was making a notch on the carriage of his gun. The sailor explained to Nelson that he was adding the notch to the other notches he had carved for previous victories, in case he should fall in battle. Nelson laughed and said, 'You'll make notches enough in the enemy's ships.' Some of Nelson's senior officers had expressed their concern for the Admiral's safety. Hardy had requested that *Temeraire*, which was stationed astern of the *Victory* should lead the weather column and Nelson reluctantly agreed. However, when that ship she came close up on the *Victory*'s stern, Nelson told her captain, 'I'll thank you Captain Harvey to keep your proper station which is astern of the *Victory!*'

At approximately 11am, only three miles separated the two fleets (5). Nelson retired below to the bare decks of his cabin, where he made the last entry in his diary – the famous prayer that he had earlier composed. He then returned on deck to 'amuse the fleet' with a signal, thinking to begin it 'Nelson confides . . .', which soon became 'England confides . . .'. However, the signal lieutenant, Pascoe, suggested substituting 'confides' with 'expects' because the word was in the Popham code and did not need to be laboriously spelt out. Nelson agreed and the famous signal 'England expects that every man will do his duty' was hoisted directly to the cheers of the companies of the British ships (6).

The scene could not have been more different from that on board the ships of the Combined Fleet. Villeneuve had cast aside any plan of attack or defence that he may have contemplated and made no attempt to sort out his confused and overlapping line, perhaps awaiting the inevitable. Believing that Nelson would certainly go for his rear division, he had told his subordinates, 'In that case, a Captain can do no better that to look to his own courage and thirst for glory rather than to the signal of the Commander-in-Chief, who himself in the thick of the fight and shrouded in smoke, may perhaps be unable to make signals.'

The two British squadrons continued their laborious advance, and at noon the first opening shots were fired from the *Fougueux* being directed at Collingwood's lee division which was ahead of Nelson's weather column. The British ship's hoisted their battle flags, White Ensigns and Union Jacks, as the *Victory* came down on the enemy line, carrying every stitch of canvas and flying Nelson's last signal, the characteristic 'Engage the enemy more closely' (7).

6

7

6. 'Nelson's Last Signal at Trafalgar', coloured photogravure by Thomas Davidson, printed by Landeker & Brown, no date. Curiously, although the phrase was adopted quickly, Nelson's signal was not immediately popular as a subject for prints, and this well-known example is Victorian. *NMM neg A752*

7. 'Battle of Trafalgar', coloured aquatint engraved by Thomas Sutherland after an original by Thomas Whitcombe, from a plan by Sir E Harvey, no date. It shows *Victory*, with stunsails set, leading *Temeraire* down on the enemy line. *NMM ref PAD5729*

The lee line

VICE-ADMIRAL Cuthbert Collingwood (1) lead the lee column with his flagship, the *Royal Sovereign*, 100 guns. Nelson had repeatedly signalled Collingwood not to take the van, to let the *Bellisle* overhaul him, but his subordinate was not going to counternance a manouevre his chief had just himself refused. Collingwood seemed intent on being the first in to action, which he achieved at approximately 12.20 when the *Royal Sovereign* broke through the allied line, firing her double-shotted broadsides into the stern of the *Santa Ana*, 112, flagship of Vice-Admiral Don I M de Alava. She also raked the bows of the *Fougueux* as she went through.

That devastating first broadside at the Spanish three-decker was said to have caused 400 casualties, but since the *Santa Ana* lost barely half that number throughout the engagement, this is clearly an exaggeration. Nevertheless, it must have been effective because Rotheram, Collingwood's flag captain, expected the Spaniard to strike before any other British ships could come up; but three-deckers could take tremendous punishment, and the battle between them, broadside to broadside, lasted two hours. In fact it was *Royal Sovereign* that was at risk in the early stages, since she was raked by the *Fougueux* and then the *San Leandro*, *Indomptable* and *San Justo*, sustaining the fight alone for nearly a quarter of an hour.

Royal Sovereign was relieved by the *Belleisle*, under the command of Captain William Hargood, which blasted the *Santa Ana*'s lee quarter as she burst through the line, then bore away to rake the stern of the *Indomptable*. *Belleisle* was then involved in a fierce duel with the *Fougueux* and was knocked about by a succession of other ships, on her way to becoming the most damaged British ship in the battle. The *Mars*, which was the third ship in Collingwood's column, had difficulty in breaking through the line. As she approached under fire, her captain believed that he would collide with the *Santa Ana* and therefore brought her into the wind, exposing her stern to raking fire. Although the *Tonnant* came to her support, the *Mars* was hit badly by the fire of the *Monarca*, and a broadside from the *Pluton* killed Captain Duff, commanding officer of the *Mars*. *Tonnant* went on to engage the *Algésiras* and the *San Juan Nepomuceno*, the *Algésiras* making a boarding attempt but her men were repelled on a number of occasions. She later struck her colours along with the Spanish *San Juan Nepomuceno* and was duly taken possession of. This early phase of the battle is shown in (4).

Bellerophon, next astern of the *Tonnant*, did not pass through the allied line until fifteen minutes after later. When she finally managed to push through, she engaged the *Monarca* which had previously struck, but having not been taken possession of had re-hoisted her colours. Captain John Cooke (5) intended to take his ship under the stern of *Monarca*, raking her as he went, and then lie alongside, but the *Bellerophon* fouled the *Aigle* and became entangled. Cooke was thus under fire on his port side from the *Monarca*, and on his starboard side from the *Aigle* (6). By 1pm the British ship had lost her main and mizzen topmasts, and shortly after that, Cooke himself fell killed in action. The *Aigle* attempted to board but was held off; she then began to fall astern of the *Bellerophon*, who raked her with as much fire as she could. The *Aigle* was then raked again, this time by the *Revenge* who was coming up to support the crippled British ship. Although badly damaged, the *Bellerophon* managed to send a boarding party over to the *Monarca*, which had once more lowered her colours.

The *Colossus* opened fired at 12.50pm and came through the line approximately ten minutes later, finding herself engaged on both sides by the French *Swiftsure* and the *Bahama*. Having almost silenced the guns of her French opponent, her fire was then directed at the Spanish ship, which exchanged her own colours for English, only to see them shot away. As the *Bahama* surrendered, the *Swiftsure*, which had previously fallen

1. 'The Rt Honble Lord Collingwood, Vice Admiral of the Red, Major General of Marines and Commander in Chief of His Majesty's Ships in the Mediterranean', mezzotint engraved by Charles Turner, published by Colnaghi & Co, 1 July 1811. *NMM ref PAG9303*

2. 'The Battle of Trafalgar. No. 1. "See how that noble fellow Collingwood carries his ship into action". This Picture represents Admiral Collingwood, Royal Sovereign ... October 21st 1805, breaking the enemy's line', brown etching by Eduardo de Martino (1838-1912) after his own original, no date. *NMM neg 8505*

2

astern, managed to come up under the stern of the *Colossus*, but Captain James Morris was quick to wear, and fortunately received very few of the rounds fired from the *Swiftsure* before engaging her with his broadside. The French ship was then also engaged by the *Orion*, firing her first broadside of the battle. This was more than enough for the *Swiftsure*, and having lost her mizzen made indications of her surrender. The *Colossus* had most her rigging shot away and had become 'quite unmanageable', but she took possession of *Swiftsure* and *Bahama*, the latter having lost her captain in the battle as well as 400 of her company killed or wounded. The *Colossus* herself had suffered 40 killed and 160 wounded, more than any other vessel in the British fleet. Unable to continue in action, the *Colossus* was later towed out by the *Agamemnon*.

Collingwood's division were less inclined to follow in their leader's wake than Nelson's, and many of the later ships made a slanting approach to pick their own breakthrough point in the enemy line (7). This tended to accelerate the process of crushing remaining resistance,

3

and within two hours of breaking through the allied line, the British lee division had effectively defeated the enemy rear.

4

3. 'Trafalgar 1pm', watercolour by P H Nicolas, no date. It shows *Belleisle* coming to the aid of *Royal Sovereign*, squeezed between *Fougueux* to the left and *Indomptable* in the centre.
NMM ref PAD8606

4. 'Plan of the Commencement of the Battle of Trafalgar', anonymous engraving, no date.
NMM ref PAD4051

5. 'Captain John Cooke', engraved by J Fittler and published by J Gold, 1 May 1807.
NMM neg D9046

6. 'Situation of the Bellerophon at the moment of the death of her gallant commander Captn Cooke', coloured aquatint engraved by Thomas Sutherland after an original by Thomas Whitcombe (born c1752), no date.
NMM neg PU5750

7. 'Battle of Trafalgar, Rear Division . . . attack on the combined Fleets of France & Spain by the British Fleet under the command of the Illustrious Lord Nelson', coloured aquatint and etching by Robert Dodd (1748-1815) after his own original, published by the artist, March 1806.
NMM neg B2581

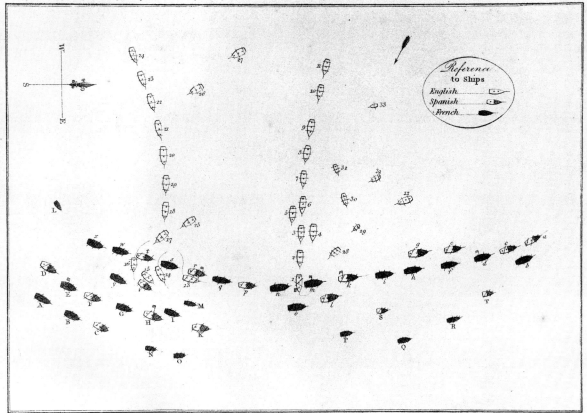

PLAN of the COMMENCEMENT of the BATTLE of TRAFALGAR.

British Fleet. Larboard or Weather line 1 *Victory*. 2 *Temeraire*. 3 *Neptune*. 4 *Britannia*. 5 *Leviathan*. 6 *Conqueror*. 7 *Agamemnon*. 8 *Ajax*. 9 *Orion*. 10 *Minotaur*. 11 *Spartiate*. 12 *Africa*. Starboard or Lee line 13 *Royal Sovereign*. 14 *Belleisle*. 15 *Mars*. 16 *Tonnant*. 17 *Bellerophon*. 18 *Achille*. 19 *Polyphemus*. 20 *Revenge*. 21 *Swiftsure*. 22 *Defiance*. 23 *Thunderer*. 24 *Defence*. 25 *Colossus*. 26 *Prince*. 27 *Dreadnought*. Frigates &c. 28 *Euryalus*. 29 *Pickle* schooner. 30 *Sirius* frig. 31 *Naiad*. 32 *Phoebe*. 33 *Entreprenante* Cutter.

Combined Fleets. a *Neptuno*. b *Scipion*. c *San Augustina*. d *Formidable*. e *El Rayo*. f *Mont Blanc*. g *San Francisco d'Asis*. h *Duguay Trouin*. i *Heros*. k *Santissima Trinidada*. l *St Juste*. m *Bucentaure*. n *Redoubtable*. o *Neptune*. p *San Leandro*. q *Indomptable*. r *St Anna*. s *Fougueux*. t *Monarca*. v *St Ildefonso*. w *Pluto*. x *Intrepide*. y *Argonauta*. ————— Squadron of observation & frigates. A *Berwick*. B *Achille*. C *Bahama*. D *San Juan Nepomuceno*. E *Algesiras*. F *Argonauta*. G *Swiftsure*. H *Principe d'Asturias*. I *L'Aigle*. K *Montanez*. L *Hermione* frig. M *Rhin* frig. N *Themise* frig. O *Argus* brig. P *Hortense* frig. Q *Furet* brig. R *Cornielle* frig. S *Flora*. T *Mercurio*. Sp frigates.

5

6

7

The weather column

I T WAS not until forty or so minutes after Collingwood had broken through the allied line that the *Victory* and her weather column got into action. Despite being under full sail—indeed she carried stunsails right up to the moment of contact, only cutting them away as she passed through the line—her approach was slow and cumbersome due to the light winds, and she received fire for forty minutes without being able to return it. At first Nelson was not clear which was the Combined Fleet flagship, but the allied ensigns and commanders' flags broke out as the allied line opened fire. Nelson then altered course slightly for the *Bucentaure*, which stood about eleventh from the van. By 12.20pm the *Victory* was receiving heavy fire, and was sustaining much damage to her sails aloft, which made her progress even slower. At approximately two and half cables (500yds) from the *Bucentaure*, she lost her mizzen topmast and had her wheel shot away. From then on she was steered from down below in the gunroom.

On the *Bucentaure*'s starboard quarter was the French *Neptune*, and on that ship's port quarter was the *Redoutable*, making a compact group. Hardy pointed out that collision was inevitable, and Nelson, concurring, told him to take his choice of which to run on board of. At approximately 1pm the *Victory* broke through the line under the stern of the *Bucentaure*, and ahead of the *Redoutable* (1). The *Victory*'s double- and even treble-shotted guns, which

had hitherto been silent, fired into the French flagship, completely destroying her stern and delivering a blow from which she could not recover. Her approach was so close that the port side of *Victory*'s main yard brushed the vang of the French ship's gaff. *Victory* then fired her starboard broadside into the *Redoutable* (2) and put her helm over to port and ran onto her.

The two ships fouled each other, and a fierce action between the two ensued. However, *Victory*'s port broadsides continued to pour into the *Bucentaure*, but her immediate efforts were concentrated on the *Redoutable*. The *Victory*'s upper deck was subjected to a torrent of musket fire from the marksmen high above in the French fighting tops, and it was at this point, about

1. 'Battle of Trafalgar – Octr 21st 1805' coloured aquatint engraved by Thomas Sutherland after an original by Thomas Whitcombe, 1 March 1817. Seen from the British side of the line, it shows the crowded space into which the *Victory* was pushing. *NMM ref PAD4059*

2. 'Battle of Trafalgar. The Victory cutting through the French line', watercolour by Nicholas Pocock (1740-1821), 1810. Seen from the other side of the line, *Victory* rakes *Bucentaure*'s stern at point-blank range, while engaging *Redoutable* to starboard. *NMM neg A917*

2

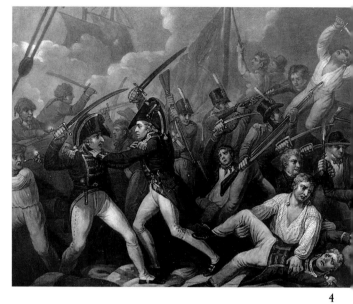

3

3. 'Commencement of the Battle of Trafalgar, October 21st 1805', engraving by James Fittler after an original by Nicholas Pocock, published by Thomas Cadell and William Davies, 15 November 1808. The viewpoint is inside and near the head of the Allied line, with the two British columns coming in from the right.
NMM ref P.AD5725

1.25pm, that Nelson whilst pacing the quarterdeck with Hardy, was mortally wounded and fell to the deck, and was taken below. Most of the men on *Victory*'s upper deck had now been either killed or wounded, and the French seeing this opportunity made several attempts to board, but were held off gallantly by sailors and marines coming up from the gun decks below.

The *Temeraire*, 98 was stationed astern of *Victory* on the approach, and like most of her consorts in the weather column, had already received a heavy fire. She had followed *Victory* under the stern of the *Bucentaure* but had been raked badly by the *Neptune* in doing so. The British 98 was left unmanageable by the onslaught, and had to con-

tend with the *Redoutable* on her port beam entangled with the *Victory*, and the *Neptune* on her starboard bow. *Temeraire* was in this situation until approximately 1.40pm when the *Redoutable* drifted on to her, the bowsprit of the French ship crashing into the main entry port on the British three-decker. *Temeraire*'s company quickly lashed down the bowsprit and with the French ship trapped, put as much shot into her bows as they could (3).

She then fired her starboard battery, which had not yet found employment, at the *Fougueux*. This ship had been previously attacking the *Belleisle* and *Mars* of Collingwood's column, but was now focusing her attention on the stricken *Temeraire*. However, her broadsides shattered

4

5

the oncoming French ship, and she crashed into the *Temeraire*'s starboard bow. Once again, Captain Harvey's men having secured the French ship to their starboard anchor, boarded her and within ten minutes she had struck (4). The *Victory* had by now managed to boom herself off from the *Redoutable*, leaving her, the *Temeraire* and *Fougueux* to drift with their bows to the south. The *Redoutable* lost her mizzen, which on crashing to the deck gave the 'Fighting Temeraires' the means for boarding, which they dutifully did and took possession of the ship at 2.20pm.

The British *Neptune*, under the command of Captain Thomas Fremantle, passed through the line ahead of the *Victory* and under the stern of the *Santísima Trinidad*, the largest vessel in the battle, whose towering four gundecks marked her out as a special prize. Undeterred by the 136 guns of the Spanish ship, Fremantle luffed up and placed his 98-gun ship alongside and fought her into submission (5).

On her approach *Neptune* had passed under *Bucentaure*'s stern, and was followed by the *Leviathan* and then the *Conqueror*, each of which fired into the flagship's already devastated stern. The scene below decks on the French ship must have been horrific, having been raked on so many occasions. When the ship eventually struck to the *Conqueror* at about 2pm, Captain of Marines James Atcherley was sent on board to collect the French Commander-in-Chief. He described the scene on the French ship's gundecks, 'The dead, thrown back as they fell, lay along the middle of the decks in heaps, and the shot passing through had frightfully mangled the bodies ... An extraordinary proportion had lost their heads. A raking shot, which entered the lower deck, had glanced along the beams and through the thickest of the people, and a French officer declared that this shot alone had killed or disabled nearly forty men.' On returning to his boat with Admiral Villeneuve—who was miraculously untouched amid the carnage—Atcherley discovered that *Conqueror* was now engaged elsewhere, so he took the French commander to the *Mars*, where he remained until the end of the battle. His flag captain, Magendie, produced a plan of the battle, which is probably the most reliable source for the order of the Allied line (6).

By now the battle was at his height, and a crushing victory was clearly within the grasp of the British fleet. Before the surrender of his flagship, Villeneuve signalled at 1.50pm to those ships of his fleet that were not in action, to take up positions to engage the enemy as soon as possible. This signal was mainly directed at Dumanoir's van division, which was still standing on. The task for the British now was to fend off any attack those ships might make, and secure as many of the battered centre squadron as possible.

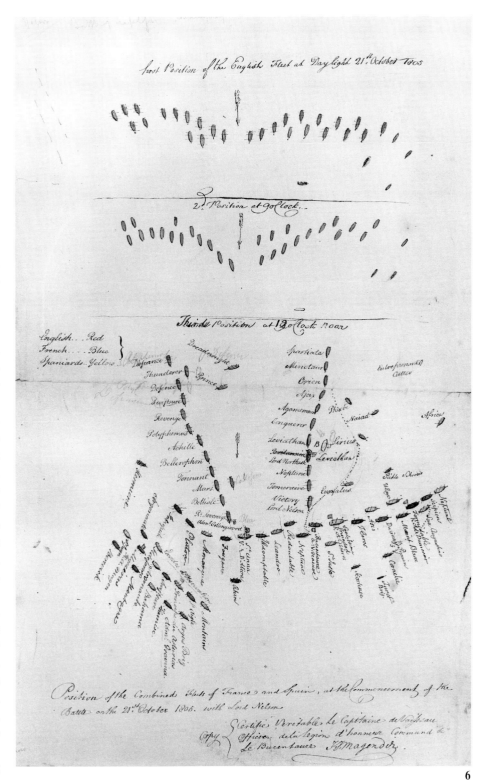

6

4. 'The Battle of Trafalgar. Captain Harvey of the Temeraire . . . clearing the decks of the French and Spaniards . . .', mezzotint engraved by H Gillbank after an original by Brown, published by J Gillbank, 15 June 1806. The printmaker seems to think that *Temeraire* was boarded (and by French *and* Spaniards), whereas it was *Temeraire* that did the boarding.
NMM ref PAG9030

5. 'The Battle of Trafalgar. This Plate representing the exact position of the Victory and of the leading Ships of each Line . . .', stipple engraving by Thomas Hellyer after his own original, published by the artist and George Andrews, 1 February 1807. The Spanish ship losing her mast appears to be the *Santísima Trinidad*
NMM neg 3167

6. 'Position of the Combined Fleets of France and Spain, at the Commencement of the Battle of the 21st October 1805 with Lord Nelson', anonymous pen and ink, copied from Captain Magendie's original drawn aboard the *Neptune* and dated 28 October 1805.
NMM neg X1875

Lone fight of the Redoutable

1

DESCRIBED EVEN by rather jingoist British historians as a 'brilliant defence' and a 'noble fight', the part played by the *Redoutable* at Trafalgar was as heroic as it was hopeless. A 74-gun two-decker of the smallest class in the French navy, under the command of Captain Jean-Jacques Lucas she had become the most efficiently officered and manned vessel in the fleet. Lucas, who was less than five feet tall, had recognised that he had little chance of winning an artillery battle, so drilled his men in the techniques of small-arms fire and grenade-throwing.

The third ship astern of Villeneuve's *Bucentaure*, *Redoutable* lay squarely between the two holes the British were trying to punch in the Combined Fleet line. As *Victory* came through that line, raking *Bucentaure*, she was herself raked by the French *Neptune* which had come ranging up, closely supported by *Redoutable*. As the latter's forward guns were fiercely plied on *Victory* her after guns hammered the *Temeraire*, the second ship in Nelson's column. *Victory* had to run aboard one or other of the opposing ships; Nelson left the choice to Hardy who, not unsurprisingly, chose his smallest opponent. At about 1.10pm she came grinding alongside *Redoutable*, fouling each ships' fore topmast rigging, and the *Redoutable*'s men lashed the ships together. Lucas, with considerable forethought, had ordered her larboard lower deck gunports closed to prevent the British from boarding through them. Now the *Redoutable*'s well-trained crew swung into the close-range action for which they had been drilled with a furious fire at her adversary: main deck guns; musketry from the decks and all three tops; brass coehorns loaded with langridge from the fore and main tops; and hand grenades (2). Although the *Victory* used her starboard 68pdr carronade to clear *Redoutable*'s gangways of her people, and pounded the Frenchman's hull at point-blank range with treble-shotted lower deck batteries, her upper deck was virtually cleared and its guns soon put out of action, by the deadly small-arms fire from the *Redoutable*. It was, indeed, a musket ball fired from her mizzen top which felled Nelson.

Seeing the *Victory*'s upper deck almost deserted, the Redoutables unhesitatingly massed in an attempt to board, but were foiled by geometry – the tumblehome of both vessels created an unbridgeable gap at upper deck level, though they were touching lower down. The *Victory*'s crew also rushed up from below once aware of the danger, although they suffered heavily from the French fire. Captain Lucas, grasping the situation immediately, ordered the main yard of his ship lowered to bridge the gap. However, just then, the two vessels had drifted down onto *Temeraire*, which fouled the French ship's other side and made fast, pouring in a hot fire causing devastating casualties (3). Trapped between two British three-deckers the French crew continued to fight on, mostly with small arms and hurling hand grenades. So great was the danger to all three ships from fire that the 'fireman' at each of *Victory*'s guns could be seen hurling buckets of water after the shot into the *Redoutable*'s sides, and at one stage a small British boat party (apparently well-received by the French) came on board through a stern port to help in the fire-fighting.

At 2pm the *Victory* managed to boom herself off and limped away to the northward – 'she seems to have done little more fighting; nor, indeed, was she fit for much', so thoroughly had she been mauled by *Redoutable*. The *Temeraire*, now with *Fougueux* lashed to her other side, drifted to the south. The *Redoutable*'s main and mizzen masts fell, the latter aboard the *Temeraire*, making a bridge between the two, whilst sporadic fires continued to break out.

Lucas, himself wounded, took stock. Of the original crew of 643, 522 were *hors de combat* (300 dead). His vessel was dismasted; tiller, helm, rudder gear and sternpost entirely destroyed, the poop and after part of the ship smashed in, hull and decks riddled, on fire astern and leaking badly with nearly all the pumps destroyed. It was enough, and he surrendered to the *Temeraire* at 2.20pm. In the evening *Swiftsure* took *Redoutable* in tow and sent a party on board to keep her afloat. By noon the following day, the leaks had gained so much that the prizemaster signalled for assistance. Boats managed to save only 119 of the Redoutables (4) before, at about 10pm on 22 October, the whole of the stern already underwater, the *Redoutable* went down with nearly all her wounded on board. The next day the *Swiftsure* rescued more survivors from wreckage. In all 169 of *Redoutable*'s company survived the battle. She, and her people, lived up to her name.

3. 'Episode du Combat de Trafalgar. Le Vaisseau Le Redoutable de 74 canons, Commande par M. Lucas, est aborde par les Vaisseaux de 120, le Victory et le Temeraire l'amiral Nelson, ou est tue dans cette action memorable, montant le Victory (le 5 [*sic*] Octobre 1805)', lithograph engraved by Charpentrier after an original by P C Causse, no date. *NMM neg B4041*

4. Another of the Lucas presentation series, this view shows the *Swiftsure* the day after the battle attempting to take off the crew before *Redoutable* sinks. The ship has just rolled out her fore mast, but by most eyewitness accounts they were not able to complete the task as the weather became 'so bad and sea running high that it rendered it impossible for the boats to pass'. *Musée de la Marine, Paris ref 10296*

1

The final stages

2

ALTHOUGH BRITISH ships were still coming into action, by about 3.30pm the battle in the centre and rear of the Franco-Spanish line had been virtually won (1). The succession and concentration of force which had come down on the Allies, had taken its toll. Many of Villeneuve's ships had either struck or were in the final extremities of resistance. The allied commander himself was being held on the British *Mars*.

However, there was one crucial element of the allied fleet left untouched: Dumanoir's van division, so far only under fire from the errant *Africa*. The British 64 had become separated from the fleet during the previous

PLAN of the RELATIVE SITUATION of the BRITISH and COMBINED FLEETS, at the CLOSE of the BATTLE of TRAFALGAR.

British Fleet. 1 Victory. 2 Royal Sovereign. 3 Temeraire. 4 Neptune. 5 Leviathan. 6 Africa. 7 Orion. 8 Conqueror. 9 Defiance. 10 Tonnant. 11 Bellerophon. 12 Mars. 13 Spartiate. 14 Minotaur. 15 Prince. 16 Sirius frigate. 17 Euryalus frigate. 18 Pickle Schooner.

Combined Fleet. a Formidable. b Scipion. c Mont Blanc. d Duguay Trouin. e Neptuno. f L'Achille burnt. g S.ta Anna. h Buxentaure i S.ta Trinidada. k Fougeux. l Redoubtable. m L'Intrepide. n L'Aigle. o Monarca. p Bahama. q S.t Augustino. r.r &c British in Chace of part of the Enemy flying to the Northward. The Enemy's Ships which were chaced to the Eastward are not introduced. s Spanish Ship bearing up cannonaded by the Leviathan & Conqueror.

night and by morning had found herself way off station to windward of the weather column. When signalled to 'Make more sail' to get her out of danger, her captain interpreted this as an order to get into action, and she ran the gauntlet of the enemy's van division in order to join her consorts. Before surrendering his flagship, Villeneuve had signalled the Allied van to come down and support the centre and rear divisions, but its response was slow due to lack of wind and boats had to be used to tow the ships' heads around.

Eventually, Rear-Admiral Dumanoir le Pelley lead five ships down the weather side of the line to relieve the centre (2), while the remaining five other ships made to support Admiral Gravina in the rear division by sailing south to leeward. The van was fired on by *Ajax*, 74 and *Agamemnon*, 64 but were not stopped. At this time the last two ships in the British weather column were the *Minotaur* and the *Spartiate*, which had yet to break the enemy line. These two 74s immediately saw the impending danger. The *Victory* and *Temeraire* were but shattered hulks and could not repel any fresh attack unsupported. *Minotaur* and *Spartiate* crossed the path of Dumanoir's ships (two 80s and three 74s) and within pistol shot open fired, raking the bows of the *Formidable*, Dumanoir's flag-

3

4

5

ship. They then stood between them and the stricken *Victory* exchanging broadsides. The Spanish *Neptuno*, 80 guns, was some considerable distance astern and to leeward of her consorts, so *Minotaur* and *Spartiate* took the opportunity of isolating her and after an engagement lasting near on an hour, the *Neptuno* struck (3).

Having been prevented from joining the action in the centre, Dumanoir, now with his remaining four ships, sought to support Gravina. Collingwood, having been informed of the death of his friend and superior by Captain Blackwood, now assumed command of the fleet. He was alerted to the situation developing to the north, and signalled the weather division to come up to the wind and sail on the port tack, forming a line to windward. Not many ships could respond to the signal, either unable to see it through the smoke which hung over the battle, or being otherwise engaged (4). However, six ships managed to form a rough line of battle and stand between the oncoming Dumanoir and his objective.

The sight of this new British line deterred Dumanoir. He could not support the rear division without having to fight his way through, and the outcome of that was most doubtful. Dumanoir finally decided that the battle was lost when he sighted Gravina's crippled flagship, *Príncipe de Asturias* bearing away and making for Cadiz. She was also flying her last signal of the battle, ordering the remaining allied ships to rally around her. The *Príncipe de Asturias* managed to escape with ten of the line and later successfully put into Cadiz. Not being willing to fight his way through the new British line to join Gravina, Dumanoir made southeast for the Gibraltar straits, and then decided to head for Rochefort. The threat of the allied van had been successfully countered.

The last significant event of the battle was the destruction of the French *Achille*. The French 74 had been in action with the *Prince*, 98 when her fore top caught fire, and the next broadside from the *Prince* brought the *Achille*'s blazing main mast down, engulfing the ship in flames. At this point, knowing that her opponent's fate was sealed, Captain Grindle, the *Prince*'s captain, ceased firing and wore round to clear the burning 74. She then placed boats in the water in a bid to rescue the French seaman (5), but this proved hazardous as the *Achille*'s abandoned but loaded guns were set off by the intense heat now raging below decks. The *Achille*'s ordeal was brought

to a swift end when at 5.45pm she blew up with an incredible explosion. Only some 100 French sailors were rescued by the surrounding British ships out of 499 on board.

An officer serving in the *Defence* wrote, 'It was a sight the most awful and grand that can be conceived. In a moment the hull burst into a cloud of smoke and fire. A column of vivid flame shot up to an enormous height in the atmosphere and terminated by expanding into an immense globe, representing for a few seconds, a prodigious tree in flames, specked with many dark spots, which the pieces of timber and bodies of men occasioned while they were suspended in the clouds.'

The end of the *Achille* symbolically marked an end to the battle. As flotsam and debris lifted and fell with swell, and the bodies of dead sailors littered the waters, the din of battle faded.

The Royal Navy had won a crushing victory, capturing or destroying eighteen of the thirty-three ships of the Franco-Spanish line. Not a single British ship had struck, although many were severely damaged, some little more than hulks (6). More significantly, the British had lost their finest fighting admiral, whose tactics and leadership had secured the most complete victory in the era of sail.

---

1. 'Situation of the Temeraire at half past 3pm October 21st 1805', coloured aquatint engraved by J Baily after an original by Thomas Whitcombe (born c1752), no date.
NMM neg 8408

2. 'Victory of Trafalgar, in the Van . . . Action with a view of the French Admiral Dumanoir and the ships of his Division, making their escape to Windward', aquatint and etching by Robert Dodd (1748-1815) after his own original, published by the artist 1 March 1806.
NMM neg C764

3. 'Plan of the Relative Situations of the British and Combined Fleets, at the Close of the Battle of Trafalgar', anonymous engraving, no date.
NMM ref PAD5716

4. 'To the Right Honble Lord Barham . . . This Print representing the Glorious Victory obtained by Admiral Lord Nelson, on the 21st Oct 1805 over the combined French & Spanish Fleets off Cape Trafalgar . . . ', coloured aquatint and etching by John Hall after an original by John Thomas Serres (1759-1825), published by C Wigley, 25 August 1806.
NMM neg 5381

5. 'Battle of Trafalgar – Octr 21st 1805', coloured aquatint engraved by Thomas Sutherland after an original by Thomas Whitcombe, 1 March 1817.
NMM ref PAD4046

6. 'A view of the British and Combined Fleets at the conclusion of the Battle of Trafalgar. Engraved for Brenton's Naval History', etching by J Walker after an original by Herbert, no date.
NMM ref PAD5755

6

160

1

Ordeal of the Belleisle

HMS *BELLEISLE*, 74 guns, Captain William Hargood, was the second ship in the leeward column to break the Franco-Spanish line, 10-15 minutes after Collingwood's *Royal Sovereign*. A good sailer, she had easily passed *Tonnant* and *Mars* to take up her new station, and made the long approach to battle in silence, not replying to the broadsides of the eight or ten of the enemy ships whose guns bore. These had already caused casualties among her crew, lying on deck between their guns, and had begun the ruin of her sails and rigging. Her colours had been thrice shot away and replaced, but Hargood rebuffed his First Lieutenant's suggestion that they bear up and show their broadside: 'We are ordered to go through the line, and go through she shall, by God!'

She passed through the gap between *Santa Ana* (closely engaged with *Royal Sovereign*) and the French *Indomptable*, firing her port broadside, double-shotted with grape on top, into the stern of *Santa Ana* and bore up for *Indomptable*, who wore away. The *Belleisle* was then engaged by the *San Juan Nepomuceno*, losing her fore topmast to her fire. The

Fougueux then ran aboard her, her port bow striking the starboard gangway, and in the following sustained battering fight *Belleisle*'s main topmast and mizzen mast were shot away. When the French *Achille* took a position off the *Belleisle*'s port quarter, the wreckage of the mizzen hanging over the side impeded *Belleisle*'s answering fire; then the *Neptune* began to rake her from ahead and the *Aigle* arrived off her starboard bow, adding to the passing broadsides of the *San Leandro, San Justo*, and Admiral Gravina's *Príncipe de Asturias*: the *Fougueux* had at last sheered off, under fire from *Mars*.

At 2pm the main mast fell, blanketing many of the portside guns; half an hour later the fore mast went. With the loss of her bowsprit she was, in the words of a Lieutenant in HMS *Swiftsure* 'an immovable log'; but the *Belleisle* still kept up a defence, firing whenever a gun would bear, whenever the enormous wreckage of her masts, sails and rigging encumbering the decks and hanging over the sides allowed a shot, her colours nailed to the stump of the mizzen and a Union flag held aloft fixed to a boarding pike (1).

At half past three 'to our great joy . . . the *Swiftsure*, English 74, came booming through the smoke. . . shortly afterwards the *Polyphemus* took the enemy's ship off our bow and thus we were happily disengaged after nearly four hours of struggle.' Hargood's log records: '3.25. Ceased firing, and turned the hands up to clear the wreck.' The *Belleisle* had been shot to pieces; under the fire of the succession of passing Franco-Spanish ships she had lost her masts, bowsprit and figurehead, her anchors, and 'ports, port-timbers, channels, chainplates, all exhibited unequivocal marks of the terrible mauling she had received', as one historian recorded. The loss in men was also severe: 2 lieutenants, 1 midshipman, 22 seamen and 8 marines were killed; Captain Hargood, the Marine Lieutenant Owen and 93 officers, petty officers, seamen and marines wounded – Hargood did not mention his injury in his report.

At least nine enemy ships had at various times brought the *Belleisle* under sustained and concentrated fire, and her part of the 'pell-mell battle' was the thickest – cannonballs were seen to strike each other in mid-air – now, when finally the centre of the action had moved away, the men on deck watched as the French Rear-Admiral Dumanoir's division filed past within gunshot 'and as we lay in a helpless and solitary situation, our apprehension was much relieved by seeing them proceed silently on their course'.

Now, with the battle everywhere coming to a conclusion, *Belleisle* was able to take her one prize. The Spanish *Argonauta*, 80 guns, had hoisted English colours as a token of surrender: somehow, a seaworthy boat was found and returned with her Second Captain (de Pareja had been wounded), and joined *Belleisle*'s officers having tea in Captain Hargood's cabin, as the guns of the two fleets at last fell silent (2).

The *Belleisle* had survived the heart of the battle, and the fighting spirit and resolution of her crew had not broken: now their seamanship and will to survive would be tested. Under tow of the frigate *Naiad*, the battered ship laid a course for Gibraltar. Through the night and the next day, the exhausted men cleared decks, improvised jury masts from salvaged spars, and repeatedly passed anew the hawser, which several times parted in the rising swell and increasing wind – the latter task a considerable risk to the *Naiad*, having repeatedly to approach the ungovernable hulk of the *Bellise*. By the afternoon some fore and aft sails could be set, steadying the ship in the squalls, and the pumps were in continuous use. By evening the Fleet was out of sight.

In the gale that came on that night, the hawser again carried away and could not be repassed, and at half past three breakers were seen to leeward. Any touch on this lee shore would have been the end. A jibboom was set up as a foremast, and with a boat's sail set from it the ship managed to wear away from the danger – at daylight the *Naiad* was able to take the tow again (3). Captain Hargood's log entry for 24 October somehow conveys the relief of a safe arrival after such a trial: 'AM Standing through the Straits of Gibraltar. At 12 made our number and the signal for assistance. PM Cast off the tow. Made signal for assistance with a gun. At 1, repeated the signal. Boats came to assist us. Cheered occasionally. 1.20 Let go the best bower anchor.'

1. 'Belleisle 4h. 15m. P.M. Octr 21st 1805', aquatint engraved by E Duncan after an original by William John Huggins (1781-1845), no date. Dumanoir's squadron is seen to the far left, with the frigate *Naiad* astern, while to the right *Achille* burns. *NMM neg A5859*

2. 'Situation of His Majesty's Ship Bellisle, Wm Hargood Esqr Captain, with the Naiad Frigate, Captain Thos Dundas, taking her in Tow at the close of the Action off Trafalgar 21st October 1805', aquatint published by G Andrews, 12 August 1806. *NMM neg X1884*

3. 'His Majesty's Ship Bellisle, Wm Hargood Esq Captain, in Tow of the Naiad Frigate Captain Thos Dundas, near Gibraltar on the morning 24th October 1805 . . .', coloured aquatint published by G Andrews, 12 August 1806. *NMM neg X1886*

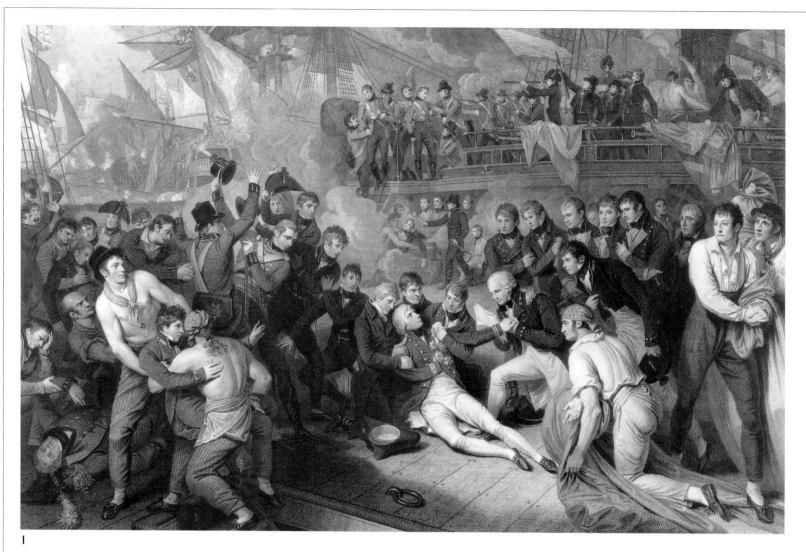

1

The death of Nelson

THE DEATH of Nelson has become the central event of the Battle of Trafalgar. Even at the time, it overshadowed all other aspects of the great drama. Ordinary seamen broke down crying when the news spread through the victorious British fleet. Collingwood's official dispatch began with the words 'The ever to be lamented death of Vice Admiral Lord Viscount Nelson . . .'. When the news reached England, the customary forms of rejoicing were muted by sorrow for the death of the hero.

Artists rushed to depict the scene, usually inaccurately. Benjamin West—whose 'Death of Wolfe' had been one of Nelson's favourite paintings—showed him dying heroically on his quarterdeck (1), surrounded by all the ship's officers improbably frozen in attitudes of horror, and all identified in an accompanying key (2). He later produced a more realistic painting, this time set accurately in the *Victory*'s cockpit. But he had been pre-empted by the lesser-known Arthur Devis whose almost photographic rendering of the same scene has become by far

the most famous—indeed, the most hackneyed—version (3).

Like all great heroes, Nelson attracts myths, and none more potent than those surrounding his death. Some started at once, such as the still-common misconception that he was wearing a splendidly decorated full-dress coat, which made him an easy target for the French marksmen. Others arose later, such as the tight-lipped Victorian dismissal of his touching request for a kiss from Hardy and the inane alternative suggestion that he suddenly began talking Turkish: 'Kismet [fate] Hardy'! In fact, the details of Nelson's final hours are well-documented by reliable witnesses and can be reconstructed with some precision. Three men were close to him as he lay dying: the Surgeon, William Beatty; the ship's Chaplain, Alexander Scott; and the Purser, William Burke. All three wrote accounts—in Beatty's case a slim book of some 100 pages—and they tally remarkably well.

At about 12.45pm, the *Victory* smashed her way through the Allied line, firing a murderous double-shot-

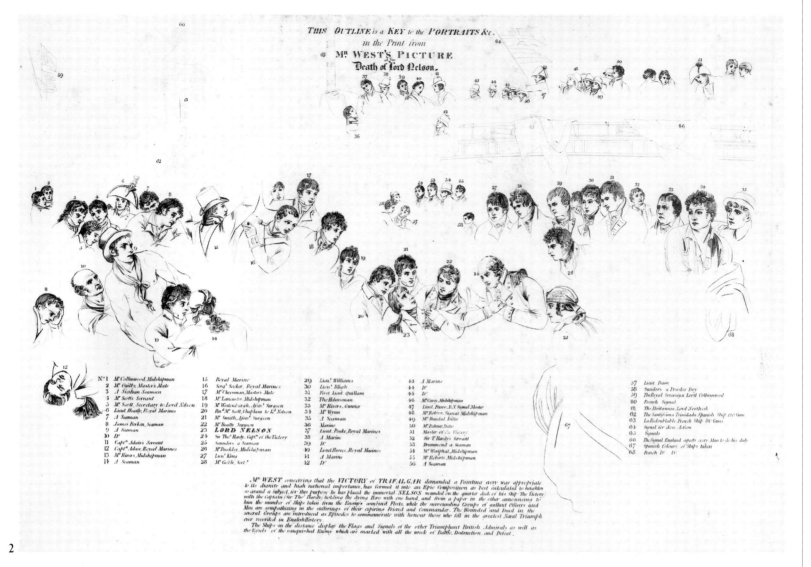

2

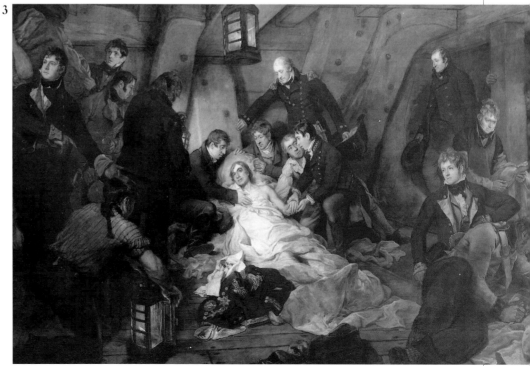

3

ted broadside into the stern of the *Bucentaure* as she did so. She then became locked with the *Redoutable* and the two ships drifted gradually to leeward. The *Victory*'s starboard guns were still firing; but Captain Jean Lucas of the *Redoutable* had withdrawn most of his men from his guns to form boarding parties, hoping to capture his opponent by storm. As a prelude to this attack sharpshooters posted in the tops began sweeping the *Victory*'s decks with small-arms fire, trying to thin down her crew. It was during this phase of the battle, at about 1.15pm, that Nelson was shot while pacing the *Victory*'s quarterdeck, accompanied by Captain Thomas Hardy. As was his invariable custom when at sea, he was dressed in a rather shabby, workaday undress uniform coat. On the left breast were sewn sequin facsimiles of his four orders of chivalry, tarnished by constant exposure to the elements. In the swirl of gunpowder smoke covering the deck, they would not have presented a particularly obvious target.

Indeed, it is doubtful that the fatal shot was deliberately aimed at all. It was fired from an ordinary musket, rather than a rifle, from a constantly moving platform some 20

4

metres above its victim, who from that angle would have presented a very narrow target. More likely it was a stray bullet – or even a ricochet from the *Victory*'s rigging. An account of the incident was published in France in 1826, purporting to be the reminiscences of 'Sergeant Robert Guillemard', the man who shot Nelson. The story was challenged by John Pollard, one of the *Victory*'s midshipmen, who claimed he and some colleagues had deliberately shot every man in the *Redoutable*'s mizzen top in an attempt to avenge their chief. Later research established that the French account was indeed a clever work of fiction – but the myth has persisted.

Whether an unfortunate stray or a deliberately aimed shot, the musket ball nevertheless had a devastating effect. Striking Nelson on the left shoulder it smashed two ribs, tore through his left lung, severing a major artery on the way and, having fractured his spine, lodged underneath his right shoulder blade. Nelson felt death enter with it for, when the horrified Hardy knelt beside his stricken friend, he heard the rueful words, 'They have done for me at last Hardy, my backbone is shot through.'

Hardy ordered Sergeant Secker of the Royal Marines and some seamen to lift Nelson (4) and gently he was carried down to the orlop deck below the waterline,

where the surgeons carried out their operations in action. He was laid against the port side of the ship and Beatty began an examination, which quickly revealed that the case was hopeless. Thinking he was going to die very soon, Nelson breathlessly gave out messages to his mistress Emma Hamilton and their daughter Horatia. In fact, he survived for almost $2\frac{3}{4}$ hours and for the most of that time he was in very great pain. But he clung tenaciously to life, waiting impatiently to hear news of the battle. Finally, at about 3.30pm, Hardy was able to assure him he had achieved a great victory and, satisfied, he then composed himself for death. He gave his last directions for the fleet – an order to anchor which Collingwood did not follow – another series of loving messages to Emma and Horatia and then, finally, took his leave of Hardy.

His famous request for a kiss, which so embarrassed the Victorians (and continues to embarrass some of his less imaginative enthusiasts today) was recorded not only by Beatty but also by Scott and Burke, both of whom were within inches of him as he spoke. And, as Beatty records, Hardy responded not with a single kiss but with two: the first on the cheek and, after a brief reflective pause, a second on the forehead. 'Who is that?' Nelson asked. 'It is Hardy'. 'God bless you Hardy.'

Nelson now asked to be turned on his right side; an act which probably hastened his death, since blood which had already flooded his left lung now drained into the right. Almost at once his breathing became oppressed and shortly afterwards he uttered his last words, 'Thank God I have done my duty.' He slipped away so quietly that no-one knew exactly when he died.

The spot where he had lain became a shrine (5). Every 21 October, wreaths are laid there to honour his memory by senior naval officers, following a brief commemorative service on the quarterdeck of his flagship, now splendidly preserved in Portsmouth.

1. 'Death of Nelson', engraving by James Heath after an original by Benjamin West, no date. *NMM ref PAH8031*

2. 'This Outline is a Key to the Portraits etc, in the Print from Mr West's Picture Death of Lord Nelson', anonymous etching, no date. *NMM ref PAH8032*

3. 'The death of Nelson, 21 October 1805', oil painting by Arthur William Devis (1763-1822), no date. *NMM ref BHC2894*

4. Part of the Trafalgar panorama by William Heath showing Nelson being carried below after being shot. *NMM neg D3481-7*

5. 'The Cockpit HMS Victory', etching by R Dobson after an original by C R B Barrett, 1889. *NMM ref PAD5973*

5

1

The storm after the battle

ON THE evening of 21 October the wind was moderate from the WSW but slowly increasing in strength. The British fleet was approximately 7 miles from Cape Trafalgar. Collingwood had decided not to anchor as Nelson had wished but took the fleet out to sea. It is most probable that some of the ships were unable to anchor, having had their anchors and cables shot to pieces. With the elation of victory receding the crews of the British fleet could not relax, but were forced into further effort putting their ships and prizes in a seaworthy state. Many of the ships most heavily engaged had lost some if not all of their masts and had to be taken in tow. Others were crawling along under jury rigs, wallowing heavily in the ominous swell (1).

'Jack Nasty-Face' Robinson, an Able Seaman wrote, 'Orders were now given to fetch the dead bodies from the after cockpit, and throw them overboard; these were the bodies of the men who were taken down to the doc-

tor during the battle, badly wounded and who by the time the engagement ended, were dead. Some them perhaps could not have recovered, while others might, had timely assistance been rendered, which was impossible; for the rule is, as order is requisite, that every person shall be dressed in rotation as they are brought down wounded and in many instances, some have bled to death.'

On the morning of the 22nd the wind was blowing fresh from the south and increasing in strength; by the evening a full gale was in force. On board the prizes the captured French and Spanish were turned loose to assist the prize crews in preventing the ships from foundering. The seamen who were only the day before fighting against one another, were now working side by side against a greater enemy. Midshipman Henry Walker serving in the *Bellerophon* had been appointed to the prize crew of the *Monarca*. He later wrote:

1. 'The battle of Trafalgar, 21 October 1805: evening', oil painting by William John Huggins (1781-1845), no date. *NMM ref BHC0542*

2

2. 'The day after Trafalgar. The Victory trying to clear land. The Royal Sovereign in tow by Euryalus', watercolour by Nicholas Pocock (1740-1821), 1810.
NMM neg 8501

3. 'Victory . . . in the Gale that succeeded the Battle of Trafalgar, the remains of . . . Nelson on board', coloured aquatint and etching by Robert Dodd (1748-1815) after his own original, published by the artist August 1806.
NMM neg 2788

3

I felt not the least fear of death during the action, which I attribute to the general confidence of victory which I saw all around me; but in the prize, when I was in danger of, and had time to reflect upon the approach of death either from the rising of the Spaniards upon so small a number as we were composed of, or what latterly appeared inevitable from the violence of the storm, I was most certainly afraid, and at one time, when the ship had made over three feet of water in ten minutes, when our people were lying almost drunk upon deck, when the Spaniards, completely worn out with fatigue, would no longer work at the only chain pump left serviceable; when I saw the fear of death so strongly depicted on the countenances of all around me, I wrapped myself up in a Union Jack and lay down upon the deck.

However, *Monarca* was lucky in being attended first by Codrington's *Orion* and then the newly arrived *Donegal*, and against all the odds was brought in safe to Gibraltar.

On the other side of the equation, on that night the British fleet lost the *Fougueux*, the *Redoutable* and the *Algésiras*. The first broke away from the frigate *Phoebe*, and went ashore taking most of those on board, including thirty men of *Temeraire*'s prize crew, to their deaths. *Redoutable*'s fate has been described previously (pages 154-155), but aboard the *Algésiras* the fifty-man prize crew from *Tonnant* was forced to release the French crew to help save the dismasted and drifting hulk; by a fine feat of Anglo-French seamanship the vessel was brought into Cadiz, but the British thereupon found the positions reversed and themselves prisoners.

Collingwood, his flagship herself under tow by the *Euryalus* (2), later wrote to William Marsden of his concerns for the fleet's safety during the days after the battle, 'The condition of our own ships was such that it was very doubtful what would be their fate. Many a time I would have given the whole group of our capture, to ensure our own . . . I can only say that in my life I never saw such efforts as were made to save these ships, and would rather fight another battle than pass through such a week as followed it.' One of his chief worries was the *Victory* still bearing the body of his late friend and commander, but towed by *Polyphemus* the fleet flagship

4

weathered the storm (3), and Fremantle's *Neptune* eventually brought her into Gibraltar on the 28th.

The gale continued to blow and when threatened by Cosmao-Kerjulien's sortie from Cadiz on 24 October, Collingwood reluctantly ordered the prizes to be scuttled and burnt. The prize crew aboard the *Bucentaure* were lost when in obedience to this order she was abandoned by the *Conqueror*; the former Allied flagship then drifted ashore but not before most of the crew were rescued by two of the French ships.

Lieutenant John Edwards of the *Prince*, which had taken in tow the great *Santísima Trinidad*, described the problems of removing the wounded from the prizes: 'Tis impossible to describe the horrors the morning presented, nothing but signals of distress flying in every direc-

tion. The signal was made to destroy the prizes. We had no time before to remove the prisoners; but what a sight when we came to remove the wounded, of which there were four hundred. We had to tie the poor mangled wretches round their waists, and lower them down into a tumbling boat, some without arms, others no legs and lacerated all over in the most dreadful manner' (4). Sadly, not all of the wounded could be removed from the crippled ships. Some survived to be rescued from the sea, but many perished on the orlop decks, where they had lain since being struck down in battle.

Those that were able to anchor fared better; the *San Ildefonso*, tended by the *Defence*, road out the storm and survived (5), one of only four prizes, one French and three Spanish, to do so.

4. 'The battle of Trafalgar: prizes in a gale the day after the action, 22 October 1805', oil painting after the style of the Tudgay family (nineteenth century), no date. It purports to show the last hours of the *Santísima Trinidad*, with a boat off her port quarter taking off survivors. *NMM ref BHC0567*

5. 'Situation of His Majesty's Ship Defence and her Prize the San Ildefonso', coloured aquatint engraved by Hall after an original by John Theophilus Lee, published by Joyce Gold, 31 January 1806. *NMM ref PAD5735*

5

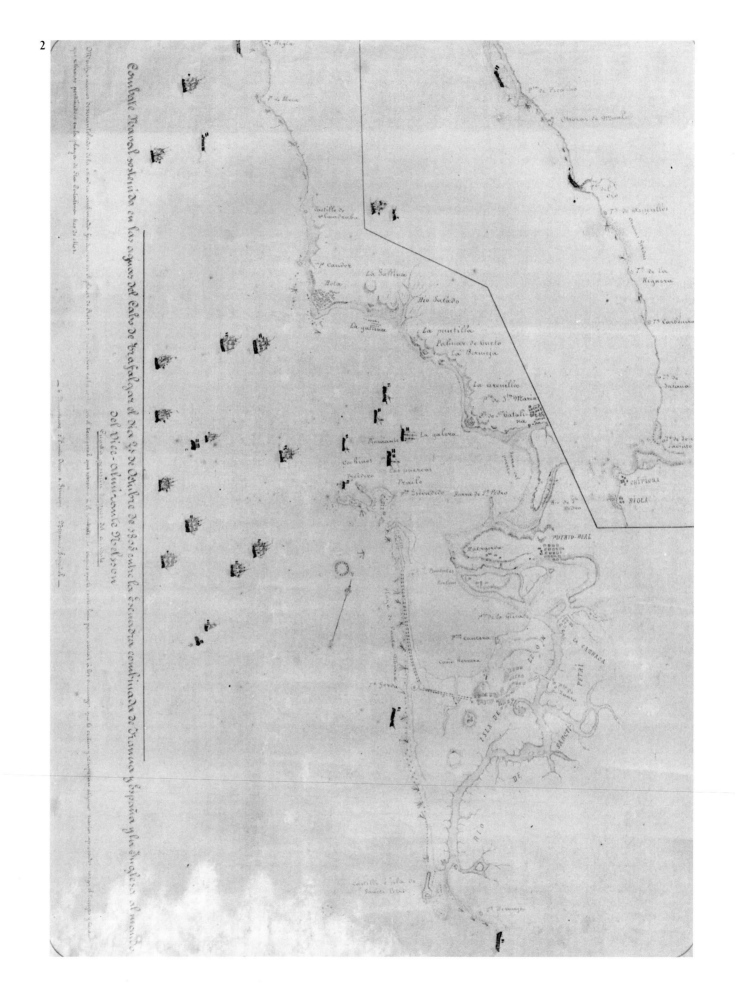

Counterattack

THE AFTERMATH of Trafalgar throws up two mysteries. The first is why Collingwood, a good and experienced seaman, failed to obey Nelson's dying, and eminently sensible, command to anchor the fleet. This, in view of what happened during the ensuing storm, seems to have been absolutely sensible and totally justified. No doubt some of the damaged ships would have had trouble complying, but they had a better chance of contriving some ground tackle that would hold before the storm rather than during its height. It seems especially unfortunate that this was not done when one considers the results of a totally unexpected sortie from Cadiz by a squadron from the apparently crushed Franco-Spanish fleet. The sortie caused the British to abandon their attempts to salvage the prizes at a crucial point as the weather worsened, because they had to prepare to fight again, and which therefore combined with the storm to deprive the British of much of the fruit of their victory.

This, too, is something of a mystery. How was it that a small fragment of a totally defeated force, which consisted of ships of two different nations with much mutual dislike and distrust, could possibly be galvanised into leaving harbour to tackle a numerically superior enemy; an enemy, moreover, who had just conclusively proved his superiority in skill and aggressiveness? It is difficult to find another example of such a counterattack in this, or any other war, in the period of sail. Yet Commodore Baron de Cosmao-Kerjulien (1) of the French navy, the senior allied officer at Cadiz, since Gravina was dying of his wounds, contrived to do just this. And he did so in the face of conditions that were likely to prove only a lull in a fierce storm.

He was, as were so many French naval officers, a minor Breton nobleman, and one who had seen service before the Revolution (he was born in 1761). His *Pluton* was one of the most efficient ships of the Combined Fleet, and he had been chosen to command the successful assault on Diamond Rock earlier in 1805. It is probably of significance when considering the fact that Spanish as well as French ships followed him to sea, that during Calder's action it was he in the *Pluton* who had launched a determined and partially successful attack on the British ships which were overwhelming the Spanish ships of the Allied van. He was clearly a leader of considerable ability and force, not to mention determination and aggression.

The immediate inducement which caused him to sortie on the morning of 23 October was the NW wind which was favourable for an attempt to recapture some of the crippled prizes drifting off Cadiz with prize crews and prisoners alike trying to raise jury rigs and claw off an increasingly threatening lee shore (2). He sailed with his own ship, the *Pluton*, 74, and the French *Indomptable*, 80 and *Neptune*, 84, with the Spanish *Rayo*, 100, and *San Francisco de Asís*, 74, plus the five French frigates and two brigs which had been present at the battle. The other ships of the line in harbour were in no state to sail (3), whilst the *Pluton* herself had already been badly knocked about on the 21st. Soon after he had cleared Cadiz, the wind veered to WSW and blew harder than ever. At noon he found himself near the British ships. Up till then those British vessels whose rigging was comparatively intact had been towing the worst damaged of the prizes, many of which were mere hulks. The threat of Cosmao's squadron caused the ten or so most mobile British ships to cast off the vessels in tow, and form line of battle to screen their prizes (4). With an unfavourable wind, Cosmao did not venture to attack this formidable

1

3

1. Commodore Julien-Marie, Baron de Cosmao-Kerjulien, plate from E Fraser, *The Enemy at Trafalgar* (London 1908).
Chatham Collection

2. 'Combate Naval sostenido en las aquas del cabo Trafalgar el dia 21 de Octobre 1805 . . . Cuatro posicion despues del combate', reproduction and watercolour by Manuel Sestelo y Jimanez and R Millan, 3 January 1906. This is one of a series based on contemporary official charts from the archives of the Captain General of Cadiz; in engraved form they were published in E Desbrière, *La Campagne Maritme de 1805: Trafalgar* (Paris 1907). In stylised form it shows the dispersed nature of the fleet around Cadiz on 23 October, and depicts the rescued *Neptuno* (marked 'g') and *Santa Ana* ('c') under tow; the dismasted *Príncipe de Asturias* ('e') lies off Cadiz, while *Bucentaure* ('b') is shown wrecked on the rocks at the entrance to the harbour.
NMM ref PAI6140

3. A contemporary view of the shattered remnant of the combined fleet in Cadiz harbour on 22 October. Despite the stylised nature of the depiction there is a real attempt to differentiate the damage to the individual ships, which are keyed (left to right) as follows: 1. *Héros* 2. *Montañes* 3. *Pluton* 4. *Indomptable* 5. *San Leandro* 6. *Algésiras* 7. *Príncipe de Asturias* 8. *San Justo* 9. *Neptune* 10. *Argonaute* 11. *San Francisco de Asís*; for some unknown reason, the *Rayo* is missing.
By courtesy of John Harbron

4. 'Combats Maritimes. Le Lendermain de Trafalgar, Capitaine Cosmao Commandant le Pluton poursuit l'escadre victorieuse et reprendre plusieurs vaisseaux', tinted lithograph engraved by De Laplante and Jean Baptiste Henri Durand-Brager after his own original, printed by Lemercier and published by the Anaglyphic Company, 20 August 1844. Despite the bombast of this print, there was no actual fighting between Cosmao's squadron and the British.
NMM neg B2584

5. The recaptured *Santa Ana* under tow by the French frigate *Thémis.* Anonymous contemporary watercolour.
Chatham Collection

6. 'Destruction of the Prizes, on the 28th [*sic*] Oct 1805', coloured lithograph engraved by R H Nimmo after an original by A Masson, no date.
NMM ref PA17643

force; but his frigates managed to cut off and retake the two nearest of these prizes, the *Neptuno* and the *Santa Ana* (5). The frigates contrived to get these two back under tow and returned with them to Cadiz. At the same time the remaining vessels which had been under tow were blown towards the hostile shore. With the worsening weather it would prove impossible for the British to get them under tow again.

The weather was to be the real victor. On the following day, the *Indomptable*, having grounded off Rota, went to pieces; the *San Francisco de Asís* went ashore in Cadiz Bay; and the *Rayo*, anchored off San Lucar to escape going ashore, rolled away her masts, and was forced to surrender to the *Donegal*, which had rejoined the British fleet a few hours earlier from Gibraltar, having missed the battle. The newly made prize, however, did not remain British for long, for she went ashore and was wrecked on the 26th. The *Indomptable*'s loss was particularly harrowing, since she had over 1000 men on board, including many of the survivors of the *Bucentaure*, and only about 100 of this total got ashore.

Cosmao's counterattack, therefore, on balance made a loss. Two Spanish ships of the line were recaptured at the expense of one French and two Spanish lost. On the other hand he had forced the British to suspend salvage operations to see off the threat posed by his ships, and must have had a bearing on Collingwood's decision to scuttle or fire the most exposed prizes (6). However, this is only on the material plane. In moral terms Cosmao's was an important gesture, and shows that, if the French and Spanish navies were at this stage inferior to the British, it was not for want of gallantry, determination and, at least in this case, of aggressive and admirable leaders.

1

Strachan's Action

THE STORY of Trafalgar has an important appendix in the fate of Rear-Admiral Dumanoir Le Pelley's four ships which had escaped to the southward. He would have made for Toulon had he not known that several British sail of the line were near Gibraltar, so he decided to make for one of the French Atlantic ports.

The Rochefort squadron under Allemand was still at sea, raiding British commerce, and several British squadrons and detached ships were looking for it. At the end of October, the *Phoenix*, 36, learnt from some neutrals that a squadron had been sighted in the Bay of Biscay. Captain Baker took his frigate in search of the enemy, and on 2 November, in the latitude of Cape Finisterre, he sighted and chased four large ships; and, when he in turn was chased, he steered south, hoping to lure the enemy into Captain Strachan's squadron, which was looking for Allemand off Ferrol. In the afternoon Baker sighted four

2

Sr RICHd. J. STRACHAN's ACTION with the FRENCH, off ROCHEFORT: Novr. 2.1805.
in which the four French Ships were taken.

1. 'Sir Richard Strachan's Action, Novr. 5th 1805', coloured aquatint engraved by Thomas Sutherland after an original by Thomas Whitcombe, no date.
NMM ref PAD5756

2. 'Sir Richard Strachan's Action, Novr. 4th 1805', coloured aquatint engraved by J Jeakes after an original by Thomas Whitcombe, 1 September 1810.
NMM ref PAD5757

3. 'Sir Richd. J Strachan's Action with the French off Rochefort: Novr. 2. 1805 in which four French ships were taken', coloured aquatint published by Laurie and Whittle, 12 December 1805. Despite the diagram-like nature of this print, the wrong date is a fair indicator of its accuracy; if mirror-imaged it might represent the final stages, with the frigates to leeward, but there seems to have been no moment when the British line was formed in the order shown.
NMM ref PAD5758

4. 'Lord Nelson's Victory over the French & Spanish Fleets off Trafalgar Octr 21st 1805', coloured aquatint published by John Fairburn, no date. Despite the title to the print—and sometimes claimed to depict Dumanoir's escape from Trafalgar—the ships are identified, left to right, as *Hero, Duguay Trouin, Mont Blanc* and *Caesar*; Strachan's ships were not, of course, present at Trafalgar. It must represent the last stage of the 5 November engagement.
NMM neg X1881

5. 'HMS Implacable', anonymous coloured lithograph, no date but postwar.
NMM neg A1945

other large ships to the southward, and a little later the vessels which had been chasing him turned away.

Baker had discovered Dumanoir's squadron, which, at about the same time, had also been sighted and chased by the *Boadicea*, 38, and the *Dryad*, 36, although these were soon left behind. *Phoenix* persisted, despite being fired at, and hailed the *Caesar* with her news of the enemy. The British squadron at that point was scattered, so Strachan directed Baker to bring up the stragglers, and himself pursued the enemy. He lost contact more than once during the night, but the next morning despite the dirty weather he again saw the French in the NNE. He had then with him three ships of the line besides his own, together with the *Santa Margarita*, 36, and he instantly chased under all possible sail. In terms of line of battle-ships, the forces would be theoretically equal, since the *Bellona*, 74 could not keep up and did not rejoin in time to take part in the ensuing battle. Both sides had one 80 and three 74s (*Caesar, Hero, Courageux* and *Namur* against *Formidable, Duguay Trouin, Mont Blanc* and *Scipion*), but Dumanoir's flagship, *Formidable*, had had three guns dismounted at Trafalgar, and had thrown overboard twelve of her quarterdeck 12pdrs during the chase, so that she effectively had only 65 guns. Rather more to the point, the British also had four frigates: *Santa Margarita*, 36, *Æolus*, 32, *Phoenix*, 36 and *Revolutionnaire*, 38 and used these to very good effect to slow down the fleeing enemy.

At noon, with a strong wind, the French were about 14 miles distant; at about 3pm, the fast-sailing frigates *Santa Margarita*, and, later, the *Phoenix*, began to catch up with the enemy's rear. It was at this stage that the *Bellona*

dropped behind. By dawn on 4 November, the wind had dropped to a moderate breeze and the leading British ship of the line was about 6 miles astern of the rearmost Frenchman, the *Scipion*, which, earlier in the morning, had begun to be engaged by the *Santa Margarita*, and then the *Phoenix*, and which was from then on continually harassed by the frigates hanging on her quarters, yawing to fire broadsides, dodging the enemy's heavier broadside and inexorably slowing him down. Soon afterwards, the *Caesar, Hero*, and *Courageux* formed in line ahead, and aided by a shift of wind, closed so rapidly that, at 11.45, realising that he could not avoid an action, Dumanoir Le Pelley ordered his ships to reduce sail, and to form line themselves on the starboard tack a little more than a mile from the British. The *Namur* and the *Revolutionnaire*, were still respectively 14 miles, and 7 miles astern of the *Caesar*.

Strachan told his two consorts that he proposed to attack the centre and rear of the French and, at about noon, the three British ships moved towards the three rearmost French ones, the *Caesar* steering towards the *Formidable*, the *Hero* the *Mont Blanc*, and the *Courageux* the *Scipion*. The *Caesar*, followed shortly by the other ships, opened fire at 12.15 (1). At about 12.55pm, five minutes after Strachan had hoisted his signal for close action, the *Duguay Trouin* attempted to tack to cross the *Caesar*'s bows and rake her; but the latter moved to counter this, and, the *Duguay Trouin* having been taken aback, both the two leading British ships were able to pound her very severely at close range (2). The *Formidable, Mont Blanc*, and *Scipion* tacked in support of the *Duguay Trouin*, but, in the course of the manoeuvre, the French flagship, being somewhat crippled aloft, lost her place in the line and became second instead of third. The French, however, finally got round on the port tack; and at 1.20pm the British came round in chase. The *Namur* was by then on the weather bow of the French, and Strachan, whose own *Caesar*, with damaged rigging, was falling behind, signalled to her to attack the enemy's van, and, to the *Hero*, to lead on the port tack. He then made sure the *Namur* obeyed his order by the drastic expedient of firing two loaded guns at her! A little before 2pm, the *Hero* restarted the battle by firing her starboard battery into the *Scipion*, bringing down her main topmast, and to causing her to fall to leeward, where she was quickly engaged by the *Courageux*, from windward, and by the *Phoenix* and *Revolutionnaire*, from leeward. The *Hero* by that time, having placed herself on the *Formidable*'s weather beam, gradually drew up, until she was on the French flagship's port bow. At 2.45, the *Namur*, arriving astern of the *Hero* (3), also engaged the *Formidable*, whereupon the *Hero* made sail to close with the *Mont Blanc*. The *Caesar*, having repaired her rigging, was about to open fire on the *Formidable* when she surrendered. Some five minutes later

4

the *Scipion* also struck, just as the *Duguay Trouin* and *Mont Blanc* were trying to form a fresh line ahead of her. It was then obvious to them that the day was hopelessly lost; and they tried to escape, but were quickly overhauled by the *Hero* and *Caesar*. After 20 minutes of heavy firing, both of them struck (4).

The losses on the British side were 24 killed, 111 wounded. The *Hero* and the *Caesar* had suffered most severely aloft. The French ships lost 750 killed and wounded, including among the wounded Dumanoir Le Pelley himself. Dumanoir was later to be criticised for not engaging the British earlier when he would only have had to fight three ships of the line. This was neither fair nor sensible. As the survivors of Trafalgar his crews can have been in little doubt of the relative fighting quality of the British forces, and it was already clear that the British would make skilful and aggressive use of their frigates to even the odds, whilst the *Formidable* had already had her fighting capabilities reduced. The sensible thing to do was to escape and preserve ships and crews for another day, not to attempt to act aggressively against an enemy who was, even on the best interpretation, not much inferior on paper, and who had a very great advantage in morale and skill. Had it not been for the aggressive and skilful handling of two British frigates it is quite probable the French would have achieved their escape.

The four prizes, all of them terribly mauled, were carried to Plymouth, and all of them were eventually added to the Royal Navy, the *Formidable* as the *Brave*, the *Duguay Trouin* as the *Implacable*. The *Implacable* (5) survived as the last of the numerous prizes of the Napoleonic War until finally scuttled in the Channel flying both white ensign and tricolour in 1949.

5

1

Ships of the Royal Navy: the 74-gun ship

SINCE THE beginning of the eighteenth century the standard line of battle ship in every major navy was a two-decked Third Rate of around 70 guns. By about 1750 the number of guns was increasingly set at 74, a number which has no particular logic but which often came about by increasing the length of the standard 70 and adding two extra ports on each gundeck to make twenty-eight per broadside, the armament of the upperworks remaining at eighteen guns.

The first British 74s were mainly the work of Sir Thomas Slade, the designer of the *Victory,* Anson's favoured naval architect, and one of the very best ship designers of the age of sail. Introduced from about 1755 onwards, 74-gun ships quickly fell into a pattern of about 168ft on the gundeck with twenty-eight 32pdrs on the lower and the same number of 18pdrs on the upper gundeck, with 9pdrs on the forecastle and quarterdeck (1). Slade and his successors experimented with the hull forms but the basic dimensions remained in use until the end of the American Revolutionary War, and occasionally even later. Generally known as the 'Common Class', these 74s still formed the backbone of the battlefleet in 1793, although numbers declined steadily in the 1790s before staging a recovery after Trafalgar.

Year	No in Sea Service	No in Ordinary or Repairing
1793	18	40
1796	48	8
1799	41	8
1801	39	11
1805	30	13
1808	47	4
1811	56	6
1814	64	3

The reasons for the reversing trend were twofold: firstly, most ships built and captured in the 1790s were of the new 'Large Class', whose increase tended to offset the decline in 'Common' 74s; but after 1800 there was a return to more moderate dimensions for new construction (particularly the infamous 'Forty Thieves' of the Surveyors' class), and the widening of the theatre of war required the commissioning of every battleship that would float.

2

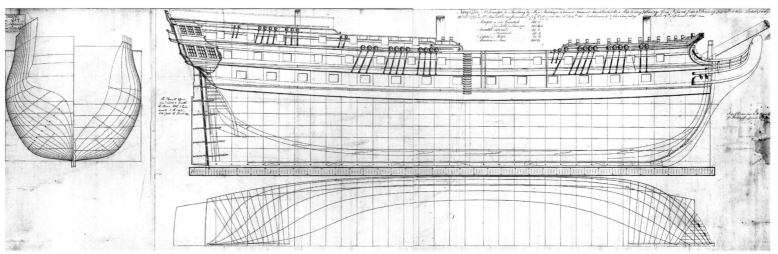

3

The 'Large Class' could trace its ancestry to the *Valiant* and *Triumph* (2) of 1757, based on the lines of the French *Invincible* captured in 1747, which introduced 24pdrs on the upper deck. Compared with around 1650 tons for the standard 74, they were 1800 tons and were seen as unnecessarily large and not followed-up by the conservative administrations of the American War period—although it is only fair to point out that numbers rather than individual quality were far more important in this conflict than was the case earlier or later in the century.

The relative success of the French navy in the American Revolutionary struggle inspired much admiration in the British service, and one important factor was considered to be the size and quality of French ships. A few large 74s were laid down after the war, concentrating initially on increased length for greater speed, and

the process gathered pace under Spencer's forward-looking Admiralty in the 1790s (3). Some of these ships returned to 24pdr secondary batteries, and with French prizes being regularly added to this class, numbers grew quickly (4).

Year	No in Sea Service	No in Ordinary or Repairing
1793	1	2
1796	6	2
1799	17	3
1801	17	3
1805	19	5
1808	29	1
1811	24	4
1814	21	9

4

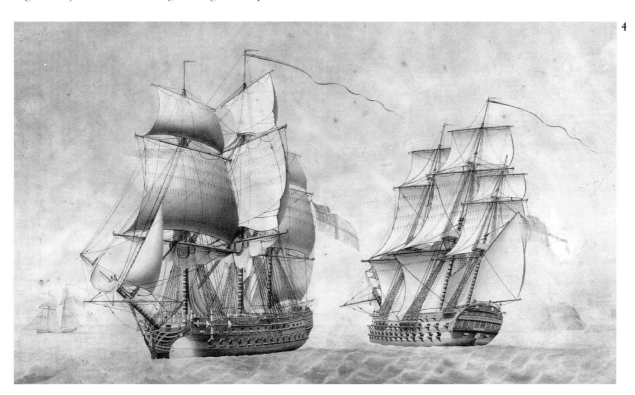

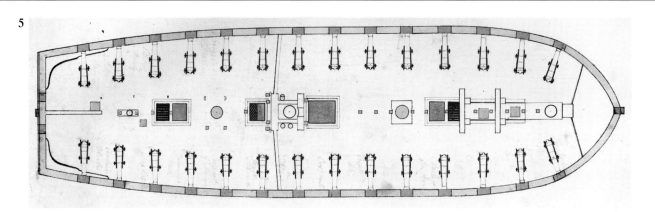

5

1. 'His Majesty's Ship Audacious of 74 Guns & 600 men. Drawn by Richard Hawes anno 1793', watercolour by Richard Hawes, 1793. A Common Class 74 of 1600 tons belonging to one of Slade's earliest designs dating from 1758, although this ship was not built until 1785.
NMM neg B4871

2. 'Sketch of His Majesty's Ship Triumph of 74 guns 1808', water-colour by William Latham, *c*1820. One of the original pair of Large Class 74s, this ship had a long career, serving from 1764 until being hulked in 1813; the hulk was not broken up until 1850.
NMM neg 6160

These bigger ships, of 1850-1900 tons or more, have been associated with the distant blockade policy of Howe and Bridport, which presumed that the main fleet would spend much of its time in sheltered home waters and not exposed to damage or loss off a hostile coast. They would chase the French once an inshore squadron of observation had reported any sortie, and for this fast—which usually meant large—ships were necessary. If this were the case, it would reveal very muddled thinking on the part of both Admiralty and Admirals, because the strategic mobility of the fleet—its ability to get into a position to encounter the enemy—would depend on the speed of the slowest ship, in all probability one of the three-decker flagships that could not be left behind. The inspiration for the larger ships is far more likely to have been a general desire for improvement, since both the

Chatham and Spencer Admiralties invested heavily in frigates and sloops of significantly greater size as well as bigger battleships.

In fact, the large 74 had a tactical advantage in that it could act as a fast division of the battlefleet. Not unlike the battlecruiser force in the First World War, these ships could be detached either to cut off the rear of a retreating enemy line or to delay the main force until the rest of the British fleet could come up. The separate division was merely defined as 'fast-sailing two-deckers', and could include the better Common Class 74s, but the Large Class provided the majority of such ships—certainly out of all proportion to their numbers. When combined with 80-gun two-deckers the large 74s made ideal flying squadrons: Calder's detachment in pursuit of Ganteaume in 1801 was an early, if flawed, example since

he still had a three-decker flagship; but Duckworth's victory at San Domingo in 1806 was largely the work of big two-deckers, assisted by one Common 74 and the famously fast-sailing 64 *Agamemnon*.

As the tactics of blockade became more sophisticated, the Large Class was found increasingly useful on the more demanding stations, especially inshore. They tended to be powerful and weatherly under sail, so could be risked as a link between the frigates and the main fleet, and eventually came to comprise whole squadrons: off Rochefort in 1808, for example, Sir Richard Strachan commanded a homogeneous force of seven large two-deckers from the *Caesar*, 80. To blockade Rochefort was particularly demanding, and the Large Class took a major share of this duty. A spectacular proof of their value came in September 1806 when Sir Samuel Hood in the *Centaur* (5) led the Rochefort squadron, which included three other large 74s, in the pursuit and capture of four 40-gun frigates; in heavy weather even frigates could be overhauled by Large Class 74s.

These ships were plum commands, so generally fell to the lot of senior captains. Therefore, they often became senior officers' ships when detached, and in due course became flagships, sometimes even in preference to 80s: Borlase Warren chose the *Renown* to carry his flag rather than the *Gibraltar* in 1801, and *Kent* was Sir Richard Bickerton's flagship for the Egypt expedition in the same year. Like all first-class ships, there was a strong tendency to keep them at home or in the Mediterranean, but it is significant that with his well-known prejudice against large ships Jervis had neither 80s nor Large Class 74s in his fleet in 1797. A few large ships served in the West Indies, but they were not to be found further afield before the renewal of war in 1803, nor with the odd exception in the North Sea.

Despite their obvious advantages, large ships fell from favour towards the end of the 1790s. The victories at St Vincent, Camperdown and the Nile were almost exclusively the work of Common Class 74s, and resources—in both the general financial sense and in the specific area of shipbuilding capacity—were stretched very thin. In this climate the big 74 did not look like good value, costing about 25 per cent more than a Common Class vessel, and making greater demands on scarce supplies of 'grown' timber. Furthermore, doubts began to be expressed about the strength of the long-hulled two-deckers, especially when employed on near-continuous blockade duty. Even before St Vincent's retrenchment-minded administration took office in 1801, there had been a return to moderate dimensions (around 1700 tons), and a move away from small numbers of single ships or pairs towards once again building classes of substantial numbers to a single draught (6).

This process reached a climax with the 'Surveyors of the Navy' class, a collaborative venture between the three chief designers intended to produce what might be called a 'war emergency' standard battleship. It was as small as could be considered viable (at 1740 tons it rated as a Middling 74), with a flattened sheer to maximise gunport freeboard amidships, and was meant for construction in large numbers in merchant yards. Like all ships 'designed down to a limit', they could not stand comparison with larger and more expensive equivalents, and as such they quickly became the target of unfair criticism. The building programme was to reach forty ships, and some journalistic wag christened them 'The Forty Thieves', a soubriquet that was unjustly bequeathed to history (7).

Some ships of the class undoubtedly suffered problems, but more often constructional than design-related. To execute a programme of this size the Navy Board was forced to turn to many builders with little or no experience of large warships, and the Board clearly had difficulty overseeing construction in the depth required. Ships were certainly badly finished, and in a few well-publicised cases there was more than a suspicion of fraud, but many of the ships were also subjected to experiments with systems of fastening designed to alleviate the great shortage of natural 'grown' knees. Complaints of structural weakness were certainly exaggerated, and the vast majority of the class survived for decades after the end of the war. Under sail they were not outstanding, but they were not noticeably inadequate either; most importantly, they were available, and in large numbers, when they were needed.

3. Design sheer elevation and body plan for the *Spencer*, dated 19 October 1795. As well as utilising the lines plans of captured French ships, the Royal Navy also employed a French designer, the emigre *constructeur* Barrallier from Toulon to build a few ships, including this large 74. *NMM neg DR937*

4. 'An English ship in stays and another close hauled', anonymous black and wash, grey pen and ink, no date. Despite the caption, the fifteen lower deck ports and the French-style stern suggests a prize rather than a British-built 74, although a few classes built to the lines of French ships had fifteen ports. *NMM neg A5841*

5. 'Plan of ye Centaurs Lower gun Deck', anonymous black and wash, grey pen and ink, no date. One of the first of the revived Large Class with upper deck 24pdrs, this ship was ordered in 1788 and launched in 1794. *NMM ref PAH5197*

6. 'HMS Aboukir', anonymous grey graphite and wash, no date. This ship represented the return to moderate dimensions, ordered in 1802 to a 1779 design, itself based on the lines of a French prize taken in 1761. *NMM neg X78*

7. 'HMS Duncan at Mahon', oil painting by William Anderson (1757-1837), no date. One of the standard Surveyors' class, the so-called 'Forty Thieves'. *NMM ref BHC3297*

7

1

Securing the Victory

2

NELSON'S FLAGSHIP had borne the brunt of the fighting in the allied centre. Having lead the weather column, she had been engaged by the enemy for approximately half an hour before being able to return fire, and her casualties had been the highest in the British fleet.

The remarks of Midshipman Roberts, who was serving in *Victory* at the time of the battle, creates a vivid picture of what the great ship must have looked like on the evening of 21 October 1805.

The Hull is much damaged by shot in a number of different places, particularly in the wales, strings and spirketting, and some between wind and water. Several beams, knees, riders, shot through and broke; the starboard cathead shot away; the rails and timbers of the head and stern cut by shot; several of the ports damaged and the port timbers cut off; the channels and chain plate damaged by shot and the falling of the mizzen mast; the principal part of the bulkheads, half ports and port sashes thrown overboard in clearing the ship for action. The mizzen mast shot away about nine feet above the deck; the main mast shot through and sprung; the main yard gone; main topmast and cap shot in different places and reefed, the main topsail yard shot away; the foremast shot through in a number of different places and is at present supported by a topmast and a part of the topsail and crossjack yards; the fore yard shot away; the bowsprit jibboom and cap shot, and the spritsail, spritsail yards, and flying boom are gone; the fore and main tops damaged; the whole of the spare topmast yards, hand mast and fishes shot in different places and converted into jury gear. The ship makes in bad weather 12 inches an hour.

The *Victory* was indeed in bad shape, and consequently one of the British ships in most danger from the storm. But for a fleet which had just lost their commander, saving the flagship was a top priority, and no effort was spared by her crew or the ships around her. However, it became clear that she might not survive on her own, and at about 11am on 24 October she was taken in tow by the *Polyphemus*; but *Victory* had to be cut loose again when she became uncontrollable in the heavy weather, risking a collision with the towing ship. The three-decker was adrift until the *Neptune* picked up the tow on 27 October; this ship, commanded by Nelson's old friend Fremantle, conducted *Victory* safely into the bay of Gibraltar the following day (1). For the weary crew, respite was short, for the ship was rapidly made ready with temporary repairs for her voyage to England bringing Nelson's body home.

The gales that had swept over the fleet had prevented Collingwood from immediately sending news to England of their great victory and of the death of Nelson. It was not until 26 October that Collingwood was able to turn over his despatches to Lieutenant John Richards Lapenotiere (2) of the schooner *Pickle* (3), which sailed the thousand miles from Cape Trafalgar to Falmouth in eight days. A few days later Collingwood sent a duplicate set in the cutter *Entreprenante* (4) to Faro in Portugal for the Ambassador in Lisbon to forward to the Admiralty. It was a close race between the schooner and the diplomatic courier but first news of the battle arrived in England with the *Pickle*, and with the aid of fast horses Lapenotiere covered the 265 miles to London in 37 hours.

He arrived at the Admiralty at 1am on 5 November, two weeks after the battle. Lord Barham, the First Sea Lord, was roused and Lapenotiere delivered his despatches. The following morning King George III was informed of the great victory, but both he and his Queen were more inclined to mourn the loss of England's great fighting sailor than celebrate the end of the invasion threat. This set the tone of mixed emotions that greeted the news throughout the country. The *Times* spoke for the nation when it opined: 'We know not whether to mourn or rejoice. The country has gained the most splendid and decisive Victory that has ever graced the naval annals of England: but it has been dearly purchased. *The great and gallant Nelson is no more.*'

---

1. 'H.M.S. Victory towed into Gibraltar', watercolour by W Clarkson Stanfield (1793-1867), no date.
NMM neg D2575

2. 'Captain John Richards Lapenotiere, 1770-1834', oil painting of the nineteenth-century British school, no date.
NMM ref BHC2829

3. The schooner *Pickle*, detail from 'Victory of Trafalgar, in the Rear. This view of the total defeat of the combined Fleets of France and Spain . . . is most respectfully inscribed to the Right Honble Lord Collingwood . . .', aquatint and etching by Robert Dodd (1748-1815) after his own original, published by the artist, 1 March 1806.
NMM neg B2582

4. The cutter *Entreprenante*, detail from Trafalgar panorama by William Heath.
NMM neg D3481-8

1

Nelson's funeral

'DON'T THROW me overboard,' whispered Nelson to Hardy just before their final farewell. 'Oh no,' came the reply, 'certainly not.'

Certainly, there was no question that the hero of Trafalgar would be buried at sea; Hardy and his colleagues knew that the country would wish to bury him with full honours. But the *Victory* had been very badly damaged in the battle and ensuing storm, and would have to put into Gibraltar for repairs before making the voyage home to Britain. So the first problem they faced after the battle was the preservation of Nelson's body. The largest type of barrel on board, a 'leaguer', was lashed on its end on the main deck and into this the body was placed head first. The cask was then filled with brandy (*not* the rum of persistent naval tradition) and a Royal Marine sentry posted to guard it. At one point, a

2

discharge of air from the body raised the lid of the cask, to the considerable alarm of the sentry.

The original intention was that the body would be transferred to a frigate at Gibraltar for the journey home. However, as one of the *Victory*'s marines laconically put it, 'we told Captain as we brought him out we would bring him home: so it was so' – a delightful expression of the way in which officer/men relations worked in the Nelsonian navy. But even after her repairs, the ship was still very slow and she also encountered blustering weather and successive gales on her voyage north. As a result, she did not reach Britain until 4 December, almost one month after the news of Trafalgar had arrived.

That news had caused a remarkable outpouring of public grief, in which Nelson was mourned in an intensely personal manner: in the memorable words of Robert Southey, the Poet Laureate, 'Men started at the intelligence, and turned pale, as of they had heard of the loss of a dear friend.' So, the decision had been made to give Nelson a full State Funeral and a tomb in St Paul's Cathedral. The *Victory* was therefore ordered to take the body round to the Thames. Various artists, including J M W Turner, sketched her during her voyage. Robert Dodd (1) cheated and re-issued a print of the *Victory*, dating from some years before, with a new caption claiming that it showed her with Nelson's body on board.

At the Nore, the great naval anchorage at the mouth of the Thames, she was met by the Commissioner's yacht *Chatham*, bearing a curious cargo. Six years before, in the Mediterranean, one of Nelson's captains, Ben Hallowell had presented him with a simple, plain coffin. Made from wood taken from the wreckage of *L' Orient*, the French flagship at the Battle of the Nile which had caught fire and blown up at the height of the action, it suited Nelson's slightly macabre sense of humour and he carefully preserved it. Now he was to be laid in it, as Hallowell intended.

On 22 December the body was finally transferred from the *Victory* to the *Chatham* and taken up river to the Naval Hospital at Greenwich. There, the plain trophy coffin and its leaden shell were encased in a magnificent casket, specially designed by the Ackermen brothers (2). Covered in gilded heraldic devices and other symbolic decorations such as crocodiles and seahorses, it was so impressive that the organisers of the funeral left it displayed to the public gaze, instead of covering it with a heavy black pall as custom required.

Custom was to play a large part in the ceremonial that followed. It was one of the last full heraldic funerals ever staged in Britain and all the details were in the hands of the College of Arms, under Garter King at Arms, Sir Isaac Heard. So, for example, the coffin was accompanied throughout by the hero's helmet, surcoat, shield and gauntlets. Of course, none of these had been actually worn by Nelson; they were all specially made for the occasion. It was almost as if a medieval knight was going to his rest, an analogy made at the time by Chaplain Alexander Scott who, half demented with grief, insisted on remaining with his friend and commander until the last moment. Writing to Emma Hamilton from his post beside the body, he said, 'So help me God as I think he was a true knight and worthy the age of chivalry.'

By the turn of the year, all was ready for the spectacle.

3

On 4 January the gold-encrusted coffin was placed on a catafalque in the Painted Hall of Greenwich Hospital, which had been transformed into a grand mortuary chapel (3): black hangings covered the vivid wall-paintings which gave the hall its name; heraldic devices gleamed in the rich glow from hundreds of candles in wall sconces. The first mourner admitted was the Princess of Wales who paid a private visit that afternoon. The following day, a Sunday, the doors were thrown open and a steady stream of people flowed through.

On Wednesday 8 January, there was a grand river procession from Greenwich to London (4). A large flotilla was assembled, including eleven barges owned by City Livery Companies, resplendent with their ornately carved and gilded decoration and distinctive banners. The coffin was placed in one of the royal barges, origi-

4

5

nally made for King Charles II, its gilding and paint obscured by black velvet, with a large canopy erected over its stern surmounted by black ostrich plumes. It became a Nelson trophy, lovingly preserved on board HMS *Victory* and is now displayed in the Royal Naval Museum. Slowly, the huge long line advanced up-river, its passage marked by the dull thuds of minute guns fired from the naval escort boats. The weather was fine, but a strong wind was blowing from the southwest, setting up a heavy chop on the river and forcing the oarsmen to struggle to keep the unwieldy barges on station. Eventually, after passing through London (5) the procession arrived at Whitehall Stairs. The coffin was unloaded and taken to the Admiralty, where it lay overnight.

The following day, the coffin was placed on an ornate funeral car, designed to look like the *Victory* and hung with more heraldic devices and trophies (6). It was escorted by a huge procession, made up mainly of soldiers. The only naval contingents were some of the Greenwich pensioners and members of the *Victory*'s crew who proudly carried their ship's enormous battle

ensigns, opening them up from time to time to display the shot-holes to the admiring crowd. The procession was so long (7) that its head had reached St Paul's before the funeral car had even left the Admiralty and, as the sea of red flowed endlessly past, the crowd began to get restive. But once the huge plumes above the car finally came into sight they fell silent and then, one eyewitness remembered, there was a noise like the rushing of waves on the shore as the men removed their hats.

So, finally, the body arrived at St Paul's Churchyard (8) where every nearby building was packed with spectators and a special stand had been erected above the great west portico. Inside, the cathedral had been transformed into a huge amphitheatre by the erection of more stands in the nave and underneath the great dome. By now, the short January afternoon was drawing to its close and darkness was gathering, so a special lantern, mounted with 130 individual lamps, had been suspended from the dome (9).

The service that followed was striking both for simplicity and for highly-charged emotion. It had been decided that the Burial Service would be performed within the context of Evensong, said or sung daily, then as now, in churches and cathedrals throughout the land. So Nelson, the parson's son, was sent to his rest with the ringing words of the Book of Common Prayer, familiar to him since very early boyhood—so familiar, indeed, that his own fine prayers often echo the language and cadences of Thomas Cranmer. The music, too, was extremely effective: a special selection put together by Revd John Pridden, one of St Paul's vicars choral. It included well-known pieces such as, 'Thou knowest Lord the secrets of our hearts' by Henry Purcell, composed for the funeral of Queen Mary in 1689; the lesser-known and starkly sombre anthem, 'Lord let me know mine end' by Maurice Greene, a former organist of St Paul's and at least one new composition—a Grand

6

7

Funeral Dirge by the current organist, Thomas Attwood.

So, at last, the final act in the great drama arrived. The coffin was placed on a catafalque directly beneath the dome and all the main participants gathered around. There were officials such as Garter King at Arms and the Bishop of Lincoln who officiated at the service (in those pluralist days he was also Dean of St Paul's). There were service friends such as Captain Thomas Hardy and Sir Peter Parker, one of Nelson's earliest patrons who, as the Admiral of the Fleet, was acting as Chief Mourner. And there were personal friends and family: Nelson's prize agent Alexander Davison; the new Earl Nelson, his ungainly and undignified elder brother, William; and his young nephew, George Matcham, who later described the spectacle in his diary as 'the most aweful sight I ever saw.'

The last words were read, the 'Committal'; the last anthem sung—a glorious Handel chorus, 'His body is buried in peace; but his name liveth evermore!'—and Sir Isaac Heard read out the titles of the deceased, ending with the unscripted words, 'The hero, who in the moment of Victory, fell covered with immortal glory.' Then, at a given signal, the body began to sink slowly from sight to the crypt below. As it did so, the rubric required that the *Victory*'s sailors should reverently fold up the shot-torn colours and place them on the disappearing coffin. But in a moment of spontaneity, which sent a *frisson* of emotion round the spectators beneath the dome, the sailors first ripped off a large portion of one of the flags and then subdivided it into smaller pieces to be kept as mementoes. Mrs Codrington, wife of the captain of the *Orion* at Trafalgar commented, 'That was *Nelson*: the rest was so much the Herald's Office.'

The *Naval Chronicle* reported proudly, 'Thus terminated one of the most impressive and most splendid solemnities that ever took place in this Country, or perhaps Europe.' There have, perhaps, been others more splendid; but few have matched Nelson's funeral for symbolic significance. It was in a very real sense an apotheosis: marking the moment when he passed from mortal man to immortal hero.

8

9

POSTSCRIPT

IN THE Battle of Trafalgar the loss in life and limb was small compared to the scale of the battle. In the British fleet, 37 officers and 412 men were killed; 102 officers and 1112 men were wounded. In the Combined Fleet, although the French did not declare their casualties, nevertheless from the information available we know that while 34 officers were killed and 58 wounded, probably over 6000 men of all other ranks became casualties by ships blowing up, foundering and becoming wrecks as well as by action with the British fleet. The casualties of the Combined Fleet were a measure of the defeat for France and Spain. Counting the four losses to Sir Richard Strachan off Cape Finisterre on 3 November, the Combined powers lost 21 ships of the line, 13 French vessels and 8 Spanish. Against these losses, Britain lost no ships at all.

For the Spanish navy, Trafalgar was a catastrophe. At the beginning of 1805 she had over 30 ships of the line fit for sea. A quarter of her best vessels had been destroyed and the pick of her officer corps had been ravaged: 12 of the 15 captains who commanded Spanish vessels were killed or wounded; four Spanish admirals were also wounded and Gravina would die later from his wounds. Moreover this was in a campaign into which Spain had been drawn by force of diplomacy rather than because Spain's own interest demanded war with Britain. Spanish morale was as badly hurt as the material of her navy. The news of the battle and of the wreckage strewn along the coast between Cadiz and Cape Trafalgar could not be suppressed. The Spanish people might have recovered from this, but the battle also undermined their economic strength. Her navy weakened and blockaded in its ports, Spain was cut off from her Central and South American colonies where independence movements grew to deprive her of much of her mineral and trade income. Trafalgar ended Spain's naval resurgence.

For the French, Trafalgar was not such a defeat, logistically, economically, or in terms of morale. At the beginning of 1805 France had over 70 ships of the line to call upon, and the loss of 13 of them did not deprive Napoleon of seapower had he chosen to use it. Nevertheless, the French fleet had been reduced by nearly one-fifth and, divided between the Atlantic and Mediterranean ports, it remained only as strong as its largest individual squadron. Blockaded even more carefully after 1805, the dispersed squadrons failed to constitute a serious threat until late in the Napoleonic War and only then on account of their potential power should any squadrons have united.

Nevertheless, Napoleon refused to abandon the strategy he had conceived to bring about the invasion of Britain. The subjection of his enemy across the Channel remained always at the back of his mind, and to achieve that aim he continued to build ships of the line in every port that fell under his control from the Adriatic to the Baltic. It was a policy he maintained until the very end of the conflict. He set a target of 150 ships of the line: by 1813 he had 80 completed and 35 still building. Sir Thomas Byam Martin observed that as late as 1814 Britain had 'to strain our efforts to the utmost to keep pace with French building; and, had the war continued, the French . . . would in a short time have outnumbered us, so . . . determined was Bonaparte to try and master us on our own element'.

The French continued to believe Napoleon was capable of pursuing an effective naval strategy because most Frenchmen in 1805 were not subjected to the demoralising impact of the news of their defeat off Cape Trafalgar. French newspaper propaganda emphasised the death of Nelson at Trafalgar, the presentation of which was represented as very far from a defeat. On top of that, the French people could celebrate the victories Napoleon had begun to inflict on his continental enemies in southern Europe. In August 1805, as soon as he heard that Austria had joined the Third Coalition,

Napoleon signed a defensive agreement with the Elector of Bavaria. On 26 August he himself abandoned the invasion camp at Boulogne and began preparations to march his army into Germany. Austrian armies began to mobilise early in September, and Napoleon ordered the withdrawal of the bulk of his troops from the invasion camp. They crossed the Rhine on 25 September and, led by Napoleon, in October crossed the Danube and surrounded the Austrian army under General Mack at Ulm. On 22 October Mack agreed to an unconditional surrender with 23,000 men. Fighting his way further along the Danube, Napoleon entered Vienna without resistence in mid November, and on 2 December inflicted a crushing defeat on the combined armies of Austria and Russia at Austerlitz. In a single campaign of two months, Napoleon had destroyed the Third Coalition.

Nevertheless, for those at the head of the French government, propaganda and Napoleon's victories on land could not disguise the lessons of the Trafalgar campaign for France: that Napoleon could achieve far more on shore than his admirals seemed capable of at sea; that the English Channel presented a great obstacle to any attempt by France to invade Britain, and yet provided France with security on that side too; that her continental enemies presented greater threats to the security of France and had to be defeated before a realistic attempt could be made again to invade Britain; and that the British Navy was still superior at sea and would not surrender that superiority.

The campaign underlined these lessons for the British people as well as for Napoleon. Befitting their great victory, they celebrated Trafalgar just as the French celebrated Ulm and Austerlitz. Henceforward, to an even greater degree than previously, the British people regarded their navy as superior to any other, and their ascendency at sea to bring with it an authority which to many, like the Americans, would soon be regarded as arrogance. Their confidence, however, encouraged them in ever greater amphibious operations. Napoleon was eventually to be defeated only by the joint campaigns of allied armies, of which Wellington's in Iberia owed its success to the support provided by the Royal Navy.

Yet after Trafalgar the British people also had to mourn the death of Nelson. He had become their hero and was now regarded as their saviour. Everywhere rejoicing at the victory was muted by news of his death. In the heightened feeling of the time, Nelson and his victory became identified as one. Indeed, it was with Nelson that Trafalgar and the whole naval war against Napoleon was largely identified in the century and a half to come. 'What would Nelson have done?' became the question that bound British naval officers to their common legacy. Even with the transition of the sailing navy into that of the Dreadnought era, the tactics to be employed in a big battle like that of Trafalgar remained the central issue of all quarterdeck officers. Destruction on the scale achieved by Nelson seemed the primary objective to aim for. By this criterion, Jutland was a failure for Jellicoe, but Beatty was the man who, with a panache comparable to that of his great predecessor, might have succeeded where Jellicoe failed.

Trafalgar, through Nelson, accordingly entered the thinking of military men in Britain and her empire for longer than that empire lasted. The latter was of course crucial to the cast of mind that could contemplate the wholesale destruction of an enemy in a single big battle like Trafalgar. Rivalry for control over large shares of the world's surface was produced by economies generating navies far greater than internal national resources could fund. Nelson was fortunate in that Britain at the time of Trafalgar possessed the most powerful maritime economy then in existence. He could afford to take risks with the ships under his command. A century later the shift to steam, steel and shell made the loss of battleships economically less easy to bear.

Although naval technology and economics thus changed, the Trafalgar campaign inspired generations of naval officers, in Japan, the United States of America, and indeed throughout the rest of the English-speaking world. For them, Trafalgar signified a superiority in tactics, training, professional competence and morale that distinctly separated Britain from any other power at that time. That Napoleon did not again risk another major defeat at sea during the course of the Napoleonic War, even though he possessed the ships, indicated the difference he himself drew between the capabilities of the French and the British at sea. Trafalgar established a standard that remained fixed in the mind of the Emperor as well as in that of every seamen who was aware of what that victory implied. Through the vicissitudes of time, that standard has remained. Although all else might have changed, the assumption that the British Navy, or any other imbued with the Nelsonic spirit, was capable of again achieving that standard has repeatedly proved an inspiration.

Sources

Introductions
Ian R Christie, *Wars and Revolutions. Britain 1760-1815* (London 1982)
William Laird Clowes, *The Royal Navy. A History from the Earliest Times to 1900*, 7 vols (London 1897-1903, reprinted 1996-97)
Patrick Crowhurst, *The Defence of British Trade 1689-1815* (Folkestone 1977)
Edouard Desbrière, *The Naval Campaign of 1805: Trafalgar*, translated and edited by Constance Eastwick, 2 vols (Oxford 1933)
Clive Emsley, *Napoleonic Europe* (Harlow 1993)
Richard Glover, *Britain at Bay. Defence against Bonaparte 1803-14* (London 1973)
John Harbron, 'Spain's forgotten Naval Renaissance', *History Today* (August 1990)
David Howarth, *Trafalgar. The Nelson Touch* (London 1969)
William James, *The Naval History of Great Britain*, 6 vols (London 1837)
Roger Morriss, *Nelson. The Life and Letters of a Hero* (London 1996)
C Northcote Parkinson, *The Trade Winds. A Study of British Overseas Trade during the French Wars 1793-1815* (London 1948)
Tom Pocock, *Horatio Nelson* (London 1987)
———, *A Thirst for Glory. The Life of Admiral Sir Sidney Smith* (London 1996)
Alan Schom, *Trafalgar. Countdown to Battle 1803-1805* (London 1990)
Nicholas Tracy, *Nelson's Battles. The Art of Victory in the Age of Sail* (London 1996)
Julian de Zulueta, 'Trafalgar - the Spanish View', *The Mariner's Mirror 66* (1980)

America's Barbary Wars
James A Field, *America and the Mediterranean World 1776-1882* (Princeton, NJ 1969)
Leonard F Gutteridge and Jay D Smith, *The Commodores* (New York 1969)
Dudley W Knox (ed), *Naval Documents related to the United States Wars with the Barbary Powers*, 6 vols (Washington, DC 1939-1944)

East Indies and Africa 1803-1804
C Northcote Parkinson, *War in the Eastern Seas 1793-1815* (London 1954)

Cruise of the *Marengo*
Duclos-Legris journal, NMM LOG/F/2
C Northcote Parkinson, *War in the Eastern Seas*

Dance's Action
Jenny Wraight, 'Dance's Action', *Les flottes des Compagnies des Indes 1600-1857* (Vincennes 1996)

West Indies 1803-1804
William Laird Clowes, *The Royal Navy*, Vol 5
William James, *Naval History*, Vol 3
Olivier Troude, *Batailles Navales de la France* (Paris 1867)
The Naval Chronicle

HM sloop of war *Diamond Rock*
Poacher turned gamekeeper
Vivian Stuart and George T Eggleston, *His Majesty's Sloop-of-War Diamond Rock* (London 1978)

Privateering actions
Privateering vessels
Patrick Crowhurst, *The Defence of British Trade*
John Knox Laughton, *Studies in Naval History: Biographies* (London 1887), Ch XII
David Lyon, *The Sailing Navy List* (London 1993)
C Northcote Parkinson (ed), *The Trade Winds*

An epic of convoy defence
William Laird Clowes, *The Royal Navy*, Vol 5
William James, *Naval History*, Vol 3
Nicholas H Nicolas (ed), *The Dispatches and Letters of Lord Nelson*, Vol VI (London 1846)

The convoy system
Patrick Crowhurst, *The Defence of British Trade*
C Northcote Parkinson (ed), *The Trade Winds*
Owen Rutter, *Red Ensign: A History of Convoy* (London 1942)

Frigate actions
William Laird Clowes, *The Royal Navy*, Vol 5
William James, *Naval History*, Vol 3

Ships of the Royal Navy: the 12pdr frigate
Jean Boudriot, *The History of the French Frigate 1650-1850* (Rotherfield 1993)
Robert Gardiner, *The First Frigates* (London 1992)

Invasion craft - the nightmare
Invasion craft - the reality
Edouard Desbrière, *Projets et Tentatives de Débarquement aux Iles Britanniques*, 5 vols (Paris 1900-1902)
David Lyon, *The Sailing Navy List*

The National Flotilla
Edouard Desbrière, *Projets et Tentatives*
Richard Glover, *Britain at Bay*

The Downs Command
C Lloyd (ed), *The Keith Papers* Vol III (London 1955)

Anti-Flotilla operations: the Channel
William Laird Clowes, *The Royal Navy*, Vol 5
William James, *Naval History*, Vol 3
C Lloyd (ed), *The Keith Papers* Vol III

Vencejo **at Quiberon**
William Laird Clowes, *The Royal Navy*, Vol 5
William James, *Naval History*, Vol 3
Tom Pocock, *A Thirst for Glory*
The Naval Chronicle

The invasion defences
Richard Glover, *Britain at Bay*
C Lloyd (ed), *The Keith Papers* Vol III
Andrew Saunders, *Fortress Britain* (Liphook 1989)
Sheila Sutcliffe, *Martello Towers* (Newton Abbot 1972)

Torpedoes and rockets: the attacks on Boulogne
Christopher Lloyd & Hardin Craig, Jnr (eds), 'Congreve Rockets 1805-1806', in *The Naval Miscellany*, Vol IV (London 1952)

Fulton's Infernals
Wallace S Hutcheon, Jr, *Robert Fulton: Pioneer of Undersea Warfare* (Annapolis, MD 1981).
C Lloyd (ed), *The Keith Papers* Vol III

Anti-Flotilla operations: the North Sea
C Lloyd (ed), *The Keith Papers* Vol III
Tom Pocock, *A Thirst for Glory*

French naval bases: Boulogne and the invasion ports
Edouard Desbrière, *Projets et Tentatives*

The blockade of Brest
William Laird Clowes, *The Royal Navy*, Vol 5
G Cornwallis-West (ed), *Life and Letters of Admiral Cornwallis* (London 1927)
William James, *Naval History*, Vols 3 & 4
John Leyland (ed), *Dispatches and Letters Relating to the Blockade of Brest 1803-1805*, 2 vols (London 1899 & 1902)
The Naval Chronicle

'Dangers of the sea': shipwreck
David Hepper, *British Warship Losses in the Age of Sail* (Rotherfield 1994)
Michael Lewis, *A Social History of the Navy, 1793-1815* (London 1960)

Nelson takes over in the Mediterranean
William Laird Clowes, *The Royal Navy*, Vol 5
Nicholas H Nicolas (ed), *The Dispatches and Letters of Lord Nelson*, Vols V & VI (London 1845-46)

Ships of the Royal Navy: gunboats and gunbrigs
David Lyon, *The Sailing Navy List*

Watching Toulon
William Laird Clowes, *The Royal Navy*, Vol 5
William James, *Naval History*, Vols 3 & 4
The Naval Chronicle

Spanish gold
William Laird Clowes, *The Royal Navy*, Vol 5
William James, *Naval History*, Vol 3

Missiessy's raid
William Laird Clowes, *The Royal Navy*, Vol 5
William James, *Naval History*, Vol 3
Olivier Troude, *Batailles Navales de la France*
The Naval Chronicle

A naval officer's view
William O'Byrne, *Naval Biographical Dictionary* (London 1849)

Villeneuve's first sortie
Villeneuve escapes
Nelson in the West Indies
Julian S Corbett, *The Campaign of Trafalgar* (London 1910)
William Laird Clowes, *The Royal Navy*, Vol 5
William James, *Naval History*, Vol 3
Nicholas H Nicolas (ed), *The Dispatches and Letters of Lord Nelson*, Vols V & VI

Ships of the Royal Navy: the 50-gun ship
Rif Winfield, *The 50-Gun Ship* (London 1997)
Public Record Office Adm 8/- series, Station Lists

Calder's Action
Julian S Corbett, *The Campaign of Trafalgar*
William James, *Naval History*, Vol 3

Anti-Flotilla operations: the North Sea

Ship decoration
L G Carr Laughton, *Old Ship Figure-heads and Sterns* (London 1925)
H C Bjerg and J Erichsen, *Danske Orlogsskibe 1690-1860* (Copenhagen 1980)

The blockade resumed
Trafalgar - the opening moves
The lee line
The weather column
The final stages
Storm after the battle
Securing the Victory
Julian S Corbett, *The Campaign of Trafalgar*
Edouard Desbrière, *The Naval Campaign of 1805*
Edward Fraser, *The Enemy at Trafalgar* (London 1906)
T Sturges Jackson (ed), *Logs of the Great Sea Fights 1794-1805*, Vol II (London 1900)
Stuart Legg, *Trafalgar: An Eye-Witness Account of a Great Battle* (London 1966)
R H Mackenzie, *The Trafalgar Roll* (London 1913)
Nicholas Tracy, *Nelson's Battles. The Art of Victory in the Age of Sail* (London 1996)

Ordeal of the *Belleisle*
Joseph Allen, *Memoir of the Life and Services of Admiral Sir William Hargood, GCB, GCH* (London 1861)

Death of Nelson
Sir William Beatty, *The Authentic Narrative of the Death of Lord Nelson* (London 1807)
Colin White (ed), *The Nelson Companion* (Stroud 1995)

Lone fight of the *Redoutable*
Counterattack
Edward Fraser, *The Enemy at Trafalgar*
William James, *Naval History*, Vol 4
Olivier Troude, *Batailles Navales de la France*

Strachan's Action
Julian S Corbett, *The Campaign of Trafalgar*
William James, *Naval History*, Vol 4

Ships of the Royal Navy: the 74-gun ship
Brian Lavery, *The Ship of the Line*, Vol 1 (London 1983)

Nelson's funeral
Colin White (ed), *The Nelson Companion*
The Naval Chronicle XV (1806)

Artists and printmakers
E H H Archibald, *Dictionary of Sea Painters* (Woodbridge 1980)
E Bénézit, *Dictionnaire critique et documentaire de Peintres, Sculpteurs, Dessinateurs et Graveurs* (Paris 1976)
Maurice Harold Grant, *A Dictionary of British Etchers* (London 1952)
Ian Mackenzie, *British Prints: Dictionary and Price Guide* (Woodbridge 1987)
Lister Raymond, *Prints and Printmaking* (London 1984)
Ronald vere Tooley, *Tooley's Dictionary of Mapmakers* (New York and Amsterdam 1979)
Jane Turner (Ed), *The Dictionary of Art* (London 1996)
Ellis Waterhouse, *The Dictionary of 18th Century Painters in Oils and Crayons* (Woodbridge 1980)
Arnold Wilson, *A Dictionary of British Marine Painters* (Leigh-on-Sea 1967)

NOTES ON ARTISTS, PRINTMAKERS AND THEIR TECHNIQUES

These brief notes cover most of the artists and printmakers who appear in the volume, as well as the principal printing techniques. They are intended only to put the artists in context with the period and readers wanting further information on their art and lives should turn to the sources; in many cases there is little more to tell.

Abbott, Lemuel *(1760-1803)* English portrait painter, known principally for his portraits of Nelson.

Alexander, William *(1762-1816)* English watercolourist and architectural illustrator known mainly for his series on China which he visited in 1792. In 1807 he was appointed Professor of Design at the Military College at Great Marlow.

Anderson, William *(1757-1837)* Scottish marine painter who trained as a shipwright. He is known principally for his small river and estuarine scenes around Hull, but he also executed large-scale set pieces such as 'The battle of the Nile' and 'Lord Howe's Fleet off Spithead'. The British Museum hold sketch books of the battles of the Nile and Copenhagen.

Andrews, George Henry *(1816-1898)* English marine watercolour painter who was, by profession, an engineer. A number of his works were produced in the *Illustrated London News* and the *Graphic*.

Aquatint A variety of etching *(qv)* invented in France in the 1760s. It is a tone rather than a line process and is used principally to imitate the appearance of watercolour washes. The process involves the etching of a plate with acid through a porous ground of powdered resin. The acid bites small rings around each resin grain and gradations of tone are achieved by repetition of the biting process and the protection of areas of the plate with varnish.

Bailey, John *(fl late eighteenth and early nineteenth centuries)* English engraver of acquatints *(qv)* of topographical views and naval subjects after his contemporaries.

Barnard, William S *(1774-1849)* English mezzotint *(qv)* engraver of decorative subjects and portraits after his contempories.

Baugean, Jean-Jérôme *(1764-1819)* French painter and prolific engraver best known for his collection of shipping prints, 'Collection de toutes des Especes de Batiments' which went through numerous editions in the early nineteenth century. Also well known is his depiction of 'The Embarkation of Napoleon on board *Bellérophon*'.

Beechey, Sir William *(1753-1839)* English portrait painter who studied under Zoffany. He was made portrait painter to Queen Charlotte in 1793 and for the rest of his career produced a steady output of fashionable subjects. A contemporary portraitist, James Opie, said of his picture that they 'were of that mediocre quality as to taste and fashion, that they seemed only fit for sea captains and merchants'.

Bluck, John *(fl early nineteenth century)* English aquatint *(qv)* engraver mainly of topographical subjects as well as marine scenes, after his contemporaries.

Buttersworth, Thomas *(1768-1842)* English marine painter who served in the Royal Navy from 1795 until he was invalided out in 1800. His vivid watercolours of the battle of St Vincent and the blockade of Cadiz, painted while he was at sea, suggest first-hand experience. After leaving the Navy he devoted himself full-time to his painting and created a very considerable body of work.

Cartwright, Joseph *(1789-1829)* English landscape and marine painter and member of the Society of British Artists who was also a naval paymaster. He was made marine painter to the Duke of Clarence and painted a number of naval scenes particularly of actions in the Mediterranean including 'The Battle of the Nile' and 'The *Euryalus* Frigate Becalmed in the Channel of Corfu'.

Cleveley, Robert *(1749-1809)* English marine painter, son of John Cleveley the Elder *(qv)* and twin brother of John Cleveley *(qv)*. He was Captain's Clerk in the *Asia* and served on the North American and West Indies stations in the 1770s. He is known mainly for his history paintings of the American Revolutionary War.

Daniell, William *(1769-1837)* English draughtsman, watercolourist and aquatint *(qv)* engraver of topographical, marine and architectural views. He was the nephew of Thomas Daniell with whom he travelled to India when he was sixteen. Apart from his *Oriental Scenery* he is probably best known for his plates for *A Voyage around Great Britain*.

Devis, Arthur William *(1762-1822)* English history and portrait painter and landscape artist and the nineteenth child of the painter Arthur Devis. He travelled to the East Indies on board the *Antelope* and when the ship foundered he took the opportunity to work in Canton and later India. He returned to England in 1795 hoping to receive commissions for history paintings but he had little luck and was declared bankrupt in 1800. He is perhaps best known for his *Death of Nelson* which was exhibited in 1809.

Dodd, Robert *(1748-1815)* English marine and landscape painter and successful engraver and publisher, best known for his portrayals of the naval battles of the American Revolutionary and French wars. His is also known for his formal portraits of ships in which three views are included in a single image.

Dowman, John *(1750-1824)* English portrait artist and pupil of Benjamin West *(qv)* who, as well as working in oils, was particularly revered for his chalk sketches and watercolours, but while he is sometimes regarded as the most important watercolour portraitist of the late eighteenth century, the pretty style of some of his work has been described as 'cloyingly effeminate'.

Drypoint Intaglio *(qv)* engraving *(qv)* technique in which the image is scratched into a copper plate with a steel needle which is held like a pen. Ridges – burr – are created around the lines which give drypoint its characteristic fuzzy effect. The burr is delicate and quickly wears away during the printing process so that print runs are short.

Dutton, Thomas Goldsworth *(c1819-1891)* Prolific English draughtsman and lithographer of ships and shipping scenes, after his own watercolours and those of his contemporaries. His huge and varied body of work gives a vivid impression of nineteenth-century shipping.

Eckstein, John *(fl late eighteenth and early nineteenth centuries)* English sculptor who exhibited regularly at the Royal Academy.

Faden, William *(1750-1836)* English catographer and publisher, and the partner of Thomas Jeffereys *(qv)* whose business he ran in the Charing Cross Road after the latter's death in 1771. He is best known for his *North American Atlas*, published in 1777, *Battles of the American Revolution* and *Petit Neptune Français*, both of 1793.

Fairburn, John *(fl late eighteenth and early nineteenth centuries)* London publisher and geographer and map seller whose works include *North America* (1798) and *Spain and Portugal* (1808).

Fittler, James *(1758-1835)* English line engraver of naval scenes and topographical views, after his contemporaries. He was appointed marine engraver to George III.

Garneray, Ambroise-Louis *(1783-1857)* French marine painter whose early life was spent at sea in the French navy and ashore as a shipwright in Mauritius, before being taken prisoner by the British in 1806. Confined on a prison ship at Portsmouth he made an income painting portraits. Returning to France in 1814 he exhibited his first shipping scenes in 1815. He is probably best known for his work illustrating the ports of France which was published in *Vues des côtes de France dans l'océan et dans le Mediterranée* (1823).

Gilbert, Pierre-Julien *(1783-1860)* French marine painter and the pupil of Nicholas Ozanne. He was appointed professor of drawing at the school of the *Marine Royale* and travelled as the official artist on the expedition to capture Algiers in 1830.

Gillbank, Henry *(fl late eighteenth and early nineteenth centuries)* English engraver of aquatints (*qv*) and mezzotints (*qv*) of decorative and historical subjects, known particularly for his *Lord Nelson Mortally Wounded . . . at Trafalgar* (1806) after Mather Brown.

Gold, Joyce *(fl early nineteenth century)* English printer and publisher whose works included Rowe's *English Atlas* (1816). Also the publisher of the *Naval Chronicle*.

Greatbach, William *(born 1802)* English engraver of historical and more sentimental subjects such as *Alpine Mastiffs Reanimating a Traveller* after Landseer.

Heath, William *(1795-1840)* English engraver of military subjects, mainly after his own designs., though his depiction of *The Death of Lord Viscount Nelson* (1811) was after Benjamin West (*qv*).

Hellyer, Thomas *(fl late eighteenth and early nineteenth centuries)* English line and aquatint (*qv*) engraver of naval and decorative scenes such as his plates of *The Battle of the Nile* after Captain James Weir.

Hoppner, John *(1758-1810)* English portrait painter and engraver of German descent, regarded in his time as the foremost portraitist and the natural successor to Sir Joshua Reynolds.Throughout the 1770s, when his reputation was at its highest, he painted ever increasingly distinguished sitters. His vibrant use of colour and almost abstract brushwork, shown to good effect in *A Gale of Wind*, look forward to Turner.

Huggins, John William *(1781-1845)* English marine painter who spent his early years at sea with the East India Company until around 1814 when he established himself as a painter. He produced an enormous number of ship portraits, many of them engraved by his son-in-law, Edward Duncan (*qv*), as well as a number of large-scale naval battles, in particular the battle of Trafalgar. In 1836 he was made marine painter to King William IV.

Intaglio printing The method of printing using metal plates which can be worked as aquatints (*qv*), drypoints (*qv*), engravings (*qv*), etchings (*qv*), or mezzotints (*qv*). Once the lines have been made on the plate, by whatever method, printing is done by pressing damp paper hard enough against the plate so that the ink is lifted out of the incised lines. This explains why prints done by this method have slightly raised lines, a distinct characteristic of the process.

Jeakes, Joseph *(fl early nineteenth century)* English engraver of aquatints (*qv*), notably of topographical scenes and naval engagements after his contemporaries, particularly Thomas Whitcombe (*qv*) and his own designs.

Jukes, Francis *(1747-1812)* English painter and etcher of aquatints. As well as his popular 'Views of England' and his sporting prints he was a prolific exponent of marine subjects.

Justyne, Percy William *(1812-1883)* English landscape painter and engraver, born in Rochester, who painted both European and English views and exhibited in the Royal Academy.

Laurie & Whittle *(fl late eighteenth and early nineteenth centuries)* English publishers and engravers who amalgamated with Imray, Norrie & Wilson. Works included *American Atlas* (1794) and *East India Pilot* (1800).

Lee, John Theophilus *(fl early nineteenth century)* English marine painter.

Lithograph A print made by drawing a design on porous limestone with a greasy material. The stone is then wetted and ink applied to it which adheres only to the drawn surfaces. Paper is then pressed to the stone for the final print. Lithography was discovered only at the very end of the eighteenth century but quickly developed into a highly flexible medium.

Livesay, J *(fl late eighteenth and early nineteenth centuries)* English marine watercolour painter.

Livesay, Richard *(1750-1823)* English landscape and genre painter and pupil of Benjamin West (*qv*). He was appointed the drawing master of the Naval Academy, Portsmouth, in 1796, and his first marine painting, 'Cornwallis's Retreat', was exhibited at the Royal Academy that year.

Martino, Eduardo de *(1838-1912)* Italian marine painter who moved to England in 1875 where he settled at Cowes and became painter to Queen Victoria. The Royal Collection houses his four compositions of *The Battle of Trafalgar*.

Maynard, Thomas *(fl 1777-1812)* English portrait painter.

Medland, Thomas *(1755-1822)* English draughtsman and aquatint (*qv*) engraver of landscapes, topographical views and naval subjects, who taught drawing at the East India College.

Meyer, Henry *(1782-1847)* English painter and engraver of portraits, after his cotemporaries, such as *Lady Hamilton as Nature* by Romney (*qv*). He was the nephew of John Hoppner (*qv*)

Mezzotint A type of engraving (*qv*) in which the engraving plate is first roughened with a tool known as a rocker. The rough surface holds the ink and appears as a black background and the design is then burnished onto it by scraping away the rough burr to create lighter tones and by polishing the surface for highlights. Thus the artist works from dark to light, creating a tonal effect which was particularly suited to reproducing paintings and had its heyday in eighteenth-century England.

Mitchell, Thomas *(1735-1790)* English marine painter who was by profession a shipwright at Deptford. He is known principally for his depictions of naval battles.

Moses, Henry *(1782-1870)* English draughtsman, engraver and sometime painter. While he engraved mostly classical subjects after his contemporaries, he also made engravings of marine subjects after his own designs and published several booklets such as *The Marine Sketch Book* (1826) and *The Cruise of the Experimental Squadron* (1830)

Pocock, Nicholas *(1740-1821)* Foremost English marine painter of his day. He was apprenticed in the shipbuilding yard of Richard Champion in Bristol before being appointed to command the barque *Lloyd*, setting sail to Charleston in 1768. This was the first of a number of voyages for which there are illustrated log books, some of which are at the National Maritime Museum. He was present at the West Indies campaign in 1778 or '79, and completed an oil painting in 1780, receiving helpful criticism from Sir Joshua Reynolds. Thereafter he devoted himself to his art and painted numerous depictions of the struggles with Revolutionary France

Pollard, Robert *(1755-1838)* English line and acquatint (*qv*) engraver of naval and historical subjects, as well as of portraits and architectural scenes. He set up business in London in 1781 and is known to have collaborated with Francis Jukes (*qv*).

Ponce, Nicholas *(1746-1831)* French publisher and engraver to the Count of Artois, based in Paris.

Pugin, Augustus Charles *(1760-1832)* Architect, illustrator, designer and watercolourist, born in Paris, who settled in England during the French Revolution. He worked for John Nash and was one of the best architectural draughtsmen of his day as well as an expert on Gothic detail. His son, Augustus Welby Pugin, is now best known for his interiors of the Houses of Parliament.

Reynolds, Samuel William *(1773-1835)* English painter and engraver of landscapes, topographical views and portraits. Though not related to Sir Joshua Reynolds, he engraved many plates after that artist's work. Under the patronage of Samuel Whitbread he expanded his interests to include architecture, landscape gardening and collecting.

Ridley, William *(1764-1838)* English engraver of bookplates and portraits, mainly after his contemporaries.

Romney, George *(1734-1802)* English portrait painter who made his early reputation with his depiction of 'The Death of Wolfe' (1763). His reputation today rests mainly on his series of portraits of Emma Hart who later became Emma Hamilton, Nelson's mistress.

Rood, Jan *(fl late eighteenth century)* Dutch draughtsman who specialised in marine subjects.

Roux, Joseph Ange Antoine *(1765-1835)* French marine painter of naval battles, and ship portraitist.

Sabin, Joseph F *(fl late nineteenth century)* French watercolourist and illustrator who spent much of his working life in New York.

Sartorius, Francis *(fl early nineteenth century)* English marine painter from a family of painters better known for their sporting scenes. No paintings are known after 1808 which suggests that he died thereabouts. As well as a number of naval scenes he executed a pair of paintings depicting the rescue of a crew from a wrecked ship using Captain Manby's rocket and line.

Schetky, John Christian *(1778-1874)* Scottish marine painter from a cultured background whose early interest in the sea led to his joining the frigate *Hind* in 1792. He soon returned to land and in 1801 embarked on a continental tour. He was drawing master at the Royal Military College, Great Marlow, and later Professor of Drawing at he Royal Naval College, Portsmouth, where he remained for 25 years. His painted subjects ranged from ship portraits to reconstructions of naval battles of the Nelsonic era. He continued to paint until his death at the age of 95.

Serres, John Thomas *(1759-1825)* English marine painter and elder son of Dominic Serres, the elder. Though he painted a number of dramatic naval battle scenes in the manner of de Loutherbourg whom he greatly admired, his main activity was drawing the coasts of England, France and Spain in his capacity as marine Draughtsman to the Admiralty. A selection were subsequently published in *Serres' Little Sea Torch* (1801). He died in debtors' prison as a result of the pretensions and wild extravagances of his wife, the self-styled 'Princess Olive of Cumberland'.

Smith, John Thomas *(1766-1833)* Draughtsman and etcher of mainly architectural subjects and topographical views. He studied under the sculptor Nollekens and in 1816 was appointed Keeper of Prints and Drawings at the British Museum.

Stadler, Joseph Constantine *(fl late eighteenth and early nineteenth centuries)* A prolific aquatint *(qv)* engraver, of German extraction, who was based in London between 1780 and 1812. His subjects ranged from decorative designs to topographical views and military and naval scenes.

Stanfield, Clarkson (Frederick) *(1793-1867)* English artist who was considered to be the greatest marine painter of his day. He spent his early life at sea, variously in a collier, the Royal Navy and again in the merchant navy, until 1816. He then became a theatre scene painter while at the same time building a reputation as an easel painter. His most impressive work was probably the huge *Battle of Trafalgar* in which he combined his knowledge of ships with an ability to compose on the large scale. He was also a fine watercolourist. He is often wrongly referred to as William Clarkson Stanfield.

Sutherland, Thomas *(fl late eighteenth and early nineteenth centuries)* English acquatint *(qv)* engraver of sporting, naval and military subjects and portraits after his contemporaries.

Turner, Charles *(1773-1857)* English acquatint *(qv)* and mezzotint *(qv)* engraver of portraits, military and sporting subjects and topographical views. His engraving of J M W Turner's 'A Shipwreck' in 1805 was the first one after a Turner painting.

Turner, Joseph Mallard William *(1775-1851)* English painter and printmaker who dominated British landscape painting in the first half of the nineteenth century and could be judged to have raised it to the status of a serious art form. He regarded his painting as being in direct line from the seventeenth-century classicists such as Poussin, and certainly his early marine subjects pay homage to the earlier tradition of Dutch marine art. *Dutch Boats in a Gale* (1801) was executed as a pendant to Willem ve de Velde the Younger's *Kaag Close-hauled in a Fresh Breeze* while his *Calais Pier* (1803) looked back to the work of van Ruysdael. He was a natural candidate to be commissioned by King George IV to paint the battle of Trafalgar to hang alongside de Loutherbourg's *Glorious First of June*, but the result was not regarded as a happy one by many of his contemporaries, especially in regard to the depiction of technical detail. However, his historical paintings, as with all his output, increasingly aimed towards the sublime, so successfully achieved in marine form in *The Fighting Temeraire Tugged to her Last Berth to be Broken up 1838* (1839). His extraordinary understanding of natural phenomena made him a supreme painter of the effects of light and water his depictions of rivers, estuaries and the sea and the array of craft which sailed on them are unsurpassed.

Uwins, Thomas *(1782-1857)* English genre painter and engraver whose main work was a book illustrator.

Warren, Charles Turner *(1762-1823)* English line engraver, mainly of portraits and figure subjects after his contemporaries. He is credited with the development of steel plates for engraving.

West, Benjamin *(1738-1820)* American painter who is now regarded as the founding father of the American school. He settled in London in 1763, and though he retained his contacts with his native land, he remained there for the rest of his life. His history paintings, as personified by 'The Death of General Wolfe', became an inspiration for young American painters depicting the history of their young nation.

Whitcombe, Thomas *(born c1752)* English marine painter who, like Pocock *(qv)* and Luny *(qv)*, was celebrated for his huge output of paintings depicting the French Revolutionary Wars. He contributed some fifty plates to the *Naval Achievements of Great Britain* and also painted numerous works for engravings. There is no record of his death.

Willyams, Cooper *(fl late eighteenth and early nineteenth centuries)* English amateur engraver who made illustrations of his travels abroad.

Yates, Lt Thomas *(c1760-1796)* English marine painter who entered the Royal Navy in 1782, leaving a few years later to become a painter. With the outbreak of the French Revolutionary Wars he began to engrave and publish from his drawings of celebrated naval actions. He was shot in a family dispute and few works remain from his short life.

INDEX

All ships are British unless otherwise indicated in brackets following the name. Page numbers in bold indicate tables.

Abbreviations

Cdr =	Commander	Fr =	France	Neths =	Netherlands	USA =	United States of
Cdre =	Commodore	GB =	British merchant	R/A =	Rear-Admiral		America
Den =	Denmark		ship	Sgt =	Sergeant	USN =	United States Navy
		Lt =	Lieutenant	Sp =	Spain	V/A =	Vice-Admiral